WARNING SIGNALS?

Johnny won't eat his dinner—again!
Susy has just had another nightmare.
Bobby is ten. He still wets his bed.
Ralph's teacher says he is out of control.

All these children may—or may not—need professional help. How can you know? And what can you do?

A practicing child and family therapist, Dr. Bush looks at the problems that baffle and concern parents. He explores the various kinds of therapy and counseling that are available. He provides specific resources for help in special problem areas.

Gathered together in one authoritative, indispensable handbook, here is all the information you need in order to make intelligent, informed choices.

WHEN A CHILD NEEDS HELP

"A valuable contribution to the tools parents have when coping with emotional difficulties."

—Dr. Burton White,
Center for Parent Education,
Newton, Mass.

"Direct and demystifying . . . informative and supportive."

—*Kirkus Reviews*

WHEN A CHILD NEEDS HELP:
A Parents' Guide to Child Therapy

Richard Bush, Ph.D.

Published in hardcover as
A Parents' Guide to Child Therapy

LAUREL

A Laurel Book
Published by
Dell Publishing Co., Inc.
1 Dag Hammarskjold Plaza
New York, New York 10017

Originally published under the title:
A PARENTS' GUIDE TO CHILD THERAPY.

ISBN: 0-440-39574-7

Reprinted by arrangement with Delacorte Press
Printed in the United States of America

First Laurel printing—October 1982

Contents

Acknowledgments		7
Introduction		9
Part One	**WHEN, WHERE, AND HOW TO GET HELP**	13
Chapter 1	DOES MY CHILD NEED HELP?	15
Chapter 2	EMOTIONAL PROBLEMS OF CHILDHOOD AND ADOLESCENCE	21
Chapter 3	HYPERACTIVITY AND LEARNING DISABILITIES	79
Chapter 4	PLACES TO GO FOR HELP	99
Chapter 5	THE MAJOR MENTAL HEALTH PROFESSIONS	119
Chapter 6	THE MAJOR SCHOOLS OF PSYCHOTHERAPY	137
Chapter 7	THE USE OF DRUGS IN THE PSYCHOTHERAPEUTIC TREATMENT OF CHILDREN	171
Chapter 8	PSYCHOLOGICAL TESTING	181
Part Two	**A STEP-BY-STEP GUIDE TO GETTING HELP**	197
Chapter 9	OBTAINING HELP FROM A THERAPIST IN PRIVATE PRACTICE	199
Chapter 10	OBTAINING HELP IN A CLINIC SETTING	221
Chapter 11	THE GROUND RULES OF PSYCHOTHERAPY	225
Chapter 12	EVALUATING THERAPY	247
Chapter 13	OBTAINING HELP THROUGH YOUR CHILD'S SCHOOL	263
Chapter 14	OBTAINING HELP IN AN INPATIENT OR RESIDENTIAL SETTING	279

Chapter 15 PSYCHIATRIC EMERGENCIES 303

Appendix A NATIONAL ORGANIZATIONS 313
Appendix B NATIONAL DIRECTORIES 317
Appendix C SOME HELPFUL READINGS 319

Notes 323
Index 333

Acknowledgments

I had originally intended this book to be relatively brief, and in it to present some ideas on how to choose a therapist for a child or family. Over time this work seemed to take on a life of its own, and has evolved into a comprehensive volume about mental-health services for children and families.

This evolution could never have taken place without the generous assistance of many friends and colleagues. Indeed, so many people have helped, in so many ways, that I don't know how to thank them sufficiently, and whom to thank first.

I'll begin with Fredric Coplon, whom I called upon again and again for his knowledge and advice. He helped me formulate or revise many chapters of this book. I am also indebted to Joan Axelrod, Helen Broskowski, Al Cain, Peter Musliner, and Myron Stocking, who graciously shared their time and expertise each and every time I needed them.

In addition, I'd like to thank Daniel Palant for his pediatrician's-eye view of Chapter Two. Not only did he carefully review this lengthy chapter, but he devoted an entire evening to helping me revise it. For their help with Chapter Three I'd like to thank Mel Levine and Penny Axelrod, and for her assistance with Chapter Four, Beverly Dudek. For help with Chapter Five I'd like to thank Miles Johnson, Ralph Kolodny, Arthur Mutter, Lester Rudy, Roma Lee Taunton, Diane Vines, Anne Wissink, Henry Work, and Joan Zaro. For help with Chapter Six, my thanks to Charlie Rice, Carter Umbarger, and John Markoff; with Chapter Eight, to Celia Schulhoff, Barbara Miller, and Anne McGloin; with Chapter Nine, to Michael Singer, Judith Singer, and Jessica Hammann; with Chapter Ten, to Leslie Brody and George Lussier; with Chapter Thirteen, to Celia Schulhoff, Barbara Miller, John Freedman, Martha Zigler, Noreen Curran, and Joanne Driscoll; and with Chapter Fourteen, to Lloyd Price, Matthew Friedman, Maryanne Perrichini, and Rita Williams.

I owe a special debt to Joan Axelrod, Helen Broskowski, and Mitch Wangh, for the excellent job they did as coauthors of chapters of this book.

I'd like to thank Lorraine Loviglio, who did the early editing of this book, and Jay Howland, who did all the rest. They made this work far more readable. Thanks also to Norma Panico who runs one heck of a typing service.

Special thanks to Cynthia Vartan of Delacorte Press who provided me with help and support, and, most importantly, gave me free rein to write this work as I saw fit. Thanks also to Peter Skolnik for being such a marvelous agent.

In closing I'd like to thank a number of people who were instrumental in my writing this book: my clients, both youngsters and parents, who have taught me a great deal about the helping process; my teachers and supervisors, who provided me with models for being a therapist: Al Cain, Larry Gusman, Myron Stocking, Carter Umbarger, and Jodi Veroff; my friends, who supported me through these long years of writing: Judy Druker, Michael Dvorkin, Al Goodstadt, Kathleen Herr, and John Markoff; and my parents, who taught me to care and to persevere.

Introduction

Mr. and Mrs. Cook felt confused, guilty, and despairing. Their twelve-year-old son, Frank, was causing so much trouble in school that it was uncertain whether he could remain there. Neither the Cooks nor the school had been able to help him control his bad temper, and after Frank threatened to hit his teacher, it was clear that something more had to be done. At the urging of the school psychologist the Cooks called me to ask if I could be of assistance.

The Cooks had tried getting help for Frank a few years before, at their local mental health clinic, but had been frustrated and bewildered by that experience. They had vowed not to seek help again, but their son's problems had grown to such proportions that they felt they had no other choice.

When I saw them in my office, the Cooks told the following story:

Frank's troubles had begun in first grade. He had been in almost constant difficulty, fighting with his classmates and defying his teacher. The teacher had first tried reason and patience with Frank, but when this approach proved unsuccessful, she deprived him of privileges, and eventually began to send him to the principal whenever he misbehaved. At first the visits to the principal seemed to calm Frank, but this effect soon wore off, and he was "as impossible as ever." The Cooks also had tried everything they could imagine to get Frank to behave in school; but all to no avail. Finally the principal told the Cooks that Frank had an emotional problem and that they should take him to the local mental health clinic for counseling.

Sitting in my office, years later, Mrs. Cook still seemed stunned by the thought that her son "had an emotional problem." For his part, Mr. Cook remembered saying that he didn't believe in psychiatry, but since he had been unable to help his son, he would reluctantly agree to let someone else try.

Mrs. Cook remembered how hard it had been to build up the courage to call the clinic and how disappointed she was to hear that there would be a "short wait" before an appointment could be arranged. The short wait turned into four weeks, and the Cooks had almost forgotten about the clinic when a Mr. Hermann called, apologizing for the long delay and offering them a time to come in to talk about their son's problems. No, he didn't want to see Frank quite yet, just Mr. and Mrs. Cook.

The Cooks described Mr. Hermann as a young man who didn't look much older than their own son. Worse than that, he seemed far more interested in how they were getting along than in Frank's problems. After spending three hours talking with them and one hour with Frank, Mr. Hermann announced that Frank's problems were caused by tension in the home and that Mr. and Mrs. Cook were in need of counseling.

Since Frank's misbehavior occurred at school, not at home, the Cooks couldn't understand how *their* talking with someone could do much good. They decided not to follow Mr. Hermann's suggestion, and instead had been trying to handle things on their own. Indeed, Frank had settled down at school, until this year, when his behavior was proving worse than ever.

As they talked about their experience at the mental health clinic, the Cooks remembered how hurt and angry they had felt at being told that they were the cause of Frank's problems. Maybe they had done some things wrong, but they had tried everything the school had told them to do, and nothing had worked. After all, the teacher and principal couldn't get Frank to behave either. The Cooks wanted me to know that they had been reluctant to come to someone else for help and that they definitely didn't think they were the only reason that Frank misbehaved. In a blend of defiance and pleading, they wanted to know what I thought should be done.

I began by telling the Cooks that if Frank's problems were easy to remedy, they and the school would have done so already. I told them that just as it would be unproductive for them to blame themselves for Frank's behavior, so too it would be unhelpful to place the blame on the school, the mental health clinic, or mental health professionals in general.

I told the Cooks that their unfortunate experience might have been avoided if they had known what to expect when they first called for help. They certainly would have been less disappointed if they had known beforehand that many clinics have waiting lists, and that (except in cases of emergency) it may take anywhere from a few weeks to a few months before an initial appointment can be scheduled. They probably would have felt more receptive to the idea of counseling for themselves, if they had known that many therapists attempt to help children by providing assistance to parents; and that this does not imply that the parents are "to blame" for the youngster's difficulties. And finally, they would have been relieved to know that their son's problems were not uncommon, and that no one was suggesting that Frank was "seriously disturbed." Perhaps if they had known these things before they sought help, the Cooks might have been able to take advantage of the services offered by the clinic.

The Cook's story was such a familiar one that I decided to formulate some guidelines for other parents who found themselves needing help, but not knowing how to find or use it. Thus, this book is an attempt to provide parents with all the information necessary to locate and utilize the mental health services available to them. It is written with consumers' interests at heart, but from the perspective of a therapist. In it I share the suggestions I have given to my clients and to my friends.

Parents should realize that the information contained herein represents my understanding of a still evolving and ever-changing body of opinion and knowledge. Although as a group mental health professionals tend not to agree on many things, most would accept the statement that what has yet to be discovered in this field far overshadows what is already known. Thus I'd suggest you use this book to enhance, but not replace, your own experience and common sense.

It is my intention that this book be used as a reference volume; that readers will refer to those sections or chapters which are of special interest to them. Indeed, in its entirety this work contains far more information than any given parent will need in order to help his or her child or family.

Finding appropriate mental health services and getting the maximum benefit from them are not simple matters, and I have no magic formulas or secret recipes to offer. I do believe, however, that knowing about therapy and therapists will increase the likelihood that you and your child will use such treatment wisely and benefit from it.

Part One

WHEN, WHERE, AND HOW TO GET HELP

Chapter 1

DOES MY CHILD NEED HELP?

It would be nice if childhood were a blissful time, free of any cares or worries. Yet as you know from your own growing up or from raising your children, childhood experience is a mixture of achievement and failure, pleasure and disappointment, conflict and resolution. As much as you may wish to shield your youngsters from emotional upset, they will inevitably go through some periods of significant psychological stress. Indeed, such periods of turmoil are often necessary stages, preceding important times of emotional growth.

Temper tantrums, nightmares, irrational fears, fighting with siblings, and rebellion against parental authority, to name just a few, are all problems which are considered to be a normal part of childhood development. Such difficulties are expected to be relatively short-lived, and to be resolved as a result of maturation or in response to parental support or discipline.

However, some problems persist over long periods of time and may be an indication of more abiding distress. In such circumstances parents often find themselves with the following unanswered questions:

1) Are my child's problems serious or relatively minor?

2) Will the problems go away on their own or, if left unattended, will they stay the same, or get worse?

3) Is there something that I or my spouse can do to help?

4) Should we get some professional assistance?

Any parent who has wrestled with these questions knows how difficult they are to answer. The following general guidelines are offered to help you determine if your youngster's difficulties are serious enough for you to consider obtaining some kind of outside assistance.

GUIDELINES FOR DETERMINING THE NEED FOR HELP

There are six interrelated factors to consider when trying to decide if your child may need professional help. These are as follows:

1) Age: How old was your youngster when the problems started?

2) Duration: For how long have the problems existed?

3) Nature of the problems: Are the problems relatively serious or relatively minor?

4) Context of the problems: Can the problems be understood as a reaction to some external stress or did they begin when things appeared to be relatively calm?

5) Previous attempts to resolve the problems: Have you, your spouse, or others tried to help your youngster resolve his or her problems? Did such attempts help, make things worse, or have no effect? Are you and your spouse in agreement about how to help your child or are you in conflict about what to do to help?

6) Your reaction to the problems: Do you or your spouse feel that your child's problems are leading to

a significant disruption in your family's equilibrium?

Age

Experience has taught parents and people who work with children that, at certain ages, youngsters typically evidence certain behavioral or emotional difficulties. For example, it is considered normal for two- to four-year-olds to become upset by even a very brief separation from their parents, and it is not surprising to find four- or five-year-olds getting into frequent squabbles when they try to play together. In addition, it is not uncommon for children anywhere from age six to sixteen to have a teacher or two whom they don't get along with, and for this to negatively affect their schoolwork; and finally, it is a rare adolescent who doesn't rebel or defy his or her parents from time to time.

On the other hand, there is reason for concern when a six-year-old continually refuses to separate from her mother in order to go to school, or when a ten-year-old doesn't have any friends because he's constantly fighting with his agemates. A fourteen-year-old who can't get along with any of her teachers and is failing all of her classes is obviously in need of some help. And a sixteen-year-old who defies all parental rules is probably experiencing some important emotional upset.

Duration

If your child has had some problem for a relatively long period of time, and he or she and you have been unable to resolve that difficulty, then obviously you should be more concerned than if the problem has just begun. For example, if your four-year-old has trouble separating from you when it's time for her to go to nursery school, you can reasonably expect that her anxieties will diminish over time. However, if her crying and protests persist or get worse over many months, you should begin to think of getting some help.

Nature of the Problem

Some problems, because of their very nature, are only of minor concern to parents—even when they persist over long periods of time. For example, nail-biting or thumb-sucking are rarely, in and of themselves, reason for parents to seek outside assistance. On the other hand, a child's persistent refusal to eat (when this is not caused by something like a stomach flu) presents a very serious problem, after a very short period of time.

Context of the Problem

Problems need to be looked at in the context of a child's circumstances. For example, it is not uncommon for a six-year-old to begin wetting his or her bed again after a family move or after the birth of a sibling. However, if such bedwetting were to begin without any clear external reason, it should be of more concern to parents.

Previous Attempts to Resolve the Problem

In most instances the most reasonable first step to take when concerned about some aspect of your child's behavior is to see if it will change of its own accord, or with a little help from you or your spouse. A large majority of childhood problems are resolved in this way. If the problems still persist, many parents wisely seek the advice and guidance of their own parents or other relatives, or talk with friends, neighbors or co-workers. They might also seek the opinion of the family doctor or pediatrician; or the counsel of a priest, rabbi, or minister; or if their youngster is in school, they might think to turn to their youngster's teacher, principal, or guidance counselor. Oftentimes people who do not live with a youngster from day to day will be able to offer parents a new perspective, and thus new ideas, for resolving a child's difficulties. However, if problems still persist, after all these avenues have been tried and proven unsuccessful, then it is reasonable to turn to a mental health professional for assistance.

In addition, professional help is especially indicated if you and your spouse disagree about how to help your child. In general, if parents are unable to resolve such differences, they will probably have limited success in helping their youngster solve his or her problems.

Your Reaction to the Problem

If either you or your spouse feels that your child's problems are beginning to seriously interfere with your family's sense of well-being, or if they seem to have aggravated problems between the two of you, then professional help may well be indicated.

Summary

In summary, there are a number of interrelated factors to consider when determining your child's need for help. It is important to note that you don't have to be completely convinced of the need for therapeutic help before contacting a mental health professional. Rather you might want to call such a person with the express request that he or she evaluate your child's need for treatment. Indeed, many therapists, before they will agree to treat a child or family, will themselves wish to conduct an evaluation in order to determine if therapy is necessary or likely to be of help.

DOES THERAPY ALWAYS HELP?

I do not want to give you the impression that psychotherapy is a solution to every child's or family's difficulties. Indeed, I have seen children, parents, and families invest time, energy, and money in a treatment which was not at all useful or that was even destructive.

However, I am biased in that I believe psychotherapy and related treatments can provide invaluable assistance for some people. My primary motivation for writing this book is to provide parents with a variety of information about this field, in the hope that this knowledge will enable them to locate the most appropriate therapist or agency, and the most beneficial treatment, for their child or family.

Chapter 2

EMOTIONAL PROBLEMS OF CHILDHOOD AND ADOLESCENCE

Children's and adolescents' development can be hampered by any of a variety of emotional difficulties. These range from relatively minor problems which seem to go away of their own accord to severe problems which prove to be quite long lasting and difficult to remedy.

In the sections which follow I will provide you with information about the most common emotional difficulties of childhood. I have divided all such problems into eleven general groupings,[1] as follows:

1) Disorders of Biological Functions
2) Physical Complaints with Possible Psychological Components
3) Disorders of Habit
4) Neurotic Disturbances
5) Suicide
6) Problems Associated with Speech and Language
7) Antisocial Behavior or Conduct Disturbances
8) Child Neglect or Child Abuse
9) Childhood Psychosis (Childhood Schizophrenia)
10) Problems Associated with Physical, Neurological, or Intellectual Handicaps
11) Special Problems in Adolescence

This division is not based on any particular theory of how childhood problems develop, nor do I attempt to rank order problems in terms of their severity. Rather, problems are grouped together because they have some important similarities.

I. DISORDERS OF BIOLOGICAL FUNCTIONS

This group of disorders encompasses a wide array of problems, whose primary similarity is that they involve difficulties in one or another area of basic biological necessity; namely, eating, sleeping, elimination, or sexual functioning.

Eating Disturbances

Parental instinct, common sense, and expert advice all agree that eating is not only a basic survival requirement but a profoundly important psychological event for children and their parents. Thus it is not surprising that when children evidence difficulties associated with eating, parents can become particularly distraught. At such times it is easy to lose sight of the fact that eating difficulties are quite common in infancy and childhood. I doubt if there is a parent who has not had some periodic concern about his or her youngster's eating behavior.

Some of these concerns are relatively minor, such as periodic misbehavior at the dinner table. Some, such as persistent refusal to eat, are quite serious and life threatening. In general, the less serious eating disturbances involve what can be called "difficulties associated with eating" such as: disruptive behavior at the dinner table or in restaurants, eating very slowly or too quickly, or wanting to eat at times other than those scheduled for family meals. The more serious disturbances can generally be categorized as "difficulties with what is eaten or not eaten" such as: self-starvation, chronic overeating which leads to obesity, and the ingestion of dangerous or poisonous materials.*

DIFFICULTIES ASSOCIATED WITH EATING

In general, these problems can be dealt with by parents alone or with the help of a pediatrician or family physician. Such problems need not be brought to the attention of a mental health professional unless they: 1) persist over long periods of time, 2) lead to serious deficiencies in a child's diet, or 3) are part of an overall pattern of friction between a child and his or her parents.

Causes

As is the case with any behavioral problem of infancy or childhood, difficulties associated with eating can be caused by any or all of the following factors:

1) Maturational forces: These are problems brought about as a result of expectable changes in a child's intellectual or emotional development. For example, the period from eighteen months until approximately three years of age is often referred to as the "terrible twos." Many, though not all, youngsters at this age (enamored of their burgeoning abilities to walk and talk) become insistent on doing everything for themselves; or they may insist that a parent do something for them in a manner exactly according to their wishes.

In terms of feeding behaviors, toddlers will often insist on feeding themselves, regardless of their competence at it. Other common problems range from the two-and-a-half- to three-and-a-half-year-old's insis-

* This classification system for eating disturbances is not ideal —since finicky eating, although properly included as a "difficulty in what is eaten or not eaten," is usually not a serious disturbance.

tence on eating the same small variety of foods, day after day, to the adolescent's perpetual dieting despite the fact that he or she is of normal weight.

2) Temporary situational factors: Transitory problems with eating can be caused by physical illness or by such emotional upsets as the birth of a sibling, the beginning of school, or a family move.

3) Resistance to parental wishes: In answer to the question, "Why do so many children eat poorly?" Dr. Spock answers, "Because so many parents are conscientious about trying to make them eat well."[2]

Indeed, the most common eating disturbances are those which result from a child's general opposition to his or her parents' demands. Youngsters' wishes to be independent and autonomous may lead them to want to do all things, including eating, at their own pace, in their own way. When pushed too hard to eat when they don't wish to, or to eat foods that they don't like, youngsters can begin to develop problems about eating.

4) Temperamental Differences: It is now commonly accepted that newborns come into the world with differences in temperament which play a significant role in how they behave. Some babies are quiet, some active; some demand a great deal of attention, some prefer very little. Some are born with huge appetites which are unaffected by illness, others have small appetites which are easily influenced by their physical or psychological state. These latter youngsters are more likely to develop temporary feeding difficulties, which can, under certain circumstances, become long-lasting problems.

In summary, difficulties associated with eating can be caused by a wide variety of factors. Unless these problems persist over long periods of time, or are part of a broader pattern of difficulties, most parents will not feel the need to seek professional help.

DIFFICULTIES WITH WHAT IS EATEN OR NOT EATEN

Included under this heading are such disturbances as the ingestion of dangerous or poisonous materials, called "pica"; self-starvation, commonly referred to as "anorexia nervosa"; and obesity.

Eating Dangerous or Poisonous Materials (Pica)

The continual eating of nonnutritious or inedible materials is called "pica." In the United States the problem often involves young children eating paint chips, which may in turn result in lead poisoning.

Since it is normal during the first twelve months of life for infants to bring everything to their mouth, pica is not generally diagnosed before this age. Nonetheless, the persistent eating of inedible materials, at any age, is a potentially serious matter, and should immediately be brought to the attention of a physician.

Self-Starvation or Anorexia Nervosa

A persistent refusal to eat in spite of good appetite, which leads to extreme weight loss, malnutrition, and in the more severe cases, death from starvation, is called "anorexia nervosa." Anorexia is a disorder occurring primarily in adolescent girls, although some boys do develop this syndrome.

A leading expert on eating disorders, Dr. Hilde Bruch, writes that the oustanding feature of this condition is a "relentless pursuit of excessive thinness."[3] She continues, "the urgency to keep the body as thin as possible is so great that anorexics will resort to any means, fair or foul, to keep their weight low. In an effort to remove unwanted food from the body many resort to self-induced vomiting, enemas, or excessive use of laxatives or diuretics. . . . By whatever means and for whatever reasons the weight loss is achieved, much of the typical behavior of an anorexic patient is related to the fact that she is a starving organism. . . . Like other starving people they are eternally preoccupied with food and eating, will not talk about anything else, become excessively interested in cooking, often taking over the kitchen. However, they will not themselves eat but will force food on others."[4] In addition, as a result of their undernutrition, many anorexics stop menstruating and evidence a variety of physical symptoms, such as anemia and low body temperature.

Despite their severe weight loss and skeletonlike appearance, these youngsters "declare that there is nothing wrong with them, they feel fine, they like the way they look, [and] they would feel guilty and hate themselves if they were to gain as much as an ounce."[5]

Another characteristic of anorexics is their hyperactivity and denial of fatigue. For example, "patients who continue in school will spend long hours on their homework, intent on having perfect grades."[6] These youngsters' incredible activity level typically continues until their emaciation is far advanced.

Anorexia is clearly a serious and life-threatening condition. If your youngster is persistently refusing to eat (despite the fact that she is of normal weight or is underweight) and is losing substantial amounts of weight, you should immediately seek professional assistance.

Obesity

"Obesity is a condition characterized by excessive accumulation of fat in the body."[7] It has been traditional to diagnose a person as being obese when his or her body weight is twenty percent greater than expected for his or her height and age. Recently more sophisticated measures of overweight have been developed, involving the counting and measurement of fat cells. Nonetheless most parents can apply the eyeball test to determine if their youngster is overweight: If your child looks fat, he or she is fat.[8]

According to Dr. Hilde Bruch, "Obesity in childhood, as in other age groups, is not a uniform condition. It may range from mild degrees of overweight during periods of temporary inactivity or overeating, to severe, grotesquely deforming weight excesses. . . . It may develop gradually from infancy or in a baby who may or may not have had a high birth weight, or there may be a sudden increase in weight, as much as forty or fifty pounds during a year, in a previously big but not overweight youngster."[9]

CAUSES OF OBESITY In one sense the cause of obesity is simple: "One accumulates fat by eating more calories than is expended as energy. In another sense the causes of obesity are unknown, since little is definitively known about the mechanisms of the regulation of body weight."[10]

Parents often wonder if their youngster's overweight is caused by a glandular disorder. According to Dr. Spock, "this is rarely the case, never if the child's height is within the normal range."[11]

Rather, obesity can be caused by a number of different factors, some of which are interrelated. For instance, some infants are born with large appetites and as a result they may become overweight during their first year of life. For some of these babies this begins a pattern of high caloric intake and overweight which continues throughout their childhood. Obesity may also develop later in a youngster's development. For example, it is not uncommon for children to overeat when they feel unhappy or anxious.

Of course, not all children who overeat do so because of unusually large appetites or as a result of emotional upset. For example, "there seems to be a normal tendency for many children, including the cheerful and successful ones, to put on extra weight in the seven- to twelve-year period. . . . Most of [these youngsters] . . . slender down as they get . . . into adolescence."[12]

One of the difficulties for many obese youngsters is that they are often unskilled and inactive in games, avoid athletics, and prefer sedentary activities. This inactivity results in a lower expenditure of calories which further contributes to the child's overweight.

TREATMENT As Dr. Bruch points out, "Changing a person's weight is not an easy task, and it is not compatible with healthy living if one attempts to push the weight below what is appropriate for an individual's body build. Within these constitutional limits, however, lasting weight reduction, though often difficult, is not an impossible enterprise."[13]

There are basically two distinct therapeutic approaches to weight reduction: 1) dietary regulation and 2) psychotherapeutic intervention. The basic purpose of dietary regulation is to help the youngster reduce his food intake and increase his physical activity. The aim of psychotherapy for obese youngsters is to help them "in developing a more competent, less painful, and less ineffective way of handling their problems."[14] Of course, dietary regulation and psychotherapeutic treatment are not mutually exclusive interventions. Indeed some therapies, such as the behavioral treatments (See Chapter Six) combine aspects of both of these modalities.

In general, for any treatment approach to be successful, the youngster and his or her family must be motivated to seek help, and must be willing to accept the fact that weight reduction is best achieved in a slow but steady manner.

Disturbances of Sleep

Sleeping, like eating, is one of the necessities of life. Parents are rightfully concerned when they notice that their child is experiencing some difficulties in this area. On the other hand, since all youngsters go through periods of time when some aspect of their sleep is disrupted, it is often difficult for parents to know if any particular sleep problem is serious enough to warrant professional attention.

In general, difficulties associated with sleeping such as interrupted sleep, difficulty in falling asleep, and nightmares, go away of their own accord, or with the sympathetic help of parents.[15]

However, if your youngster's sleep problems persist over long periods of time, or seriously interfere with his day-to-day functioning, or are part of a more general pattern of disturbance, you should call your pediatrician or family physician.

RESTLESS OR INTERRUPTED SLEEP

Physical illness or discomfort, situational stresses such as family moves, the first day of school, or simply the aftereffects of an especially exciting day (such as a birthday) can all lead to temporary periods of restless sleep.

Resistance to Going to Sleep

At various ages, and in different ways, it is not uncommon for children to resist going to bed or to sleep. At younger ages a child may postpone bedtime by demanding that a parent read just one more story or by saying that he needs a glass of water. At older ages there may be bitter controversy about what's a "fair bedtime." (Youngsters always seem to know at least one classmate whose bedtime is much later than theirs.)

Nightmares

According to some experts[16] nightmares may begin as early as two years of age, although bad dreams usually are not a significant complaint in children under the age of five years. Between the ages of five and six, youngsters may be particularly upset by bad dreams and many need quite a bit of parental reassurance before they can return to sleep.

Fears Related to Sleep

Fears of the dark and/or fears that there are ghosts or monsters under the bed, in the closet, or outside of the window are not uncommon in young children. Typically such fears go away after a period of time. Meanwhile parents can be supportive and reassuring to their youngsters. Ridiculing or making fun of the child's fears, will if anything, prolong a child's period of fearfulness.

Excessive Sleep (Hypersomnia)

If your child begins to sleep for significantly longer periods of time than is normal for him, and if this excessive sleep persists over a period of time, your youngster may well be undergoing some period of emotional upset. Typically, youngsters who evidence a period of hypersomnia are depressed. (See the section of childhood depression further on in this chapter.) Excessive sleep, however, can also be caused by physical factors, and for that if for no other reason, you should contact your pediatrician.

Enuresis

In general, a youngster should be considered enuretic if he is wetting involuntarily after the age of six and if this occurs more frequently than once a month.[17] (The term "bedwetting" is often used interchangeably with the term "enuresis," but bedwetting is not a precise name for this condition since some youngsters also wet during the day.) It is important to note that enuresis is not at all uncommon. Studies have shown that about twenty percent of youngsters aged six to seven wet during the day or night.[18] Ilg and Ames write, "Many perfectly normal children are as much as eight years of age before they [achieve full bladder control]."[19]

There has been considerable research and writing about the possible causes of enuresis. Speculation has ranged from purely physiological explanations to those which are totally psychological. Many experts now believe that enuresis can be caused by any of a number of factors; that for "each child a different set of circumstances may be responsible for the symptom."[20]

It is important to note that the overwhelming majority of children who are enuretic at age six or seven are no longer wetting at age fourteen.[21] This may be one reason why many parents do not seek professional help for this problem. Another reason may have to do with the fact that many youngsters are so embarrassed about or ashamed of their bedwetting, that they unmistakably indicate their wish not to discuss it.

There are two disadvantages, however, of ignoring this

problem. The first is medical: Enuresis is sometimes, although rarely, caused by any of a number of physical problems.* The second is psychological: By the time that a youngster is seven or eight, his embarrassment about the wetting may lead to problems with self-image and self-esteem, or may result in the youngster's avoiding certain situations, such as staying over at a friend's or going away to summer camp.

On the other hand, focusing on this symptom can make a youngster more self-conscious or anxious than he is already. In summary there is no "one right thing to do" if your youngster is enuretic. In general, it is a good idea to mention this to your child's pediatrician (who can determine if a physical examination or medical tests will be necessary). In addition, if either you or your youngster is particularly upset by the wetting, you may wish to consult with a mental health professional who has experience in the treatment of enuresis.

Encopresis

A child is considered to be encopretic when, beyond the age of four or five, he or she regularly passes formed, semiformed, or liquid stools into underwear or pajamas, and when this is not caused by an organic difficulty or by physical illness.[22] While not as common a childhood problem as enuresis, encopresis affects a significant number of children; estimated at one to two percent of all youngsters.[23]

Encopresis is a particularly distressing symptom for parents, and a disabling one for children. Encopretic children may experience ridicule and ostracism from their peers, and scolding from their parents and teachers. Children with this problem typically feel embarrassed and ashamed about their soiling, and may begin to develop

* One author found that physical problems accounted for about one to three percent of enuretic difficulties.

problems with their self-image or self-esteem. In addition, encopretic children are often in some amount of physical discomfort. In one study a majority of such youngsters reported abdominal pain.

Pediatricians and mental health professionals have recently reported a number of different kinds of treatment approaches which have proven successful in helping encopretic youngsters. In general, these approaches combine 1) medical intervention, involving the clearing of any impacted fecal matter, 2) education of the youngster about normal bowel functioning, and 3) retraining of the child in proper bowel control.[24]

There is divided opinion about the necessity and benefits of psychotherapy in the treatment of encopresis. Some experts believe that therapy is indicated only if medical treatment and retraining prove unsuccessful. Others believe that psychotherapy is a helpful adjunct to whatever other methods are being employed. There is no disagreement, however, about the importance of calling your child's pediatrician, who will evaluate your youngster's physical condition before beginning a treatment program.

Problems Associated with Sexual Functioning

Many parents wonder whether or not their child's sexual curiosity, interests, or behaviors are "normal." Parental concern typically revolves around 1) their child's masturbatory activity, 2) their youngster's involvement in sexual games such as looking at, exposing, or touching the genital area, or 3) their son's engaging in effeminate behaviors. (Masculine or tomboyish behaviors of girls seem to be of little concern to most parents.)

MASTURBATORY BEHAVIOR

Masturbatory behavior begins in infancy and typically continues throughout childhood. Usually by school age, youngsters have learned that masturbatory activities are not easily accepted by adults, and they therefore stop displaying such behaviors in public. Masturbatory activity should not be of any concern to parents unless it becomes a major preoccupation of the child to the exclusion of other activities, or if he engages in such behavior in circumstances which are socially inappropriate. In such instances a pediatrician or mental health professional should be contacted to discuss whether the child's behavior requires an evaluation.

SEXUAL PLAY

Sexual play during childhood is quite common. It is also not uncommon for adolescent boys to "engage in group sexual play such as showing their genitals or touching and feeling the genitals of their friends. This form of behavior is not a precursor of later homosexuality."[25] As is the case with masturbation, sexual play should not be of concern to parents unless it becomes a major preoccupation of the child or adolescent, or if he or she engages in such behavior in socially inappropriate ways.

EFFEMINATE BEHAVIORS OF BOYS

Some parents are concerned when their sons engage in behaviors which they view as "typically feminine," such as artistic activities or playing with dolls, or when these boys avoid behaviors which their parents view as "typically masculine" such as competitive games or sports. However, there is no evidence that such youngsters will develop sexual difficulties in later life.

On the other hand, it is possible to delineate some effeminate behaviors in boys which, when continued beyond the preschool years, seem to be precursors of sexual identity difficulties in adolescence and adulthood. These behaviors are as follows:

1) Cross-gender clothing preferences (wearing girls' dresses, putting on the mother's shoes, wigs, makeup,

or jewelry, or creating dresses or skirts out of towels or other materials).

2) Verbal statements expressing the wish to become a girl or to grow up to become a woman.

3) Taking female roles in fantasy games such as that of actress, mother, grandmother, or witch, while protesting if given the role of a boy or man.

4) Imitating the gestures and mannerisms of a woman, including exaggerated swaying of the hips, effeminate gait, feminine inflection of speech, etc.[26]

If your youngster is evidencing such behaviors beyond the age of five or six, you might wish to seek professional help for him, since these activities may be the forerunners of either transsexualism or transvestism.*

HOMOSEXUALITY (GAY ORIENTATION)

A gay (the term "homosexual" has so many strong negative connotations that I will use the word "gay," instead) is defined as a person whose "strongest emotional and sexual responses are aroused by individuals of the same rather than of the opposite sex."[29] The gender identity of gays is normal, that is to say that men think of themselves as men and women think of themselves as women.

Until recently there had been substantial controversy as to whether a gay orientation, in and of itself, was an indication of emotional disorder. This issue should now be resolved since both the American Psychological and the

* Transsexualism is a "rare disorder of sexual identification in which the child, though biologically normal, fails to develop a sense of same-sex identity and indicates a desire to change sex."[27]

Transvestism is "literally cross-dressing, or putting on the garments of the opposite sex, but most commonly the term has been used to describe what would be more precisely called 'fetishistic cross-dressing' where putting on the clothes of the opposite sex 'produces clear-cut, unquestioned genital excitement, generally leading to masturbation and orgasm. . . .' "[28]

American Psychiatric Associations have officially declared that gays as a group are no more emotionally distressed than are heterosexuals.

Sexual Preferences in Adolescence

Sexual preference and sexual orientation (be it gay or heterosexual) tend to become more manifest during adolescence. Therefore, during this period of time, parents may grow increasingly aware that their youngster is interested or involved in sexual experiences with same-sexed partners. Some parents may be particularly distressed by this knowledge.* Such parents should understand that their youngsters are going through a period of sexual exploration and uncertainty, and have not yet developed a crystalized sexual orientation. In other words, not all of these youngsters will remain actively gay as adults. Nonetheless, many of these youngsters will have a gay orientation in adulthood. The knowledge that such a sexual preference is not an indication of emotional disorder will not reassure all parents and some may wish to seek professional help for their son or daughter. If you are such a parent, you should be aware of the fact that a therapist cannot (indeed, most will not try to) change a teenager's sexual preferences unless that young person is interested in such change. On the other hand, therapy may be useful for those youngsters who are confused about their sexual preferences or for those teenagers who need support in accepting their orientation. In addition, counseling may prove helpful to parents who are confused or upset about their youngster's sexual behaviors.

* If you are interested in reading further about homosexuality, I recommend a book entitled *Now That You Know: What Every Parent Should Know About Homosexuality* by Fairchild and Hayward, published by Harcourt, Brace and Jovanovich, 1979.

II. PHYSICAL COMPLAINTS WITH POSSIBLE PSYCHOLOGICAL COMPONENTS

At some point in time almost all youngsters will complain of headaches, stomachaches, nausea, or fatigue. Oftentimes these are the result of a cold, flu, or other physical illness. It is also not uncommon for parents to sometimes suspect that their child's physical complaints are either manufactured or exaggerated; this being the youngster's way to try to avoid some unpleasant task or to gain some special attention. It is usually impossible for a suspicious parent to know for sure whether or not a youngster's complaints are in any way fabricated or embellished. And, of course, an occasional instance when a child exaggerates an ache or pain is perfectly expectable. (I'm sure many readers can think of instances in their own childhood when they attempted to avoid doing something by inventing or exaggerating a stomachache or headache.)

Concern arises, however, when youngsters' complaints are commonplace and chronic. Some parents may think it wise to ignore their youngster's complaints, insisting that the child is physically fine. While this may work in the short run, it does not address the important underlying question, namely: Why does their child need constantly to invent physical ills in order to avoid normal childhood responsibilities? Therefore, I recommend, if your child is constantly complaining of one or another physical ailment, that, first, you take him to your pediatrician for a medical examination; if, as you expected, there are no medical problems, I would then recommend that you have your youngster evaluated by a mental health professional.

Psychosomatic or Psychophysiological Disorders

Psychosomatic illnesses or the more current term, "psychophysiological disorders," are quite different from the minor physical complaints which I have just discussed. These disorders are physical illnesses in which psychological "processes are believed to play an important role in the etiology and course of the disease."[30]

Researchers in the field of psychophysiological disorders believe that chronic anxiety or stress over the course of time, in certain individuals (probably because these people have some constitutional vulnerability) can indirectly lead to damage in cell tissue in various parts of the body. Commonly affected organ systems in children include: the stomach or duodenum (leading to "peptic ulcer"), the intestines (leading to "ulcerative colitis," "regional enteritis," or "irritable bowel syndrome"), and the respiratory system (leading to bronchial asthma).

TREATMENT

It should go without saying that all youngsters with psychophysiological disorders should be under the care of a physician. In addition, parents should be aware that both individual and family therapy is sometimes recommended as one part of a treatment program. (Dr. Salvador Minuchin and his colleagues have reported on the benefits of family therapy in the treatment of a variety of psychosomatic disorders.)[31]

III. DISORDERS OF HABIT

The behaviors included under the heading "disorders of habit" are those which involve the manipulation or movement of parts of the body in repetitive fashion. These include thumb-sucking, nail-biting, rocking, head-banging, hair-pulling, and tics.

The actual term "disorders of habit," although commonly used, is an unfortunate choice of words as it can give the misleading impression that a youngster is engaging in a "bad habit," from which she should be broken. Rather, some habit "disorders," such as thumb-sucking or nail-biting, are more appropriately understood as perfectly normal ways for youngsters to discharge daily tensions or frustrations. Other habit disturbances, such as head-banging or hair-pulling, may be cause for more parental concern, since a youngster may harm himself as a result of such behaviors. Finally, the less serious tic disturbances are usually left untreated, while more serious tic disorders are treated with medication.

Thumb-sucking

Thumb-sucking is a perfectly natural and normal behavior in infancy and early childhood. As a famous child psychiatrist, Dr. Leo Kanner, points out, "The notion that [thumb-sucking] is bad did not arise until the end of the nineteenth century [when] dentists and especially orthodontists asserted that thumb-sucking results in malformation of the jaws and palate."[32] Indeed, many parents' only concern about thumb-sucking is that it can possibly do some harm to their youngsters' teeth. In response to this concern, Dr. Spock writes that whatever effect thumb-sucking may have on a child's baby teeth, it "has no effect on the permanent teeth that begin coming in at about six years of age. In other words, if the thumb-sucking is given up by six years of age—as it is in the majority of cases—there is very little chance of its hurting the permanent teeth."[33]

Many authors point out that the primary difficulties with thumb-sucking result from the measures which are taken to eliminate it. Ilg and Ames's counsel to parents seems quite wise; they suggest that "the more you try to stop sucking in the early stages, that is, during the first three years or so, the stronger it may become and the harder it may be to stop later." They add that "by the time the child is four or five, if you haven't made too much fuss earlier, the behavior will usually drop out by itself or with just a little help from you."[34]

Since thumb-sucking is expected to begin to disappear at about five to six years of age, its continuance beyond that time can be viewed as a sign of immaturity. If your child evidences other signs of immaturity, such as enuresis, fears of separation, or fears of the dark—to name just a few—you might wish to consult with your pediatrician or a mental health professional.

Nail-biting

Nail-biting, like thumb-sucking, is another very common behavior in childhood. Unlike thumb-sucking, however, nail-biting does not typically disappear with age. In general, nail-biting is understood as an indication of nervous tension.

Authors generally agree that nagging or punishing nail-biters usually doesn't stop them for very long because they seldom realize that they are biting their nails, in the first place. If you would like your child to overcome this habit, you will need to help him or her find ways to reduce the underlying tensions which lead to it.

Rocking

Rocking is a tension outlet which usually starts at about forty weeks of age. This behavior typically increases until the age of two and a half or three and a half, and generally disappears at about age four. Even if rocking continues beyond the age of four,[35] it should not be a matter of concern unless it occurs in combination with other signs of tension or immaturity.

Head-banging

Head-banging is considered to be somewhat similar to rocking in that it is a stereotyped rhythmic movement whose purpose is to reduce tension. However, it is a far more distressing symptom than is rocking since it can cause bumps or welts on the front or back of a youngster's head.

In one study of head-banging, the author found that such behaviors were quite common in children under two years of age.[36] (Dr. Spock writes that head-banging typically begins during the second half of the first year of life.)[37]

In very young children head-banging is often a result of fatigue or lack of stimulation. In somewhat older youngsters it can be an angry response to some frustration.

Most authors advise parents not to scold or punish young children for head-banging, but rather to let it run its course. Of course, parents should protect their child, for example by padding the sides of a crib. In those instances where head-banging is a result of understimulation, a child should be picked up, played with, or otherwise occupied in some interesting activity.

If your child continues to bang her head beyond the age of four, especially if this behavior is frequent and continues after you provide him or her with other things to do, you should contact your pediatrician for advice.

One further note: Ilg and Ames reassure parents that it's unusual for a head-banger to do himself or herself any real harm. Of course, your pediatrician should be immediately contacted if you suspect that your child has hurt herself as a result of head-banging.

Hair-pulling

Hair-pulling is a quite uncommon symptom.[38] At times very young children will pull out a small amount of their hair, in response to some obvious upset. This behavior should not necessarily be of concern to parents. However, if hair-pulling continues for any appreciable period of time, or if it becomes disfiguring (children can pull out enough hair to create bald spots or to make themselves totally bald) parents should seek some immediate professional help. (Ilg and Ames suggest that parents provide hair-pulling youngsters with a tight angora cap to wear. This allows children "the satisfaction of pulling at something, i.e., the fuzz on the cap, but protects the hair.")[39]

Tics

Tics are defined as sudden, purposeless, and repetitive movements or utterances. They are brought about by involuntary contractions of skeletal muscles in one or more parts of the body. Tics can be voluntarily suppressed for short periods of time, but this effort cannot continue indefinitely, and the tics return.

Tics are not uncommon in children: In one study twelve percent of youngsters aged six to twelve were found to have tics; in another study five percent of all seven-year-olds were reported to have tics.[40]

The most common tic condition (called "acute transient tic disorder of childhood") is characterized by eye blinks or facial tics. Sometimes the whole head, torso, or limbs may be involved. In rare cases involuntary sounds may be uttered (these are called "vocal tics"). This condition is usually self-limiting; meaning that the tics go away without any special treatment.

For a smaller percentage of youngsters the tics are more generalized, involving movements of the head, shoulders, neck, trunk, arms, and legs. In addition, these youngsters utter involuntary sounds, either in the form of inarticulate noises or, at times, words or short sentences which may or may not be obscene. This symptom picture is generally referred to as "Gilles de la Tourette's syndrome." (Recent authors in this field have distinguished between those youngsters for whom the symptoms disappear over time—labeling this disorder "subacute tic of childhood or adolescence"—and those for whom the disorder persists into adult life—labeling this condition "chronic multiple tic" or "Gilles de la Tourette's syndrome.")

There is substantial disagreement about the causes of tic disorders. Some authors postulate an essentially psychological cause—tension and anxiety. Others feel that tics are the result of an interaction between emotional and organic factors. However, recent research seems to indicate that tics are caused primarily by organic factors.[41]

Given the transient nature of most tic conditions, treatment is usually not recommended. However, in the case of the less common but more generalized tic disorders, treatment has been found to be both necessary and helpful. The treatment of choice is drug therapy, using the medication haloperidol, trade name "Haldol." (See Chapter Seven for a discussion of this medication and its use in the treatment of tics.) It is now generally believed that psychotherapy is not an effective primary treatment for tics, although it may be useful in helping a youngster deal with his or her feelings about having this condition.

IV. NEUROTIC DISTURBANCES

In everyday conversation the term "neurotic" may be used to refer to any behavior which is considered to be atypical or abnormal. (If used in this fashion, "neurotic" could refer to almost all of the behavioral problems discussed in this chapter.)

More precisely, neurotic disturbances are characterized by the fact that 1) if left untreated, they *tend not* to disappear with age, 2) they lead the child or adolescent to experience significant emotional upset, and 3) they can lead to difficulties in many areas of a youngster's functioning. In addition, many neurotic youngsters, unlike children with other types of problems, acknowledge that they are having difficulties and are eager to get help. Psychotherapy is recommended for a large majority of children who are diagnosed as neurotic.

Phobic Reactions

A phobia may be defined as a specific recurring fear, which 1) persists over a long period of time, 2) is not affected by parental reassurance, and 3) dominates a child's feelings and external activities. Typically, phobic "children find their fears illogical and distressing and want to be rid of them."[42]

Unlike phobias, fears are considered to be a normal and universal part of childhood development. It would be difficult to imagine a youngster passing through his or her early years without experiencing at least some common childhood fears, such as separation from parents, being lost or abandoned, being in the dark, going to sleep alone at night, being frightened by bad dreams, or of being chased or hurt by monsters or other imaginary creatures.* Such childhood fears are relatively temporary and tend to diminish or disappear as a child matures.**

On the other hand, phobias, as defined above, persist for long periods of time and are experienced by the child as being unreasonable. As is the case with other neurotic disorders, phobic reactions should be brought to the attention of a mental health professional.

Many different types of psychotherapeutic techniques have proven successful in the treatment of phobic reactions. Therapy is made easier by the fact that most children are quite unhappy about their phobias and are, therefore, highly motivated to make use of professional help.

School Phobia

A somewhat special kind of fearfulness associated with leaving home to go to school is called "school phobia."

Some period of fearfulness about leaving mother to go to school is not uncommon in nursery school, kindergarten, or the first grade. Oftentimes a mother's accompa-

* Observation of normal children indicates that the specific objects or situations which they fear change as they grow older. For example, younger children may fear such things as loud noises, strangers, or unfamiliar objects; things which do not usually frighten somewhat older youngsters, who may, in turn be frightened of monsters, imaginary creatures, or of the dark.

** It is not only unhelpful but sometimes traumatic to force a child to face the object or situation which is most feared. Sensitive parents will, at times, meet with success if they gradually introduce the feared object to their child in a way that does not produce excessive anxiety; for example, by introducing a small puppy at a safe distance to a child who is frightened of dogs.

niment and the sympathetic response of a teacher will be enough to resolve this difficulty after a relatively short period of time.

However, some youngsters' fears do not disappear. At times parents and/or the school, believing that a child's fearfulness is an indication of a general level of immaturity, will decide to wait for another six months or year before expecting the youngster to attend school. This course of action may be reasonable for nursery-school- or kindergarten-aged children. However, for children much older than five, it may unwittingly serve to strengthen a child's tendency to avoid anxiety-provoking situations.

In their book on child psychiatry, Chess and Hassibi provide a vivid description of school phobia as follows: "The child begins to have vague complaints around breakfast time. He feels nauseated and has a headache, and his stomach feels 'funny.' He may begin to cry, cling to his mother, and beg to stay home. If forced to go to school, he may refuse to enter the classroom or feel miserable when sitting there. He worries about what is happening at home in his absence or about what has happened to his mother. He may call his home simply to ask if everything is fine, or he may want to be reassured that his mother will be home when he returns. He is seemingly relaxed when he is back but begins to worry at bedtime about the next morning. He may be forced to go to school, but he does not perform in the school. In the majority of cases, the child finally refuses to go to school. . . ."[43] If the child is allowed to remain at home over any period of time, he "soon becomes homebound, isolated, and fearful of venturing outside by himself."[44]

School phobic reactions are also not uncommon in older children or adolescents. In these age groups the resistance to going to school is usually not voiced directly. Rather these youngsters develop a wide variety of physical complaints which serve as their reason for not going to school. Typically such youngsters will deny any reluctance about going to school and state that they are eager to return to their classes as soon as they are feeling better.

School phobia is a disabling symptom for children and

adolescents, interfering with learning and the development of social relationships. Therefore parents are well advised to seek psychotherapeutic help for their school phobic child. This syndrome is one which is well known to mental health professionals (it has been estimated that two to eight percent of referrals to child guidance clinics are for school phobia)[45] and one for which a wide variety of treatment methods have proven successful.

Anxiety Reactions

Anxiety, like fear, is a universal experience of childhood and adolescence. In its milder forms anxiety "is experienced by children as a feeling of apprehension and general irritability accompanied by restlessness, fatigue and such [physical] components as headaches, a 'funny feeling' in the stomach, or heaviness in the chest."[46] Anxiety is of special concern to parents when it is present to such an extent that it interferes with their child's day-to-day functioning.

Anxiety can be defined as a feeling which stems from the anticipation of danger, the source of which is largely unknown or unrecognized. Anxiety can be distinguished from fear, which is defined as a response to a consciously recognized source of danger (whether such danger is real or imaginary).

It should be noted that anxiety itself and the attempts to reduce feelings of anxiety are believed to be at the root of many emotional difficulties of childhood. As was discussed in earlier sections of this chapter, most of the habit disturbances, all psychophysiological disorders, and many sleeping difficulties (as well as many problems to be discussed subsequently) are believed to result, at least in part, from a child's inability to effectively cope with what he or she experiences as overwhelming feelings of anxiety.

However, there are some syndromes in which anxiety itself is the primary manifestation of distress. For example, the chief concern of some parents who bring their children for professional help is that their youngster is generally anxious or tense. Manifestations of anxiety may include a general state of unhappiness, a preoccupation with specific worries, and an accompanying need for reassurance (for example, that the child will not be left alone). Such reassurance, however, only serves to lessen a youngster's worries for a brief period of time, as the worries typically return with equal intensity after some period of time. Overly anxious children are typically fearful of any new situation, of strangers, and of bodily injury. As a result they often have few, if any, friends. Their anxiety can be so preoccupying that they cannot easily pay attention in school and they may, therefore, function far below their intellectual potential. (Academic problems caused primarily by anxiety are sometimes difficult to distinguish from learning disabilities. See Chapter Three.) Overly anxious children are in need of therapeutic help so that they can learn to cope with the expected and unexpected stresses that all youngsters face in the course of growing up.

Anxiety Attacks

Anxiety attacks are a type of anxiety reaction which deserve separate discussion. They can occur in children with a previous history of chronic anxiety or in children who seem to be generally well adjusted.

An anxiety attack is a terrifying experience for a child and his parents. Although each child will evidence somewhat different reactions, anxiety attacks can be characterized as follows: The child becomes panic stricken, there is shallow breathing, rapid heartbeat, and trembling. Oftentimes the child becomes afraid that he is dying, or reports that everything seems "unreal" or "strange." The attacks are accompanied by physical sensations of dizziness or lightheadedness, sweating, and stomach distress, sometimes including vomiting. The attacks may last from a few minutes to an hour and may occur repeatedly over the course of a day. If such attacks occur at night, the child will awake in a state of panic and will be terrified of going back to sleep.[47]

There is not any one "right" thing to do to help a

youngster in the midst of such an attack. In general an attitude of calmness on your part and reassurance that you will stay with your child until he is feeling better is most helpful. If you are unable to handle the situation on your own, you may need to call your pediatrician or family physician for advice.

After such an attack a child may be "perplexed as to what has actually happened to him. He may accept whatever excuse or explanation is offered him, or he may half-heartedly try to find a cause in what somebody else had done to him."[48]

Obsessive-Compulsive Syndromes

Obsessive thoughts or "obsessions" are ideas, fears, or doubts which irresistibly and continuously intrude themselves into a child's awareness. Although these thoughts are experienced as being strange or foreign, the youngster cannot rid herself of them, despite a strong desire to do so.[49]

Younger children will typically evidence the presence of obsessive thinking by asking seemingly endless questions or through the repeated expression of fears and worries, often about their own or their parents' health or safety. Older children and adolescents will, at times, try to conceal such thoughts from others, feeling ashamed or embarrassed about them.

Compulsive behaviors or "compulsions" typically occur in combination with obsessions. Compulsions are defined as repetitive, stereotyped behaviors which the child feels compelled to perform; fearing that if she does not, then something terrible will happen.[50] Younger children will often involve their parents in their compulsions, demanding, for example, that the parents join with them in some bedtime or early-morning ritual. Older children and adolescents will often go through such rituals without involving or even informing their parents; for example, by secretly washing their hands compulsively. Parental attempts to stop or limit compulsive behaviors are typically unproductive or counterproductive (since such interventions only serve to increase a child's anxiety, which leads to an increase in compulsive activity).

It should be noted that such compulsive behaviors as bedtime rituals are normal in two- to three-year-olds, as is the unrelenting and repetitive questioning of three- to four-year-olds. In times of stress older children may revert to these earlier behavioral patterns.

If obsessive or compulsive behaviors persist over long periods of time in a child over six years of age, you would be well advised to have the youngster evaluated by a child therapist.

Depressive Reactions

A depressed child is one who is characteristically sad, unhappy, and either without interest in the outside world or whose interest is not easily caught. He feels rejected and unloved and is not easily comforted. He frequently suffers from insomnia or other sleep disturbances. He prefers solitary activities rather than playing with siblings or friends. If he has any complaints at all, it may be of a stomachache or headache, rarely of feeling depressed.

Periods of depression are expected and normal reactions to such external events as illness, hospitalization, separation, or loss. However, if a child is overtly depressed for any significant period of time, and if this is not in response to some clear external stress, a parent would be wise to seek professional help.

DEPRESSION IN ADOLESCENCE

Periods of depression during the teenage years are not uncommon. These periods are typically in response to a real or perceived failure, disappointment, or loss. The depression generally lifts over the course of time, as the young person meets with success in some other endeavor or relationship.

However, some adolescents remain depressed over long periods of time and their unhappiness is not affected by changes in their circumstances. For such young people depression seems to be more in response to internal distress than to external events, and outside help is indicated.

V. SUICIDE

Suicidal Thoughts and Feelings

Suicidal thoughts and feelings in children and adolescents are more common than one might expect. One author reports that approximately seven to ten percent of all referrals to child psychiatric clinics are for threatened or attempted suicide.[51]

While almost all parents would think to get immediate help for a youngster who made a suicide attempt, some parents are unconcerned when their child or adolescent simply talks of suicide. Such lack of serious concern may be reasonable if the youngster's remark is an offhanded statement made in response to some understandable disappointment, such as, "I'm so embarrassed, I wish I were dead!" A comment like that is not typically an indication of a wish to hurt oneself.

On the other hand, if a youngster is generally depressed and in this context talks of suicide, parents should take this as an indication that their child or adolescent is experiencing significant psychological distress and the parents should promptly seek professional assistance.

Suicide Threats

Suicide threats are distinguished from suicidal thoughts in that the youngster talks of planning to kill himself or herself. At times this talk is in the context of an angry interchange with a parent—"If you don't let me go out tonight, I'm going to kill myself!" In such circumstances the youngster may only be voicing a passing thought; an idea which she has no real intention of carrying out. On the other hand she may be making a statement of intent; one which she will try to carry out. If your youngster were to make such a statement, I would suggest asking her if she is making a serious threat. If she says she is, or if you suspect she is, you need to treat the situation as a potential emergency and arrange for some immediate help. (See Chapter Fifteen.)

It is even more ominous if a youngster talks of planning to kill herself, when this is not in the context of some angry interchange with a parent. In such circumstances you would be well advised to seek immediate professional assistance. You should not try to take responsibility for trying to decide if your youngster is imminently suicidal. since such a judgment is not always easy to make. (See Chapter Fifteen.)

Suicide Attempts

If your youngster has made a suicide attempt, even if it is one that could not possibly have led to serious physical harm* (for example, ingesting five aspirin) you should treat this as a psychiatric emergency and obtain immediate help. (See Chapter Fifteen.)

MYTHS ABOUT SUICIDE

All too many people still believe in myths about suicide; ideas which experts in the field have long since proved false.

The most dangerous myth is that people who talk about suicide don't commit it. The fact is that of any ten adults who kill themselves, eight have given some definite warn-

* Mental health professionals distinguish between suicide attempts which may have led to death or serious physical consequences and attempts which could not possibly have had such severe outcomes. At times the less serious attempts are called "suicide gestures." It is important to realize that even so-called "gestures" are signs of serious distress which may be precursors of more life-threatening acts.

ings of their suicidal intentions.[52] In one study of children who killed themselves, at least half of them had previously discussed, threatened, or attempted suicide.[53]

Another dangerous and erroneous myth is that children are incapable of killing themselves. Although it is true that suicide in young children is rare, the fact is that youngsters are capable of killing themselves and sometimes do. Adolescent suicide is not rare; adolescents can and do kill themselves.[54]

VI. PROBLEMS ASSOCIATED WITH SPEECH AND LANGUAGE

"Speech can be defined as the mechanism whereby sounds, when used together in certain accepted ways, produce verbal language. Verbal language refers to the symbolic meaning attached to these word groupings."[55] Children with speech disorders often manifest emotional difficulties and children with psychological problems may manifest some of their symptoms with a speech disturbance.

In this section I will discuss four problem areas associated with speech and language; namely the delayed onset of speech, problems with articulation or pronunciation, stuttering, and elective mutism.

Slow or Delayed Onset of Speech

Most babies begin "to use a few sounds that mean something when they are in the neighborhood of a year old."[56] By about eighteen to twenty months children are expected to have a small vocabulary of about fifteen to twenty words. And by about two years of age most children are able to communicate their needs and wants.

However, as with all behaviors, children can show a wide range of development and still be perfectly normal. Dr. Spock writes that "a majority of late talkers, even those who don't talk much until three, have normal intelligence and some of them are unusually bright."[57] Furthermore, many youngsters who evidence delayed or poorly articulated speech, even beyond the age of three, are perfectly normal except for their speech functioning. (These children may need speech therapy in order to catch up with their peers.) Chess and Hassibi write that the "prognosis in children with speech lag is good. Most children will have normal speech by 8–9 years of age."[58]

In general, if you have any concerns about your youngster's speech development, you should contact your pediatrician. If significantly delayed speech is found, then an evaluation will be necessary so as to rule out any medical, intellectual, or emotional difficulties.

Problems with Articulation or Pronunciation

The most common articulation difficulty in children is their use of what is commonly referred to as "baby talk." Some youngsters retain an infantile manner of speech as they grow older, while others revert to this kind of speech in response to emotional stresses such as the birth of a sibling. However, the use of baby talk is not always related to emotional factors. At times it can result from a child's difficulties in properly discriminating sounds or from delayed fine-motor coordination. In general an evaluation by a speech and language specialist is indicated if a child consistently uses baby talk beyond the age of four.

The use of baby talk in response to some clear external stress is usually accompanied by other signs of upset; for example, wetting accidents in a child who has previously been dry or by a resistance to separation from parents in a youngster who was previously more independent. Such behaviors should gradually recede with time and parental reassurance. If they do not, you should call your pediatrician or a mental health professional.

Stuttering

Stuttering is a disorder in which the flow of speech is disrupted by spasmodic blocks or repetitions of sounds or words. Stuttering generally begins either between the ages of two and four, when the child is just beginning to speak, or between the ages of six and eight, when a youngster has just begun school and is learning to read.[59]

Most youngsters who stutter simply outgrow this difficulty, without any special intervention. However, other youngsters evidence a worsening of their dysfluency and also begin to show signs that they are becoming self-conscious about their speech.

Authors and researchers disagree about the causes of stuttering; some believe it is due primarily to physical factors, others believe it is caused by emotional influences. Finally, some authors have concluded that no one factor seems to explain all stuttering and they therefore postulate that it may be caused by any of a combination of psychological and physical influences.[60]

Informed parents find themselves in a dilemma when trying to decide what to do when they suspect that their child is developing a stuttering problem. On the one hand there is the awareness that an overreaction to the symptom may lead a youngster to become self-conscious and anxious about his or her speech, thus potentially leading to a worsening of the condition. On the other hand disregard of the stuttering can delay one from obtaining needed help.

The most prudent course of action would be to have your pediatrician evaluate your child's speech during a routine checkup, or to have your child's speech evaluated during a routine preschool screening. (Such screenings are performed by most school systems, before a child enters kindergarten or first grade.) If a speech problem is found in a preschooler, the treatment usually involves parental guidance aimed at reducing the stresses in the youngster's everyday life. Speech therapy, per se, is generally not begun until a child is in school.

Traditional forms of psychotherapy, although helpful in reducing the secondary effects of stuttering such as self-consciousness and low self-esteem, have not been particularly helpful in eliminating the stuttering behavior itself. (Most forms of psychotherapy have been found to provide beneficial short-term effects, but the stuttering often returns when the child experiences a period of stress.) Thus psychotherapy, without concomitant speech therapy, is usually not indicated. The most promising treatment results are those which have been reported by investigators who have developed sophisticated speech-therapy techniques designed to remediate the underlying physical blockages leading to stuttering.*

Elective Mutism

"Elective mutism is a condition in which the child limits his verbal transactions to few or all members of his own family and stubbornly refuses to talk to other people. The situation is usually brought to light when the child enters school and fails to communicate with his teachers and peers. Some children whisper; others remain totally mute."[61] Typically such children begin to be ostracized and picked on by classmates. Attempts by teachers and other adults to encourage or force the youngster to talk are generally unproductive. Elective mutism is usually best treated with some form of psychotherapy.

VII. ANTISOCIAL BEHAVIORS OR CONDUCT DISTURBANCES

" 'Conduct disorders' are defined as those conditions in which the main problem lies in socially disapproved behavior. It can include delinquent acts such as stealing, playing truant, arson, serious mischief involving damage to other people's property, mugging, assault, or murder. It may also include nondelinquent acts such as defiance, lying, acting up in school, or not getting along with other children, as shown by bullying."[62]

Problems Associated with Aggressive Behavior

Experts in child development (and in other fields, as well)

* I am particularly impressed by a treatment program designed by Dr. Ronald Webster. Information about this program can be obtained by writing to him c/o Stuttering Project, Hollins College, Hollins, Virginia 21020.

agree that aggression is a natural part of human behavior. Some feel that aggression is based on biological instincts and is necessary for survival. Other theorists view aggression as a reaction to frustration. (These writers suggest that frustration is, itself, a normal part of human experience. They point out that infants and young children are often frustrated since they cannot meet their own needs, and because parents can never provide all a child's needs the instant that such wants are expressed.)

Whatever its cause, aggression and aggressive behaviors are found in all infants, children, and adolescents. Aggression can be detected quite early in life; in one research study it was found that mothers can reliably distinguish when their infants are crying because they are hungry, and when they are crying out of anger or frustration.[63]

As infants develop the capacity to interact more actively with their environment, their aggressive behaviors can take such forms as the biting and hitting of others. The biting of other children who are interfering with their play is not uncommon in one- or two-year-olds, but this should give way to hitting by age three or four.[64] By the time a child is going to school, teachers and parents begin to expect that a child can express his or her anger through words. Nonetheless, occasional hitting or fighting between classmates and siblings is tolerated as a normal part of childhood behavior.

The dividing line between a normal amount of aggressive behaviors and a frequency or intensity of hostile behavior that is unhealthy, is very difficult to draw, because parents and teachers have widely differing standards for acceptable amounts of such behaviors. (Things become more complicated when parents disagree amongst themselves, or when parents disagree with teachers about what is or is not acceptable.)

The following guidelines are offered to help you determine when it may be necesssary for you to seek professional help for your child's aggressive behaviors:

1) When his or her aggression is of frequent concern to you, or to other adults.

2) When the aggression continues despite various attempts you have made to help your youngster channel such feelings in appropriate ways.

3) When the aggression seems to be in response to everyday frustrations that most other youngsters seem able to cope with. Periods of aggressive behavior, in response to situational stress (such as a divorce or a family move) are not uncommon. However, if the aggressive behavior continues well after the stress has passed or if it results in dangerous or destructive behavior, then it should be of more concern.

4) When the aggressive behavior leads to physical harm to another child or adult.

5) When the aggressive behaviors are one part of a more general disturbance: for example, if your child is also involved in such activities as stealing, vandalism, fire setting, truancy, and so on.

Lying

It is perfectly normal for all children to lie from time to time. Before the age of four, deviations from the truth are not considered lies, since young children often cannot make distinctions between fact or fiction. Even at ages five to six there is still a good deal of exaggeration and storytelling, although at these ages youngsters usually can distinguish between real and make-believe. At age seven and above, youngsters will still periodically lie in order to avoid punishment or criticism or because they are embarrassed or ashamed of their actions. Distortions of the truth are also common when parents are trying to determine which child started a fight or engaged in some misbehavior.

Since common sense dictates that most children will lie, or at least distort the truth, from time to time, most parents accept such behaviors, so long as they occur only periodically. But here, as in some other situations, parental standards vary widely, and some parents may become quite concerned about even infrequent lying. If you are concerned about your youngster's lying, feel free to consult with your pediatrician or a child therapist. They will be able to tell you whether you have reason for concern, or whether your expectations for your child seem unreasonably high.

Stealing

Children between one to three years of age may often take things which don't belong to them. Such behavior is not considered stealing since youngsters at these ages have yet to fully develop the capacity to differentiate between things which belong to them and things which don't. By the time a child is four he generally does know the difference between his and others' belongings. Some preschoolers do nonetheless take others' belongings, but this is usually as a result of an inability to control their impulsive desire to have another's property and is typically not done in a secretive manner.[65]

Stealing, in which a youngster knowingly and secretly takes something which belongs to someone else, can become a problem at about age five, and seems to be most prevalent in the five- to eight-year-old range. Oftentimes such behaviors, with sensitive yet firm parental guidance, will cease. However, if such behavior is frequent and/or continues beyond the age of about eight or nine, it should be reason for concern. Child therapists generally view frequent stealing as an indication that a child is feeling that adults are not providing for his or her emotional or physical needs. (Stealing may also be one part of a more general pattern of delinquency. Delinquency will be discussed in detail later in this section.) Such feelings may reflect a true paucity of material comforts or a psychological experience of being neglected or deprived, or both. Stealing may occur despite the fact that parents feel that their child is being provided with a good deal of material and emotional support.

Fire Setting

Preschoolers who play with matches or set fires, although doing so knowing that such behavior is prohibited, usually do not fully understand the possibly dangerous consequences of their acts. School-aged children who set fires typically do know that their actions are potentially dangerous, but set fires because of, or despite, this understanding. Whatever the reasons for such behavior—and it has been found to be quite varied[66]—fire setting, in children over the age of five, is such a potentially dangerous behavior that it should immediately be brought to the attention of a mental health professional.

JUVENILE DELINQUENCY

A "juvenile delinquent" or "juvenile offender" is defined as someone whose behavior has resulted in his being brought to the attention of the juvenile court. The label "juvenile delinquent" is not used for children who commit similar anti-social acts, but who, for whatever reason, have never reached the jevenile court's attention.[67] (There is a lower age-limit to this classification, since preschoolers, regardless of their behavior, will typically not be referred to as delinquent.) "Juvenile delinquency" is a confusing label since it can be applied to youngsters who present widely varying behavior patterns: ranging from adolescents who have committed such major crimes as rape or armed robbery to younger children who are truant from school or who run away from home.

The term "juvenile delinquent" is more properly applied to those young people who 1) evidence a recurring pattern of antisocial behaviors, 2) evidence little or no regard for the rights or feelings of others, 3) have little concern for their own safety or for the consequences of their acts, and 4) tend to associate in groups or gangs with other young people who share similar values and behavior patterns. (Before adolescence these youngsters may be referred to as "predelinquent.")

Treatment for predelinquent and delinquent youth is often quite difficult. For younger children it necessitates a coordinated effort among the school system, the parents, and mental health specialists to help design and provide a closely supervised and structured environment. If such an environment, for whatever reasons, cannot be provided, out-of-the-home placement may be indicated.

For older children and adolescents who are continually

involved in delinquent acts and for whom outpatient services have proven unsuccessful, out-of-the-home placement is often necessary. In some communities halfway houses or "therapeutic communities" have been established to provide such youngsters with a well-supervised and structured therapeutic environment on a round-the-clock basis. Such programs typically focus on using the guidance and support of older adolescents who have "gotten their act together" to help younger adolescents do likewise. More traditional psychotherapy is typically only helpful with that small percentage of delinquent youth who are already well motivated to change their behavior patterns. Psychotherapy may be quite helpful to youngsters after they have had a positive experience in a half-way house or therapeutic community.

VIII. CHILD NEGLECT AND CHILD ABUSE

An "abused child" is a youngster "under sixteen years of age whose parents or other legal guardians have inflicted physical injury or sexual abuse on him, have allowed such injuries and abuses to be inflicted on him by others, or have directly or indirectly created a substantial risk to his physical safety. A "neglected child" (or a "maltreated child") is one "whose parents have failed to provide him with adequate food, clothing, education, shelter, or medical care, even though they are financially able or have been offered help to do so. Failure to provide supervision and guardianship, excessive corporal punishment, the habitual use of alcohol and addictive drugs that create substantial risk for the child or lower the parental capacity for care, and the abandonment of children are covered under this definition."[68]

"Because child abuse (and child neglect) is a nationwide problem found among all social classes, most states have passed laws requiring teachers, nurses, social workers, and doctors to report cases of suspected child abuse (and neglect). . . . In some states, failure to report a suspected case of . . . abuse (or maltreatment) is punishable by law."[69]

There is much evidence that parents who abuse or neglect their children were themselves abused or maltreated when they were young. This understanding of the cycle of abuse has increasingly led mental health professionals and legal authorities to try to provide abusive parents with support and counseling.

If you are abusing or neglecting your child (or are fearful that you may be close to doing this), you should be aware that there are many places to go for help. In addition to a variety of mental health agencies and professionals (described in Chapter Four), there is also an extensive network of local chapters of a national organization called Parents Anonymous, where parents can turn for help.

Some features of Parents Anonymous which people find particularly helpful are the following:

1) P.A. is anonymous and no one needs to use more than his or her first name.

2) There are no membership fees, dues, or other costs.

3) P.A. offers help in a group setting, where people who are concerned about their parenting share their problems, experiences, and support.

4) The group leaders of P.A. are parents who themselves have had experience with abuse.*

* For further information about Parents Anonymous, readers can write to the national headquarters:
22330 Hawthorne Boulevard, Suite 208
Torrance, California 90505
or can call toll free (outside of California) 800-421-0353 or (from within California) 800-352-0386.

IX. CHILDHOOD PSYCHOSIS (CHILDHOOD SCHIZOPHRENIA)

Childhood psychosis or childhood schizophrenia* is a general term which encompasses a wide variety of severe emotional disturbances. A youngster may evidence signs of such profound difficulties as early as three to four months of age, or may show no symptoms at all until adolescence.

The behavior of psychotic youngsters is markedly and blatantly different from that of their age-mates. Parents of psychotic children, therefore, almost invariably know that there is something wrong with their youngster (although some may understandably try to minimize or deny this painful realization). Though it is of no comfort to these parents, other readers may be reassured to learn that childhood psychosis is quite rare, significantly less than one child in a thousand receiving this diagnosis.[70]

Varieties of Psychotic Disturbance

As has been mentioned, childhood psychosis is not a uniform condition, but rather a general designation for a variety of severe disturbances. Indeed, there is substantial controversy about how to differentiate among different types of psychosis, and even whether the term "psychosis" should continue to be used as the general label for all such youngsters. For purposes of simplicity I will continue to

* Some authors believe that there are important distinctions between childhood psychosis and childhood schizophrenia. They write that schizophrenia should only be diagnosed if a youngster has delusions, hallucinations, or is incoherent. For the purposes of this book, however, I will use the terms "psychosis" and "schizophrenia" interchangeably.

use the term psychosis and will differentiate among three general types of this disturbance as follows:

1) Early infantile autism
2) Developmental child psychosis or atypical childhood psychosis, and
3) Adolescent onset psychosis

EARLY INFANTILE AUTISM

One type of psychotic disorder, signs of which are first noticeable in infancy, is called "early infantile autism."* This disturbance was first described by Dr. Leo Kanner who wrote, "The common denominator [among all these children] is [their inability] to relate in ordinary ways to people and situations from the beginning of life."[71]

Unlike most babies, autistic infants show little or no interest in people, including their parents. Almost all normal infants by the time they are three or four months of age begin to evidence an interest in, and attachment to, the important caretakers in their lives—typically their mother or mother-surrogate. For example, infants will smile to their mother's smile, follow her with their eyes, stop crying when she picks them up, protest if she tries to put them down, and lift up their arms in anticipation of being picked up.[72]

On the other hand, mothers of autistic children report that their infants showed little or no interest in them or other people, from birth on. "Almost every mother [interviewed by Dr. Kanner] recalled her astonishment at the child's failure to assume at any time the usual anticipatory posture preparatory to being picked up."[73]

(A lack of what might be considered to be a normal amount of sociability on your infant's part is, of course,

* Many researchers believe that autism is such a special condition that it should not be considered as one type of psychotic disorder. Parents of autistic children are encouraged to contact the National Society for Autistic Children for further information. (See Appendix A.)

not usually an indication of autism, nor even of any emotional or other kind of disturbance. Infants, like children, adolescents, and adults, have different temperaments, and some are simply less active and sociable than others.)

In addition to their aloofness, autistic children evidence any or all of the following difficulties:

1) Severe speech and language disturbance: Some children fail to develop any speech, while others stop talking after a period of apparently normal language development. Some youngsters evidence bizarre speech behaviors such as "echolalia" in which a child parrots back words said to him or her. For example, a girl who is asked "Would you like some milk?" will use the phrase "Would you like some milk?" each time she's thirsty. Relatedly, such youngsters typically refer to themselves as "you"; "Give it to you" meaning "Give it to me."

2) An overwhelming need to have their immediate environment remain *exactly* the same: Any change in their environment, no matter how small, can lead an autistic youngster to intense panic or anger. Such children will engage in ritualized and stereotyped behavior, apparently fulfilling their need to have everything around them, including themselves, remain the same.

3) A fascination or preoccupation with inanimate objects: Interactions with such objects are preferred over contact with parents or siblings.

4) Unusual body movements: "The autistic child often shows repetitive body movements such as rocking back and forth. There is a winglike flapping of the hands when excited which may be quite characteristic of such children. Often there is unusual body posturing."[74]

5) Diminished or heightened sensitivity to external stimulation, such as sound or pain: For example, an autistic youngster may be easily startled by a soft noise or may have absolutely no reaction to a loud,

unexpected sound. Some autistic youngsters have reportedly been exposed to situations which should have produced severe pain—for example, being accidently burned—without apparently experiencing any discomfort.

6) A total absence of a sense of personal identity.

7) A marked variability of intellectual functioning, with some areas of superior or normal capacity interspersed with areas of functioning which are so significantly below normal that the youngster is considered to be retarded.

DEVELOPMENTAL CHILD PSYCHOSIS (ATYPICAL CHILDHOOD PSYCHOSIS)

This is a very general diagnostic category which encompasses all youngsters who, between the ages of thirty months and twelve years of age, manifest "a profound disturbance in relations with people and a multiplicity of bizarre behavior."[75]

"The disturbance in emotional relation is always gross and sustained, and is evidenced by such symptoms as: lack of appropriate [emotional] interaction, social ineptitude, inappropriate clinging . . . lack of peer relationships and a lack of empathy with people in general."[76]

The bizarre behavior may be manifested by any or all of the following:

1) Continual, excessive, and seemingly illogical anxiety, evidenced by panic attacks in response to everyday occurrences and an inability to be consoled when upset

2) A variety of peculiar emotional reactions, including a lack of appropriate fearfulness, unexplained rage reactions, and extreme mood swings

3) Self-mutilation; for example, hitting or biting of oneself or severe head-banging

4) A variety of bizarre beliefs, ideas, or fantasies, and/or preoccupation with morbid thoughts or interests

In addition, these youngsters may evidence any or all of the behaviors characteristic of autistic youngsters, such as:

5) An overwhelming desire to maintain sameness in their environment
6) Any of a variety of speech abnormalities, including echolalia
7) Diminished or heightened sensitivity to stimulation
8) Peculiar body movements, including bizarre posturing or unusual hand or finger movements

Symbiotic Psychosis
This type of developmental psychosis is usually first manifested between the ages of three and five. "Generally it is ushered in by a separation from the mother, i.e., via sickness, the birth of a sibling, or placement in a nursery school. The child reacts to this separation with intense anxiety [and panic]."[77] The youngster may begin to hallucinate (see or hear things which aren't there), may talk in a very bizarre fashion, or may become very aggressive; biting or hitting parents or caretakers. In addition, these children may evidence any or all of the behaviors which characterize other psychotic youngsters.

ADOLESCENT ONSET PSYCHOSIS

Psychosis or schizophrenia in adolescence is marked by a continuing deterioration in most areas of functioning, as follows:[78]

1) Withdrawal from all outside interests, including school, work and friends
2) Decrease in energy evidenced by a general listlessness and apathy
3) Mood swings which become more and more pronounced and less and less related to external events
4) Increasing preoccupation with abstract ideas,

which eventually become clearly bizarre and dominate the adolescent's thinking

As the adolescent's functioning continues to deteriorate he or she will evidence a variety of abnormalities, the most characteristic of which are:

1) Disturbances in language or communication: The psychotic adolescent may talk in a jumbled, incoherent fashion. A listener will note that the person just isn't making "any sense."

2) Disturbances in thought: "The major disturbance in . . . thought involves delusions which often are . . . bizarre . . . for instance, [an adolescent's] belief . . . that his feelings . . . thoughts or actions are not his own . . . [but rather] are imposed upon him by some external force. . . ."[79]

3) Disturbances in perception: The most common of these are auditory hallucinations in which a person hears voices of familiar or strange people commenting on her behavior or telling her what to do.

4) Feelings of loss of identity: The sense of self that gives the normal person her feeling of individuality, uniqueness, and self-direction is frequently disturbed. The adolescent may wonder who she is and wonder in a bizarre fashion about the meaning of her existence.

What Causes Childhood Psychotic Disorders?

Although a tremendous amount of research has been conducted to understand the causes of the various psychotic disorders, there is no commonly accepted theory as to what leads to these severe disturbances.

Many authors believe that these disorders are caused by genetic, biochemical, and/or neurological factors. Others believe that many, if not all, of the psychotic disturbances are caused by psychological or social determinants. And some authors have concluded that they are caused by a combination of factors, which may vary from youngster to youngster.

Treatment

"Every weapon in the psychiatric armory has been used in the treatment of childhood psychosis."[80] These include the use of a variety of medications (See Chapter Seven), various types of outpatient psychotherapy, placement in special classes and programs, and all types of inpatient and residential treatments (See Chapter Fourteen). Oftentimes a combination of treatments is employed; for example, residential treatment and the use of antipsychotic medications. Obviously, the best treatment for any individual youngster will depend on his or her current age, the age of onset of the psychosis, and the severity and nature of the symptoms.

X. PROBLEMS ASSOCIATED WITH PHYSICAL, NEUROLOGICAL, OR INTELLECTUAL HANDICAPS

Physical Handicaps

Youngsters with physical handicaps, such as hearing impairments, visual impairments, or motor handicaps, are subject to all of the emotional and behavioral problems of childhood, plus the special psychological stresses associated with their particular disability. In addition, families, and especially parents of handicapped youngsters, also must cope with more than the usual amount of emotional stress and strain.

"Most parents with physically handicapped children do

not have easy access to guidelines for their management, particularly during infancy. Without knowing what the techniques are for compensatory stimulation or what their babies are capable of doing, the general tendency is for parents to . . . make insufficient demands for task accomplishment and/or impulse control. The child's reactions depend, in part, on his temperamental qualities. He may become passive and more helpless than necessary, or he may become a tyrant with tantrums whenever frustrated. . . . When the child's distress is expressed intensely, as in the tantrums or hostile and destructive acts, management problems and social unacceptability can become a major issue."[81]

Parents of handicapped youngsters are, therefore, well advised to seek guidance and support from people who have had experience in caring for such children. There are national and local organizations whose purpose is to help youngsters and parents cope with the special difficulties associated with various handicaps. A selected list of these organizations is presented in Appendix A.

Organic Brain Syndromes

It is important to note that behavioral deviations which might seem to be the result of emotional upset or psychological difficulties, can, at times, be caused by any of a number of brain-related injuries or disorders. Some of these symptoms might include confusion, disorientation and misidentification of objects, people, and places; illusions; hallucinations; agitation; panic; incoherent speech; the occurrence of frequent, terrifying dreams; memory disturbances; obsessive concern with details; deficiences of attention and concentration; impulsive behavior; or rage reactions.[82] The presence of any of these symptoms, of course, does not ordinarily mean that a youngster is suffering from an organic brain disorder. (Indeed, such syndromes are relatively rare.) Rather, the presence of such symptomatology should lead parents to have their child examined by a physician.

EPILEPSY

The most common type of organic brain syndrome is epilepsy. Epilepsy is defined as "a periodic, recurrent state of impaired consciousness associated with abnormal brain activities that may be clinically manifested by localized or generalized seizures."[83] Epilepsy is divided into two general categories. The first includes grand mal and petit mal varieties of epilepsy. The second includes Jacksonian seizures and temporal lobe epilepsy. In "grand mal" seizures, the person loses consciousness and has convulsions. In "petit mal" attacks, the attack is so brief (twenty to thirty seconds) that the child does not fall or lose control of himself or herself, but may just stare or stiffen momentarily. Parents may become aware of this disorder because their youngster is observed to be frequently staring into space with a dreamy look on his or her face, or because of the short period of confusion that such youngsters experience after such a seizure. "Jacksonian seizures" are "characterized by the twitching of a specific group of muscles, always in the same area [or] when the seizures are . . . sensory . . . they are felt as a tingling sensation in one part of the body."[84] Temporal lobe seizures are usually accompanied by disturbances of affect and thinking processes, and at times, atypical motor phenomena.

As Dr. Spock points out, "Every case of epilepsy should be investigated by a doctor familiar with the disease. Though the condition is usually a chronic one, there are several drugs that are helpful in stopping or reducing the frequency of the spells."[85]

Since epilepsy is a chronic illness, it can lead to a variety of secondary emotional difficulties. Chilren who suffer from grand mal seizures may avoid participating in a variety of age-appropriate activities out of a fear of unexpectedly losing consciousness, or they may become preoccupied with the reaction of their peers to their difficulty. "Children with petit mal epilepsy may go undiagnosed for long periods of time and may be accused of a lack of motivation to concentrate and learn. Their confusion . . . [may be] . . . considered a sign of strangeness, and their inability to stop 'daydreaming' an indication of defiance of authority. They may be hyperactive, have poor concentration and be generally unpredictable."[86] Children who have a variety of seizures "may present with a puzzling picture of sudden rage, unwarranted happiness, or terror that is impervious to environmental responses and vanishes as suddenly as it appears."[87]

A therapist's role in helping epileptic youngsters and their parents involves treating signs of secondary reactions to the disease such as low self-esteem and discouragement in the face of a chronic illness, as well as refusal to take, or carelessness in taking, medications. Parents may also need help to refrain from overprotecting their epileptic youngsters.

Mental Retardation

The term "mental retardation" is used to refer to a widely varying group of individuals who "by virtue of impairments in their intellectual functioning and behavior, are handicapped in coping with their . . . environment."[88]

Mental retardation is divided into four categories, based on an individual's score on an intelligence test. (See Chapter Eight for a discussion of intelligence testing.) These categories are as follows: Mild (IQ score of between 55 and 69), Moderate (IQ between 40 and 54), Severe (IQ of 25 to 39), and Profound (below 24).

It is estimated that three percent of the population of the United States—approximately six million people—are mentally retarded. About two million of these individuals are diagnosed as retarded in early childhood, while most of the remaining youngsters are identified during their elementary-school years. It is important to note that the overwhelming majority, about eighty-five percent, of retarded youngsters function within the mildly retarded range and are, therefore, capable of remaining at home during their school years, and of being productively employed and living independently in their communities in adulthood. In addition, many youngsters with more significant retardation may be educated in their local school systems, if provided with special educational services. (See Chapter Fourteen for a complete discussion of special educational services which school systems are required to provide to all handicapped youngsters.) Parents of more profoundly retarded children will have to decide whether short- or long-term residential or institutional placement is in their youngster's best interests.

SPECIAL PSYCHOLOGICAL PROBLEMS OF RETARDED YOUNGSTERS AND THEIR PARENTS

It is generally accepted that mentally retarded children are much more likely than other children to develop emotional and behavioral disturbances. Some typical problems that develop are prolonged dependency, an exaggerated need for affection, difficulties in separating from parents, and similar indications of immaturity.

For their parts, parents of retarded youngsters must cope with a tremendous amount of stress. "Even under the best of circumstances a retarded child places considerable strain on his family. . . . guilt, confusion, disappointment, denial [unrealistically high or low expectations], and some degree of rejection are [feelings commonly experienced by parents of retarded youngsters]."[89]

Because of the special difficulties faced by retarded youngsters and their families, it is usually a good idea for parents of these children to contact local chapters of the national organizations involved in the special needs of retarded youngsters (see Appendix A) for support, information, and guidance. Parents should be aware that, compared to the need for such help, there has been until recently a relative paucity of mental health services for retarded youngsters and their families. This situation has gradually been changing, and the organizations listed in

Appendix A should be able to help parents locate needed services in their geographic area.

XI. SPECIAL PROBLEMS IN ADOLESCENCE

The term "adolescence" refers to a developmental period roughly between the ages of twelve and nineteen. This period begins "with the biological changes of puberty and ends when the social status of adulthood is attained."[90] The time of onset of puberty varies widely for youngsters; generally between the ages of eleven and fifteen for girls and between twelve and sixteen for boys.

Adolescence can be divided into three subperiods, as follows:

1) Early adolescence begins with puberty. During this period of youngster's "behavior may show a disorganized, erratic quality along with a decreased willingness to accommodate to the expectations of . . . parents and others. [This period is also characterized by] wide mood swings and periodic bouts of feeling ill-treated and unloved."[91] During the period of early adolescence the young person may grow increasingly dependent on friends and schoolmates for advice and emotional support. Correspondingly, the early adolescent may spend less and less time at home and may evidence relatively little interest in his or her parents' ideas and guidance.

2) "Mid-adolescence follows puberty by about 1 to 1½ years. . . . Characteristically, this is the age when adolescent rebellion begins. . . . [There may be] . . . period(s) of irritability, [of] wide mood swings, and [of] rapidly changing feelings. Obedience to parental dictates [are often] replaced by conformity to peer-group standards and loyalties. . . . Sexual explorations [may] begin [at this time]."[92]

3) "Late adolescence is a period of transition as

> the young person consolidates his identity. . . . [The late adolescent] is able to be [more] selective and discriminating in his friendships . . . and is able to form and maintain [more] truly intimate relationships."[93]

It is important to note that youngsters' reactions to puberty and adolescence vary tremendously. Indeed, it is this variability which can make it so difficult for parents to know whether some particularly troublesome behavior is part of an expected phase or whether it is a sign of more important distress.

The "Tasks" of Adolescence

During the course of adolescence young people must face and resolve a variety of developmental issues. The nature, variety, and complexity of these issues will make it clear why adolescence can be such a stressful time of life. These issues are as follows:

BIOLOGICAL AND PHYSICAL MATURATION

"Early adolescents are preoccupied with adjusting to their new physical growth and developing sexuality. . . . Adolescents, therefore, are extremely self-conscious about their physical appearance and any deviation from 'normality.' "[94] For example, early or late maturation can exert a heavy psychological toll on adolescents. "Boys who mature later [may] not be able to compete with their peers in sports and are usually ignored by [those] girls who are interested in heterosexual relationships. Early maturing girls, on the other hand, [may be] neglected by their same-sex friends and [may be] perceived as heterosexual partners by older boys earlier than [their] emotional development would allow for such commitments. These adolescents [may] experience feelings of loneliness and depression and [may] become oversensitive in regard to their position among their peers."[95]

In addition, deviations in physical appearance which may be of little significance in early childhood or adulthood may become terribly important to self-conscious teenagers. Being skinny or short, overweight or tall, can become a reason for significant embarrassment and emotional upset.

THE DEVELOPMENT OF SEXUAL INTERESTS

As interest in sexuality develops, younger adolescents often begin to have intense fantasies or crushes, oftentimes toward people who are unavailable to them, such as movie or rock stars, teachers, or friends of older brothers or sisters. Adolescents do not typically feel comfortable talking about such feelings with their parents, and instead rely on friends to share such intimate concerns.

Over time, sexual interest and fantasy should focus on more age-appropriate and available partners. Dating, either in groups or individually, becomes the expected and accepted mode of relating. Some adolescents may choose lifemates at this time, though it is more usual for teenagers to have intense, short-lived relationships, and to develop more permanent relationships later in their lives.

Despite the relatively transitory nature of most adolescent romances, a young person may feel quite enamored with his or her current partner and will typically react quite angrily to parental comments—even if the adolescent harbors similar misgivings—about any negative qualities of the boyfriend or girl friend.

Sexual activity, whether necking, petting, or intercourse, is usually begun more as an exploration of one's masculinity or femininity than as mature, intimate love; the capacity for such love is not typically achieved until adulthood.

INDEPENDENCE AND PSYCHOLOGICAL SEPARATION FROM PARENTS

"One of the major achievements of adolescence is emotional independence. . . . Most adolescents approach independence with considerable ambivalence. They long to be self-sufficient and resent those on whom they depend.

Yet they are loath to trade the security and comforts of continued dependence for the uncertainty and responsibility of independence."[96] This inner struggle between the contradictory desires of independence and dependence are reflected in adolescent behaviors and attitudes which may appear to be amazingly inconsistent.

Some teenagers seem to want nothing more from their parents than to be provided with food, shelter, clothing, money, and transportation. Adolescents may expect such things as a matter of course (especially since they received such "basics," without arguments, when they were younger). On the other hand, teenagers expect in other ways to be treated as adults; for example, in terms of coming and going when, where, and with whom they please, and in being allowed to deal with such responsibilities as school, jobs, and household chores without any parental overseeing or "interference."

PEER GROUP RELATIONSHIPS

As one aspect of the process of achieving independence from parents, adolescents typically begin to rely on friends and acquaintances for emotional support and companionship. During this period of time the opinions and values of peers become more accepted and important than those of parents. Relatedly, parents' opinions and values may be dismissed out of hand or treated with contempt, as in "That's just not the way things are done anymore, Mother!"

FORMATION OF MORAL VALUES

Adolescents are typically intolerant of ambiguity, and therefore may be attracted to moralistic and idealistic positions on such highly complicated issues as justice, international relations, politics, and religion.

EDUCATIONAL AND VOCATIONAL CHOICES

"During middle and late adolescence a number of key decisions of lifelong importance must be made. These will be very much affected by the adolescent's earlier school or vocational achievement—or lack thereof—but will also be influenced by pressure from parents and by pervading social and cultural values."[97]

FORMATION OF "IDENTITY"

The enduring and consistent resolution of issues concerning sexual interests, friendships, values, relationships with parents and family, and educational and vocational choices leads young people to develop a sense of their own "identity." The formation of this identity, although it will go through changes in adult life, is a very crucial developmental achievement. Its successful completion generally occurs in late adolescence or early adulthood.

When Is Psychotherapy Indicated?

Adolescence is a period which can be experienced as particularly stressful by young people and parents alike. It can thus be particularly difficult for parents to differentiate age-expected emotional difficulties from problems which will prove to be more enduring and handicapping. The difficulty in deciding whether an adolescent may need professional help is complicated by the fact that many teenagers will not agree to accept such assistance, especially when it is recommended by their parents. (See Chapter Nine for a discussion of obtaining help with or for an adolescent.)

Some indications of an adolescent's need for professional help are as follows:

1) Long periods of emotional withdrawal from friends as well as from family: Although it is not uncommon for teenagers to withdraw somewhat from family involvement, it is not typical for young people to lose all interest in friendships. This "withdrawal may be first manifested as a reluctance to attend school and refusal to associate with friends [which

is] rationalized as a lack of common interest'"[98] Although many friendships in adolescence may be short-lived, a lack of interest in any friends is an indication of something other than a normal phase.

2) Lack of energy and depression: Although it is common for adolescents to become periodically depressed, especially in response to some academic failure or social disappointment, it is also typical at this age for this depression to lift, although not necessarily as quickly as it appeared. Long periods of time which are marked by lack of energy and by depression, especially when not in response to some external stress, is an indication of more basic unhappiness.

3) School-related difficulties: While it is not uncommon for adolescents to have periodic difficulties with one or two teachers or academic subjects, a more global problem with school should be taken as a sign of a more significant distress. A sudden plummeting of grades and academic interest may be an early indication of some important emotional upset.

4) Drug and alcohol use: It is common, nowadays, for adolescents to do some experimenting with such drugs as alcohol and marijuana. Although there is no evidence that such experimentation necessarily leads to alcoholism or drug abuse, some young people may begin to use these and other drugs in such quantities and with such regularity that their day-to-day functioning is impaired. Such a pattern is an indication of important underlying difficulties and should be cause for professional intervention.

5) Chronic family tension: It is not uncommon for family tension to be increased during adolescence, with protests about family rules, curfews, responsibilities, and so on. However, chronic unrelenting tension, marked by a total lack of meaningful communication, or continual defiance of parental rules, or a disregard for even minimal levels of cooperation is not typical and is reason to seek outside assistance.

In this chapter, I have discussed a wide variety of emotional problems of childhood and adolescence, as a way of helping you determine if your youngster is in need of therapeutic help. Of course, this discussion is not intended to replace the advice of a mental health professional or physician who, in consultation with you, is in the best position to make such a recommendation.

Chapter 3

HYPERACTIVITY AND LEARNING DISABILITIES*

During the past twenty years parents, educators, and mental health professionals have become increasingly aware of a group of youngsters who have a variety of academic, behavioral, and emotional difficulties. These children may evidence any combination of the following symptoms:

1) Overactivity
2) Short attention span
3) Distractibility
4) Impulsivity
5) Poor coordination
6) Difficulty in either making or getting along with friends
7) Behavioral problems at home, often resulting from overactivity and impulsivity
8) Difficulties with learning, despite average or above average intelligence

A confusing array of diagnostic labels have been applied to such children, including minimal brain damage, minimal brain dysfunction, minimal cerebral dysfunction, hyperactivity syndrome, hyperkinetic syndrome, attention deficit disorder (with or without hyperactivity), perceptual handicap, perceptual disability, educational handicap,

* Joan Axelrod, M.Ed. is the coauthor of this chapter.

dyslexia, developmental dyslexia, learning disability, or specific learning disability.

As one author has written, "If a child happens to live in the state of Michigan, educators refer to him as a perceptually disabled child. If the child is a resident of California, his education may be provided if he is classified as an educationally handicapped or neurologically handicapped child. In Bucks County, Pennsylvania, he will be placed in a class for children with language disorders. If he moves from California to New York State, he will change from an educationally handicapped to a brain-injured child. On the other hand, if he moves from Michigan to Montgomery County, Maryland, he will stop being a perceptually disabled child and become a child with specific learning disabilities."[1]

WHAT DO ALL THESE TERMS MEAN?

Minimal Brain Damage

Some professionals argue that the underlying problem of all these youngsters is that "something is wrong with their brains." This belief was originally based on the observation that adults and children who have suffered brain injuries manifested a variety of behavioral and learning difficulties. It was then assumed that similar disturbances in other children's behavior could be attributed to undetected minor brain injuries. Thus the term "minimal brain damage."[2] However, the logic underlying this assumption is faulty. The fact that demonstrable brain injury leads to such problems as distractibility and hyperactivity does not mean that distractibility and hyperacitivty are always caused by brain injury. Indeed, many youngsters who are distractible and hyperactive, or who have learning problems, are found to have absolutely no evidence of brain injuries or damage. It thus became obvious that the term "minimal brain damage" was not a useful label, and it is no longer commonly used.[3]

Minimal Brain Dysfunction

Some authors, still believing that these youngsters' problems resulted from something being wrong with their brains, substituted the label "minimal brain dysfunction" or "minimal cerebral dysfunction" for "minimal brain damage." The use of the term "dysfunction" instead of "damage" was meant to indicate that although these youngsters had no demonstrable brain injury, it was still assumed that their brains were not functioning exactly right.[4]

The use of the term brain dysfunction (or MBD) has been criticized because many children with the behavioral and academic problems outlined above, evidence no clear-cut signs that their brains are in any way malfunctioning. Thus it is argued that the term "minimal brain dysfunction" is simply inaccurate. Furthermore, the use of this term has been criticized since it can be upsetting to parents, who interpret it to mean that something is irreversibly the matter with their child's brain.

Hyperactivity Syndrome

If one accepts the previously stated criticisms of the use of the term "minimal brain dysfunction," then the question arises: What should these children be called? Many authors prefer to use terms which describe the outstanding characteristics of these youngsters, without attempting to address the underlying causes of their problems. If one focuses on the fact that many of these children are seemingly in perpetual or constant motion, then it is reasonable to label them as being "hyperactive" or "hyperkinetic" (kinetic is defined as "relating to motion"). Hyperactive youngsters usually evidence other behavioral difficulties, so that the combination of their problems has been labeled as "hyperacitivty syndrome."

Attention Deficit Disorder

Another descriptive term which has recently become popular is "attention deficit disorder." Its use reflects the belief of many experts that the problem common to all these children is their inability to selectively focus their attention for any period of time on necessary tasks. Some youngsters who evidence poor attention spans and distractibility are also constantly in motion. These children are said to have "attention deficit disorder with hyperactivity."[5]

Learning Disabilities

Many youngsters who are distractible, overactive, impulsive, and who have short attention spans experience academic difficulties. In addition, some children, even when they seem to be attending, have difficulty learning or remembering what they have learned. Educators may label these children as having "learning disabilities" (or "specific learning disabilities"). This label reflects the belief that these youngsters' academic problems are rooted in some general difficulty they have with learning. (Later in this chapter I will provide a more precise definition of learning disabilities.)

Perceptual Handicaps and Dyslexia

"Perceptual handicaps" (also called "perceptual disorders," "perceptual disabilities," etc.) and "dyslexia" (also called "developmental dyslexia") are best understood as two of a variety of different kinds of learning disabilities. Perceptually handicapped youngsters are children who have difficulty making sense of the visual or spatial relationships between objects. This difficulty often results in the youngster's having any of a number of academic difficulties and in his being poorly coordinated. "Dyslexic" youngsters are children who evidence an inability to progress beyond the earliest stages of reading skills. (Dyslexia and perceptual handicaps will be discussed in more detail in the section on learning disabilities.)

Summary

The use of a wide variety of terms to refer to youngsters with apparently similar problems reflects the fact that professionals disagree about the nature, causes, and treatment of such difficulties. Indeed, the only thing that most experts would agree upon is that "no one has any certainty about what is really wrong with these children."[6]

Do These Children All Have the Same Basic Problem?

Another reason why so many terms have been applied to these youngsters is that they probably do not all have the same basic difficulty. Rather it now seems that there are a number of similar but distinct syndromes which distinguish these youngsters. For example, some children with severe learning problems evidence no hyperactivity. Of these youngters, some have difficulty only with reading; others only with math or with handwriting. Others evidence problems in many areas of learning. On the other hand, some children are hyperactive and impulsive and yet do excellently in all their academic subjects, Of these, some seem to be hyperactive from birth; others seem to develop problems later in their lives.

Over time, as more research is done, it is likely that we will have a better idea about the nature and causes of these difficulties. Until such time, different professionals will maintain their own biases about diagnosing and treating these youngsters. My own bias is to refer to these children as either "hyperactive" or "learning disabled." It is important to note that these terms are not synonymous. Many children who are hyperactive have no learning disabilities and many learning-disabled youngsters are not hyperactive. On the other hand, some children are both learning disabled and hyperactive. In the sections which follow I will discuss in detail these two symptom pictures.

HYPERACTIVITY

Youngsters who are diagnosed as being "hyperactive" or "hyperkinetic" evidence difficulties in three general areas of functioning, as follows: 1) activity level, 2) attention, and 3) social interaction.[7]

Activity Level

A hyperactive child is one who displays "an unusual degree of motor restlessness that is purposeless and not directed toward a specific, meaningful goal."[8]

Some infants seem to be hyperactive from birth. Parents of these infants typically report that their babies were not only overactive but also had a variety of eating or sleeping problems (apparently caused by their inability to lie or sit still for any period of time).

Other children's problems are first evidenced between two to three years of age. These toddlers are reported to be "constantly on the go." Many parents will note that their youngster "never seemed to walk; as soon as he was able to stand, he ran!"

In nursery school and kindergarten these children's problems become even more apparent since they are unable to sit still or wait their turn. By the time such a youngster is in first or second grade, he or she has typically been labeled a "problem child."

To a parent or teacher a hyperactive child seems to be in perpetual motion, moving rapidly from one activity to another. Even when such a child is trying to sit still, he or she is in motion; tapping a foot, squirming, rolling a pencil, or balancing a chair on two legs.

If your youngster is hyperactive, you might notice similarities to him or her in the following example:

> Billy was sitting at the table eating dinner but he was so busy chattering that the majority of his food was falling on the table rather than going in his mouth. Finally his mother said, "Stop talking until you are done eating," which he did. However, no sooner had he stopped talking when he began eating with one hand and tapping his spoon with another. He appeared somewhat shaken when his mother said, "Put your hand in your lap," as if he were unaware that he had been tapping. He put his hand in his lap but shortly after he had done this, he began to shake his leg up and down. Finally his mother, thinking he might not be paying attention to her said, "Look at me." He looked up toward her, but within seconds his eyes seemed to be darting about the room, not focused on her at all.

This is a hyperactive child. He was probably not willfully defying his mother or attempting to agitate her but rather was unable to control his energy level.

One of the most significant characteristics of the hyperactive child is not the quantity of his or her movement but the quality of it. Studies have indicated that hyperactive children do not necessarily move more, but more of their movement is purposeless. In Billy's case, for instance, his primary activity at the moment was eating and his spoon tapping and leg shaking were unrelated, if not counterproductive, to this activity. Even when he probably intended to look at his mother, he could not direct his activity at this goal.

Parents of hyperactive children often comment: "But there are times when he can sit calmly, engrossed in television or in an activity." Indeed, it appears that hyperactive children do have periods of relative calm, but these periods do not appear to be in the children's control; they cannot willfully make themselves relax. The ebb and flow of their activity level seems more to be a matter of some internal regulator system, one which they cannot operate at will.

Many parents are reassured that their youngster's hyperactivity will begin to decrease or disappear in adolescence. Although this may be true, it now appears that the other characteristics of this syndrome, poor attention span and poor social skills, continue throughout adolescence.

Difficulties in Attending

Since no one expects infants or young children to sustain their attention for any significant period of time, difficulties in this area of functioning are not apparent until the child enters school.

In school the hyperactive child or adolescent "tends to fall behind not just in one or two subjects but in anything that requires concentration for an appreciable time. Hyperactive youngsters do not have difficulty in turning to the subject but rather in maintaining their focus. . . . The child focuses on a task but has to break off to see who is coming through the door, check on the jacket the child next to him is wearing, or wonder what is happening outside the window. These children do begin tasks. In fact, they constantly begin tasks. But they abandon them prematurely and do not finish them unless the project takes little time or the child is very bright, so that brief attention to a task may be sufficient."[9]

* * *

Social Difficulties

Hyperactive youngsters evidence difficulties relating to their schoolmates, siblings, parents, teachers, and other caretakers. One reason for this difficulty is these youngsters' impulsivity. Such children typically interrupt the play or conversation of other youngsters and have difficulty waiting their turn in games or other group situations. Such behavior generally causes these childen to be quite unpopular and may be the basis of their getting into frequent fights. A hyperactive child may be all too willing to participate in fights, partially as a result of impulsivity, and partially in response to the generally frustrating nature of his or her social interactions.

In addition, hyperactive children seem to demand an unusual amount of attention and to respond impulsively and angrily if they do not receive it. Such behavior leads to major problems with parents or teachers, who typically have many other demands on their time and attention.

Parents of hyperactive youngsters typically report that punishments, rewards, or other attempts to control or discipline their child are generally ineffective. Many such parents have periodically lost their tempers and have resorted to spankings, yelling, or various punishments, typically to no avail.

Treatment of Hyperactivity

There is as much dispute about the treatment of hyperactivity as there is about its nature and causes. One major area of controversy is the use of medications. Some physicians recommend a trial period of drug therapy for all hyperactive children. One such physician, Dr. Marcel Kinsbourne, argues as follows: "With correctly diagnosed hyperactive youngsters, the question 'Should drugs be used or not?' never arises. Instead the question is 'How much of what drug should be used?' " He goes on to state that the only way to "find out whether [medication] should or should not be prescribed for a particular child [is] by trying the drug to see if it is effective."[10]

On the other hand, many physicians believe that a diagnosis of hyperactivity is not, in and of itself, a sufficient reason to prescribe medications. These doctors remind parents that medications can have negative side effects, and should therefore only be used when necessary. They advocate the use of medications for hyperactivity only under the following circumstances:

1) If a child's distractibility and short attention span adversely affect his school performance
2) If a child's social difficulties are sufficiently severe that he has significant problems with peers, and if other attempts to remedy these problems have proven unsuccessful
3) If a child's motor restlessness presents major problems for his parents, and if attempts to help parents cope with these problems have failed. (See Chapter Seven for a discussion of the types of medication used in the treatment of hyperactivity.)

Another controversial issue is the use of dietary measures to reduce or eliminate the symptoms of hyperactivity. The most famous dietary prescription is that of Dr. Ben Feingold, author of *Why Your Child Is Hyperactive.*[11] He argues that artificial food flavorings and colorings may, in certain children, cause the symptoms associated with hyperacitivty. He advises that parents of such children place their youngsters on a diet free of synthetic food additives. Other authors suggest that parents also reduce or eliminate certain sugars from the diet of their hyperactive child. To date there is no clear evidence to confirm or discredit such dietary measures. If you are interested in attempting a trial period of dietary regulation, I suggest you discuss this with your pediatrician and then try an additive-free diet to see if it proves effective.

The third controversy revolves around the benefits of psychotherapy in the treatment of hyperactivity. Some authors believe that psychotherapy is generally not indicated because hyperactive youngsters' difficulties with movement, attention, and social interactions are not primarily caused by emotional problems. Other authors argue that (regardless of the causes of hyperactivity) youngsters with this syndrome have more than the usual amount of social and emotional difficulties and psychotherapy can, if nothing else, help them cope with their special problems.

Summary

While it is important for parents of hyperactive children to understand the controversies surrounding the treatment of this syndrome, such knowledge does not necessarily help them answer their biggest question: What should be done for my child?" The best answer that can currently be given is this: Whatever treatment makes sense to you, and is recommended to you by a professional whom you trust, is worth attempting. If such treatment proves effective, continue it. If not, reconsult your doctor so that another program can be started.

A Word of Warning About Hyperactivity

"Hyperactivity" has become one of the most overused labels in the diagnosis of children with problem behaviors. In one study, for instance, over forty percent of the entire fifth-grade population of one school were diagnosed by their teachers as "hyperactive." It is important to keep in mind that a youngster who has a high energy level or who doesn't like to pay attention in class, or who fights a lot with his friends, is not necessarily hyperactive. Emotional factors can also result in any or all of these behaviors. A diagnosis of hyperactivity can only be made after a youngster is carefully evaluated by professionals who are trained in this field.

LEARNING DISABILITIES

Most broadly defined, a learning-disabled (or LD) child is one whose level of academic achievement is lower than would be expected on the basis of his or her intellectual potential.[12] Implicit in this definition is the assumption that the youngster's poor school performance is not primarily due to emotional difficulties, mental retardation, cultural deprivation, or physical handicaps (such as blindness or a hearing impairment).

Although the symptoms of learning disability are most obvious in terms of a child's academic difficulties, she may have more general deficits in the ability to "process information." "Information processing" is a shorthand term used by learning-disability specialists. It refers to the various skills and abilities which underlie a person's ability to learn. It is generally agreed that in order to be able to learn an individual must be able to:

1) Accurately take in or receive information, whether visually, aurally, or tactilely
2) Store or retain this information for later use
3) Make sense or extract meaning from this information
4) Express what has been learned, usually through speech or writing

Thus, if a child is asked to repeat the sentence "Pretty flowers grow in our yard," and says, "Here are pretty flowers," or if a child is asked to copy a circle next to a diamond and draws an oval above a triangle, she is evidencing some problem in information processing. If a youngster has problems with tasks of this kind, she will probably also have difficulty learning that the letters "C A

T" spell "cat" or that "was" is different from "saw." Some children with learning disabilities have difficulties with only one aspect of information processing (for example, being able to remember spoken directions; this is referred to as an auditory memory deficit). Other youngsters evidence difficulties in many areas.

Different Types of Learning Disabilities

Although specialists use many different labels when describing specific areas of learning disability, it is possible to divide all such problems into the following general categories:

1) Language-processing disorders
2) Visual-spatial disorders (commonly referred to as "perceptual handicaps" or "perceptual disabilities")
3) Organizational disorders

LANGUAGE-PROCESSING DISORDERS

There are children who have difficulty processing verbal information (words). This type of deficit is often described as an "auditory" problem. The problem, however, is not that the child cannot hear, but that the child has difficulty making sense of what is said to him, remembering it, or expressing himself verbally.

There are certain symptoms which seem to be typical of children with language-processing disorders. Often such children seem to confuse what is said to them. For instance, the child is told, "Shut the window," and he opens it. Or the child is told, "Put your socks on," and he puts them in the hamper. Other such youngsters do understand what is said to them but it takes them an unusually long period of time to be able to make sense of what they hear. For example, some of these youngsters will need to repeat a question to themselves before they can fully understand it. Other children with language-processing problems display very poor grammar. Frequently, for instance, a child will say, "I'm more bigger than you," or "I bringded him a present," at an age when other children have long since stopped making such errors. Still other children with language-processing disorders will have "word retrieval" problems: difficulty in bringing a word to mind. Such a child might hesitate a lot: "Can I have some more . . . uh . . . uh . . . uh, cabbage." Or he might "circumlocute" to get around the word he can't recall: "Can I have some more of the red stuff in that dish." Finally, a child with language problems may confuse words, calling a chair a "table" or celery "salad."

Children with even mild language-processing disorders often display rather severe reading and spelling problems (probably because written language is more complicated than is spoken language). Often they can learn a basic reading sight-vocabulary, but have great difficulty sounding out a new, unfamiliar word. Thus, for instance, such a child may be able to read the words "all" or "ball," but cannot then read the word "fall." Or when they see a new word they will guess it on the basis of a few letters, reading "breakfast" as "basket." Another characteristic reading problem of children with language disorders is that they will often "forget" what sound a letter or letter combination makes. Even after a child with a language disorder begins to master a reading vocabulary, he often has great difficulty comprehending full sentences or paragraphs.

Since so much of classroom activity is based upon lisening and speaking, teachers often complain about such children: "He doesn't listen . . . he's always day-dreaming." "He doesn't understand what I say." "Sometimes Johnny is a delight, but there are days when he just doesn't seem to care."

VISUAL-SPATIAL PROCESSING DISORDERS

There is another group of learning-disabled children who seem to have difficulty making sense of the visual or spatial relationships between objects. Such disorders are sometimes referred to as "perceptual" disabilities. Again, this does not mean the child cannot see properly but merely that the way he "processes" or makes sense of what he sees is confused.

Visual-spatial disorders are often more difficult for a parent to recognize than are language disorders, but still there are symptoms that can be evident in a child's day-to-day behavior. Children with visual-spatial disorders are sometimes clumsy, and they may be extremely poor at activities such as drawing or puzzles. In addition, such youngsters may frequently misjudge space—for example, by placing a glass too close to the edge of the counter because "I thought there was room," or they may "forget" the route home from school even though they follow it daily.

For a long time it was assumed that visual-spatial disorders were at the root of most reading problems. This assumption was made because many reading errors seemed to be caused by a youngster's "seeing" a word improperly; for example reading "no" as "on," or "was" as "saw." However, it has recently been found that many reading problems are caused by language-processing disorders. In fact, research seems to indicate that by the age of eight or nine a child with visual-spatial problems may evidence little or no reading disability.

Sometimes a child with visual-spatial problems does have difficulty spelling. Such a child may spell phonetically ("light" or "lite") or may confuse the position of letters in a word ("lihgt"). In addition, their handwriting is sometimes sloppy, with uneven spacing between letters and unpredictable letter size.

Far more significant than any reading, spelling, or handwriting problems is that children with visual-spatial disorders often encounter difficulty with math. Since math concepts involve the appreciation of space and relative quantity, and since computations involve columns and different directional rules for each arithmetic operation, visual-spatial problems can be a real stumbling block.

ORGANIZATIONAL PROBLEMS

Professionals who study learning-disabled children once tried to classify every disability as either a language (auditory) processing disorder or a visual-spatial (perceptual) processing disorder. However, it is now becoming evident that these classifications may not be sufficient. There appears to be a large group of children whose learning problems are not due to specific language or visual processing disorders, but rather to an inability to develop effective and consistent strategies for problem solving. Such children seem to be strikingly disorganized and arbitrary in the way they approach tasks.

Children with organizational difficulties evidence a variety of deficits. When they speak, they seem to ramble pointlessly. If, for instance, they are telling you about a movie, they will relate innumerable minute details that seem irrelevant. Or when you tell them to do something, they will "forget" almost immediately. If you tell a child (let's say she's a girl) with this type of disorder to get ready for bed, you may come into the room fifteen minutes later and find her fully clothed and playing with a toy; and she may seem shocked when you get upset. While all children conveniently forget from time to time, this type of child seems to do it constantly and naively.

When a child with organizational problems (let's say he's a boy) sets out to do a project, the way he approaches the task may seem completely illogical—and often is. If he decides to wash the car, he may spend more time running in and out of the house than washing; one trip in for a sponge, then out, then in for a towel, then out, then in to turn on the hose, and so forth. Then, when he is finally done and proud of himself, he inevitably ends up in trouble for forgetting to turn off the hose or for leaving the washbasin out where someone can trip over it.

Like children with other types of learning disabilities, children with organizational problems may also have some trouble learning to read, but it is often not dramatic trouble. More often than not they tend to make small, apparently careless errors. Such a child might, for instance, read "difference" as "different" and then rapidly add "or something like that." In addition, when a disorganized child reads a whole paragraph, he is often able to retell many of the facts but cannot extract of summarize the main idea.

Organizational problems become even more evident in spelling than in reading. The spelling of children with such problems is often entirely unpredictable. They may spell a word right in one sentence and misspell it in the next. Even more appalling than their spelling is their written language. When they write a paragraph, it is often filled with wonderful ideas presented in a totally confused sequence, and punctuation may be either arbitrary or absent altogether. Teachers often say about such a child, "If he could only get himself organized!"

DYSLEXIA

"Dyslexia" is perhaps the most misunderstood term in the field of learning disabilities. "Dyslexia" is a term originally coined by neurologists to refer to a person's loss of the ability to read. More recently it has come to refer to a disorder in which a person has never been able to learn to read—and thus this disorder is more correctly labeled "developmental dyslexia."

Some people use the term "dyslexia" to refer to a specific group of reading problems such as letter and word reversals. However, this definition is too narrow. Others use the term to refer to any child reading two or more years below grade level. This definition is too broad.

"Developmental dyslexia" is more accurately defined as the inability to progress beyond the earliest stages of reading skill because of some disruption in one's ability to understand, store, or recall the ways in which symbols go together to represent words. For instance, a severely dyslexic fifteen-year-old boy was asked to write the word "enter" and he wrote "nxpr." This youngster demonstrates no understanding of how to translate sounds into written symbols (words).

While reading disabilities are often associated with other information-processing disorders, particularly language-processing disorders, there is a relatively small group of children who demonstrate little or no evidence of language, visual-spatial, or organizational deficits and who nevertheless have difficulty learning to read and spell. These children are perhaps the only children who are "pure" dyslexics because their reading disorder is an isolated disability apparently unrelated to any other learning disorder.

Behavioral Problems Associated with Learning Disabilities

While it is believed that the school problems demonstrated by a learning-disabled child are not primarily due to emotional factors, it is nonetheless true that learning-disabled children tend to display many behavioral and emotional problems. Many LD children appear to have difficulty learning social rules. They do not, for instance, seem to understand many of the nuances of social interaction; thus they may act in socially inappropriate ways. Often learning-disabled children are impulsive; they act without foreseeing the consequences of their behavior and then are surprised when they find themselves "in trouble" over what they have done.

In addition to the behavioral and social problems that are actually caused by a child's learning disability, there are often secondary emotional problems which develop as a reaction to academic and social frustration. A child may begin to resist going to school, may become the "class clown," or may start to act hostile and testy with others. It is not unusual for the secondary emotional problems of the learning-disabled child to become so severe that they merit psychological treatment over and above any special educational services.

Some Warnings About Learning Disabilities

Because the study of learning disabilities is relatively new and definitions are still vague, parents or teachers may be tempted to seize upon "learning disability" as the primary explanation for a child's school failure. However, there are many children who do badly in school and who do not have a learning disability. If we review the definition of "learning disability," some other factors which can also cause poor school performance should become evident.

First, a learning disability is defined as a *discrepancy* between the child's achievement and his potential. A child whose intellectual potential is lower than average for his age may have difficulty learning to read or may achieve below-grade level, but this child's achievement may be perfectly matched with his intellectual potential. A ten-year-old child with an 80 (low average) IQ who is achieving at the third-grade level when he is in the fourth grade is not displaying a discrepancy between his school performance and his intellectual potential. Or a child of average intelligence in a school where most children are above average may get comparatively poor grades in school, but his achievement may be commensurate with his potential. In none of these cases can the child be called "learning disabled."

Similarly, the definition of learning disability excludes children whose school failure is due to cultural deprivation or difference. A child who, for instance, has never been exposed to letters or reading before he enters school may take longer than other children in her class to master beginning reading skills. A child with emotional problems (lack of confidence, fear of new situations, resistance to school, or any of a number of other problems) may also perform below his intellectual potential. Finally, a blind or deaf or physically impaired child may have difficulty learning specific academic skills, and thus perform below her potential. All of these children may require special educational services and may demonstrate a level of school performance which is lower than their intellectual potential; but they are not, by definition, learning disabled.

Another faulty assumption about learning disabilities is that they can be "cured." It is more accurate to say that these problems may be remedied by special education. Even the best educational efforts, however, cannot always help a youngster correct a learning disability. He or she may need to be taught how to compensate for or work around a particular area of weakness.

You should also be forewarned that professionals disagree about how best to remedy any given learning disability. Some educators believe that it is most effective to focus on a child's underlying information-processing disorder (for example, his difficulty in remembering what is said). Others argue that one should address the specific academic difficulty (for example, a reading problem). Still others argue that since correcting the disorder is often difficult and therefore frustrating to a child, one should only help a youngster learn to work around his particular disability. There is no clear evidence that any one approach is more successful than any other in all cases. The best approach is one which proves most successful with any given child.

Getting Help

It is important to note that if your youngster is having difficulties at school, you have the legal right to request that the school conduct a complete evaluation in order to determine the nature and causes of the problems. Furthermore, the school, under certain circumstances, is also legally obligated to provide your youngster with a variety of special educational services to help overcome his or her handicaps. (See Chapter Thirteen for a detailed discussion of this topic.)

In addition, if you know or suspect that your youngster is learning disabled there are a number of local, state, and national organizations which can provide you with information, support, and guidance. (See Appendix A.)

Chapter 4

PLACES TO GO FOR HELP

In the United States there are a number of different types of facilities which provide mental health services for youngsters, parents, and families. Be forewarned that such facilities are not evenly distributed across the nation, so that some of the kinds of agencies I'll be describing may not be easily accessible to you. Nonetheless it should be helpful for you to have some idea about the different kinds of settings in which therapeutic help is provided.

One way of classifying all mental health services is to distinguish between those provided in outpatient settings and those provided in inpatient or residential facilities. "Outpatient services" include all types of help which are made available to a person while he or she lives at home. Such help is typically provided in a therapist's office, although appointments can take place in a client's home if necessary. "Inpatient" or "residential services" are those in which the patient lives away from home while receiving therapeutic help.

OUTPATIENT SETTINGS

Some of the settings in which outpatient services are provided are the following:

Private Practitioners

In most areas there are mental health professionals who provide therapeutic services for a fee. In many ways, consulting a therapist in private practice is comparable to seeing a physician or dentist, in that a client typically has one or more appointments in a professional's office, for which an agreed-upon fee is charged.

Private Clinics

Some private clinics are simply group psychiatric practices in which two or more therapists provide psychotherapeutic help, just as private practitioners do. Other private clinics offer a broader range of therapeutic services and thus are comparable to community-sponsored clinics.

Community-Sponsored Clinics

There are a number of different kinds of community-sponsored clinics which provide therapeutic services to children, parents, and families. These agencies include child-guidance clinics; community mental health centers; some hospital departments of psychiatry, including some at Veterans Administration Hospitals; family-service agencies; and an assortment of storefront and drop-in centers for troubled adolescents and/or their parents.

What distinguishes these facilities from private clinics is that fees for service are on a sliding scale based on families' ability to pay. Indeed, some agencies offer services at absolutely no cost to parents.

Community-sponsored clinics are able to provide such low-cost assistance because a substantial percentage of their operating expenses is provided by federal, state, or local funds. These agencies are also supported, in some cases, by local charities, religious or civic organizations, foundations, or research grants.

One of the first questions to ask on calling any clinic is "How will my fee be determined?" If you are told that your fee will be set according to your family's income, you have probably reached a community-sponsored clinic. If you are told that the fee is some fixed amount per hour, regardless of your ability to pay, you have probably reached a private clinic.

Public Schools

Until recently school systems varied tremendously in their willingness and capacity to provide mental health services to their students. Some schools furnished extensive services, while others provided virtually none. Since September 1978, however, under the provisions of a federal law entitled The Education for All Handicapped Children Act (Public Law 94-142), all public school systems are required to provide diagnostic and counseling services to students whose emotional problems seriously interfere with their school functioning. (Details of the provisions of this law will be explained in Chapter Thirteen.)

INPATIENT OR RESIDENTIAL SETTINGS

The major kinds of inpatient or residential settings are the following:

Hospitals

Children and adolescents can be hospitalized either in the psychiatric or pediatric units of a general hospital, or in a psychiatric hospital. Some, although not many, psychiatric hospitals or hospital programs are designed exclusively for children and adolescents. However, since the demand for such facilities far exceeds the supply, many children or adolescents who need hospital treatment must be admitted to adult units or will not be admitted at all.

Residential Treatment Centers

Residential treatment centers are non-hospital facilities which are specifically designed to treat emotionally troubled children. These centers typically provide educational services, recreational activities, and therapeutic help.

Some of these facilities refer to themselves as "residential schools for emotionally disturbed children," while others call themselves "residential treatment centers." In terms of the kind of help that such programs offer, the distinction between "residential schools" and "residential treatment centers" is often unimportant. One might think that the "residential schools" would focus more on education and the development of academic skills, but this is not necessarily the case.

In relation to the need for residential treatment centers for children and adolescents, there are only a limited number of them throughout the country.*

* Listings and descriptions of residential treatment programs in the United States are provided in *The Directory for Exceptional Children*, published by Porter Sargent. You may be able to find this directory in your library, or you can purchase it from The Exceptional Parent Bookstore, Room 708, Statler Office Building, Boston, Massachusetts 02116. In addition, the federal gov-

Group Homes

These facilities may be called "halfway houses," "group shelters," or "group residences." Such facilities are usually restricted to adolescents. They provide out-of-the-home, supervised living arrangements for youngsters who have already been hospitalized or who are at risk of needing hospitalization. Many of these facilities are affiliated with mental hospitals or community mental health centers.

LOCATING MENTAL HEALTH SERVICES IN YOUR AREA

Depending on where you live, you may have access to all of the kinds of therapeutic settings I've described, or you may have to travel long distances to receive any help at all. Wherever you live, you will need to get some idea of the different places, convenient to your home, from which you can get help. The easiest way to locate such services is to contact those agencies or professionals in your area whose job it is to know about mental health resources.

Where to Call

One place to call is your local or state branch of the Mental Health Association (MHA), formerly called The National Association for Mental Health. The MHA is a

---

ernment publishes a directory entitled *U.S. Facilities and Programs for Children with Severe Mental Illnesses.* This can be obtained free of cost by writing to the National Institute of Mental Health, Public Inquiries, 5600 Fisher's Lane, Rockville, Maryland 20857.

nationwide organization whose purpose is to represent the interests of consumers of mental health services. Your local or state branch of the MHA should be able to provide you with information about the entire range of mental health resources in your area. The easiest way to locate your local MHA is by looking under "Mental Health Association" in the white pages of your telephone directory.*

Other places to call for information about local mental health services include your town, city, or county health department; your state department of mental health; or a local chapter of the United Way or Community Chest.

You may feel that your child's or family's problems are such a personal matter that you'd prefer to talk to your clergyman or family physician. Or you might want to talk to someone at your child's school, such as a guidance counselor, principal, or school social worker All of these professionals typically have had extensive experience in referring youngsters and families for psychological help.

Other resources that you may wish to investigate are the many national organizations representing the interests of children who have special medical or emotional problems. The names, addresses, and telephone numbers of some of the more prominent of these organizations are listed in Appendix A. Local branches of these organizations can usually put you in touch with other parents who have faced problems similar to your own. These parents can often provide you with an insider's view of how and where to get effective help.

You can also talk to friends, neighbors, or coworkers who themselves have had their children or families in treatment. Of course, if you know someone who is a mental health professional, he or she may be in an excellent position to provide you with information.

Finally, you may turn to the telephone book to find out

* If you can't find a listing for your local Mental Health Association in the telephone directory you can write to: The National Headquarters, Mental Health Association, 1800 North Kent Street, Arlington, Virginia 22209. They will provide you with information about how to get in contact with the Mental Health Association nearest to you.

about mental health services in your area. Such resources will typically be listed in the Yellow Pages, under "Mental Health Services," though some may appear under the heading "Social Service Organizations."

The disadvantage of looking in the telephone book is that it can be very hard to determine which of all the agencies listed are appropriate for you. For example, the Boston Area Yellow Pages has over seven hundred entries under "Social Service Organizations" and almost one hundred listings for "Mental Health Services." Figuring out which of these agencies might be of help would seem like an overwhelming task.

What to Ask

Let's say that you've decided to call your local Mental Health Association for information about therapeutic services. Since the kind of help available will depend on your child's age and the kind of problems that he or she is having, you'll need to provide this information to the person with whom you talk.

Here is an example of what you might say:

> I'm calling to find out about mental health resources in this area. My daughter is five. She's always been difficult to handle; she's stubborn, won't share her toys, and often throws temper tantrums when she doesn't get her way. She'll be starting kindergarten next fall, and before then I wanted a professional opinion about whether she, or my husband and I, could benefit from some counseling. Can you tell me about the kinds of people or places that might be able to answer that question?

After obtaining the names of some mental health agencies or of some private therapists, you may then want to call your pediatrician or family physician to find out about the reputations of these people or places. Or you can call the agencies or therapists directly to get information about the services which they provide.

Later in this chapter I'll describe some of the potential advantages and disadvantages associated with different types of therapeutic facilities: private practitioners, private clinics, publicly sponsored clinics, and school systems. But before doing that, I'll discuss the impact of the cost of mental health services on your ability to obtain such help.

FINANCIAL CONSIDERATIONS

Unless you have unlimited funds or are covered by an insurance policy which provides for extensive mental health benefits,* financial considerations will probably play some role in your decision about where to obtain therapeutic help.

Determining how much mental health services will cost is a more complicated matter than you might imagine. First of all, when first seeking help you may have little idea how long the treatment will need to continue, or even whether any regular therapy will be necessary. You may be able to afford to consult a private therapist for one or two evaluation sessions, for example, but be unable to pay the fifty dollars per week that it would cost for ongoing treatment. That would mean that you'd want to find a lower-cost clinic—unless, of course, you have mental health insurance coverage, in which case financial considerations can become even more complicated.

Insurance coverage for mental health services is incredibly varied. Those policies which cover outpatient treatment (and not all of them do) usually pay for only some portion of the cost of therapy, typically fifty to eighty per-

* Insurance policies which provide particularly extensive coverage for mental health services include those written for civilian and military employees of the federal government. Some of the larger corporations, such as IBM, also provide excellent mental health insurance.

[illegible] a therapist's fee. There is usually a maximum [illegible]unt of coverage (for example, five hundred dollars per [illegible]erson per calendar year) and in some cases there is a deductible, typically the first fifty or one hundred dollars of a therapist's fee. In addition, insurance policies tend not to cover all settings or professionals equally. Your policy might reimburse you for treatment that takes place in a hospital, but not for outpatient treatment. Or it's possible that the community-sponsored clinic serving your region may not be eligible for insurance payments, so that going to a private therapist could actually cost you less than going to a "lower-cost" clinic. Finally, some insurance policies will reimburse you for services provided by some mental health professionals (psychiatrists, for example) but not for services provided by others (such as psychiatric nurses, unless they are supervised by someone who is eligible for reimbursement).

As you can see, insurance coverage is so varied and so complicated that you would do well to check with your insurance company, or with your firm's insurance representative, before you begin any treatment. The questions you'll want answered about your insurance coverage are the following:

1) Does my insurance cover any mental health services? If so, does it cover outpatient as well as inpatient help?
2) Does it cover one hundred percent of the cost, or some percentage of the fee?
3) Is there a deductible?
4) Is there a maximum amount of coverage per calendar year?
5) Which professionals are reimbursed for their services? Which professionals are not covered? Are these latter professionals covered if they are supervised by someone who is eligible for reimbursement?

There is one condition attached to insurance coverage for which you should be prepared. In order for an insurance company to pay a claim for mental health services, your therapist will have to provide them with so[illegible] formation about the problem for which you sought [illegible] Typically this information is in the form of a diagnosis, for example "depressive reaction" or "anxiety neurosis." I have known people who felt so sensitive about their privacy that they chose to pay for all treatment out of their own pocket rather than let their therapist give information to their insurance company. You may not feel that strongly, but you may want to ask your therapist to tell you exactly what information he or she is furnishing to your insurance company.

Throughout the rest of this chapter (and in other chapters, as well) I will periodically make general statements about the cost of mental health services. Be aware that these statements may not apply to you, either because of the particular nature of your insurance coverage, or for other reasons.

"WHERE SHOULD I TAKE MY CHILD FOR HELP?"

In the best of all worlds there would be a wide variety of mental health resources convenient to you, and you would be able to evaluate each of them carefully before selecting the one most likely to be of help to your child or family. In the real world your options will be far more limited, because of financial constraints, or because of a relative sparsity of services in your area, or because your child's or family's problems need immediate attention and you simply don't have the time to investigate different therapeutic options.

If, for whatever reasons, you have no choice in the matter, you should take your child or family to whatever facility is recommended to you. On the other hand, you may find yourself in the position of being able to choose among a number of different settings for therapeutic help. You will be most likely to find yourself in this circum-

stance if your child's or family's problems are not extremely severe and thus can be handled on an outpatient basis. (In most areas of the country, inpatient facilities are so scarce that if your youngster needed that kind of help you would probably have little or no choice as to where to take him.)

If you decide or are advised to seek outpatient treatment, you may have the choice between a private therapist and a community-sponsored clinic. The relative advantages of each of these settings are described below. The advantages and disadvantages of having your youngster receive help in a school setting present somewhat different issues and will be discussed in the subsequent section.

Relative Advantages of a Private Therapist

There are a number of reasons why you may choose to seek help from a therapist in private practice rather than obtain assistance at a community-sponsored clinic. These might include:

INCREASED CHOICE OF THERAPIST

Some parents prefer to have a choice as to who treats their child or family. They might, for example, prefer a male or female therapist, or someone of a particular age. Perhaps they're looking for a clinician who adheres to a particular *school* of treatment, such as family systems therapy of psychoanalytic therapy. (These and other schools of treatment will be discussed in detail in Chapter Six.)

In those areas of the country where there are many private practitioners, you will probably be able to find someone who meets any or all of your specifications. On the other hand, you will probably be offered no choice of therapist at a community-sponsored clinic.

INCREASED CHOICE OF TREATMENT MODALITY AND TREATMENT DURATION

Some parents have strong preferences for a particular kind of treatment, such as group therapy or individual therapy. In those areas of the country where there are many private therapists, parents can usually find someone to provide the kind of service they prefer.

In addition, private therapists are often in the best position to continue treating a child or family for as long as such help is necessary. In other settings the length of treatment may be arbitrarily restricted to a given number of sessions because of limited staff resources.

GREATER PERMANENCE OF THERAPIST

Therapists in private practice, in general, are likely to be able to stay with your child or family for the full duration of treatment. Therapists at publicly sponsored clinics, who are apt to be in training or just starting their careers, may have to turn your child's or family's treatment over to someone else because they are moving to another placement or job.

GREATER SENSE OF PRIVACY

There is generally a greater sense of privacy in a private therapist's office than at a publicly sponsored clinic. (As our society has moved more and more toward an acceptance of therapy as one constructive way of solving problems in living, the stigma of going to a therapist has lessened markedly, so that this need for privacy is becoming less of an issue for many parents.)

Some Cautions About Private Clinics

Theoretically a private clinic should offer the same relative advantages as a private therapist. And often this is the case. Indeed, since some private clinics provide a range of services comparable to those at publicly sponsored clinics, it is possible that such a facility may even be preferable to a private therapist.

However, at some private clinics, although you will be paying a high fee, you may have no choice of therapist and little or no say as to what kind of treatment you'll receive. In many private clinics relatively less experienced therapists (or graduate students) provide the bulk of the treatment. Typically they will be paid a percentage of your fee, usually about forty to sixty percent, while the rest of your money goes to the owners of the clinic. Supervision of these less experienced staff members may be excellent, but it may also be minimal or nonexistent.

If you are paying a high fee so as to be able to be in private treatment, you should be receiving full advantages for your money. In my experience this is not always the case at private clinics. (See Chapter Nine for a discussion of what questions to ask before taking your child or family to a private clinic for help.)

Relative Advantages of a Community-Sponsored Clinic

Some of the advantages of seeking help at a clinic are the following:

LOW COST

Community-sponsored clinics set fees on a sliding scale; in other words, they charge according to clients' relative ability to pay. If your income is low enough or if you have unusual expenses, you could receive help for as little as a dollar a visit. Some clinics provide services at no cost to parents.

Another financial advantage of being seen at a clinic is that some private practitioners will stop treatment if their client becomes unable, for whatever reasons, to continue to pay their fee. At community-sponsored clinics, if you were to face an unexpected financial crisis, your fee would be reduced to an amount that you could afford and your treatment could continue.

GEOGRAPHIC LOCATION

Although there is usually an overabundance of therapists in cities, there are often few, if any, private clinicians in rural areas. In such regions community-sponsored clinics are the most convenient, if not the only practical, place to take one's child or family for help.

VARIETY OF SERVICES

Clinics can provide a wider variety of therapeutic services than can be obtained from an individual therapist. This diversity of services can prove especially helpful to families who have either a multihandicapped child (for example, a youngster with physical and emotional difficulties) or to families who have more than one child in need of therapeutic help.

SPECIALIZED SERVICES

Because clinics assist large numbers of families, they can create programs for special client populations. For example, a clinic can run support or therapy groups for first-time mothers, for fathers of retarded children, or for youngsters who have had difficulty with the law, to name just a few.

EMERGENCY SERVICES

It is usually possible for clinics to have more extensive and accessible emergency services than can be provided by any private practitioner. If it is likely that a family member may need to be hospitalized during his or her treatment, some therapists will recommend that the family receive help in a clinic setting.

Some Cautions About Publicly Sponsored Clinics

Because publicly sponsored clinics are required by law to provide therapeutic services to area residents regardless of their ability to pay, such agencies typically operate on very tight budgets. Therefore they often find themselves in the position of having to assist a relatively large number of people with a small number of staff.* The imbalance between the demand for therapeutic services and the capacity of any clinic to meet that demand could result in your encountering any or all of the following problems:

WAITING LISTS

You may have to wait longer than you'd like for evaluation, treatment, or both, at a publicly sponsored clinic. A waiting list is one tool used by some clinics to handle the problem of providing high-quality services to large numbers of people with a small staff. Under the waiting-list system clients who have been accepted for treatment are provided whatever therapy is deemed necessary, even if

* Clinics do sometimes receive federal or state grants which fund some of the special programs that I described above. Therefore a given clinic might be able to provide very expensive and time-consuming help to certain special populations (e.g., retarded adolescents) even though the rest of its budget is tight.

such treatment requires many staff hours over a long period of time. All other people, except for those in crisis, are required to wait before they can be seen. Waiting periods might run anywhere from a month to six months or longer. People who are not in crisis but who are eager for more immediate help are referred to private practitioners (if they can afford it) or to other agencies (if appropriate).

TYPE AND LENGTH OF TREATMENT

You may not have a choice of the kind or duration of treatment provided to your child or family. Some clinics adopt the policy that people should not have to wait for therapeutic help. Under this no-waiting-list policy, everyone is provided with relatively rapid but often less extensive assistance—typically in the form of short-term and/or group therapy. These therapy methods allow clinics to see greater numbers of people with their existing staffs. The disadvantage of this system is that longer-term individual or family treatment is either unavailable or difficult to obtain.

LACK OF CHOICE OF THERAPIST

You may have little or no choice as to which therapist will see your child or family. Most clinics do not encourage you to select your own therapist. Rather, the clinic will assign someone to work with your child or family. This assignment can be based on any or all of the following criteria:

1) Staff availability: whoever has free time
2) Staff rotation: whichever staff member is next in line to handle a new client
3) Staff Interest or Expertise: whoever's interests and skills make them best suited to work with your particular child or family

Since most clinics serve as training agencies for psychiatric social workers, psychiatric nurses, psychiatrists, and psychologists, your child or family may be assigned to a trainee. (Student therapists are referred to either as "trainees" or as "interns." Psychiatrists in training are called "residents.") The work of each trainee is supervised by a staff member. (In Chapter Ten I'll discuss some considerations involved in working with a therapist in training.)

Advantages and Disadvantages of Counseling in Schools

Just as there are unique advantages and disadvantages involved in taking your child to a therapist in private practice or to a clinic, so there are special advantages and disadvantages that characterize counseling in a school setting. These are as follows:

SPECIAL ADVANTAGES

Proximity to the Child's Problems:
Since school mental health personnel are situated in the school, they are able to intervene quickly when a youngster is having difficulty. In addition, a school counselor or psychologist is in a good position both to help a youngster understand and accommodate to some of the realities of school life, and to represent the youngster's interest and viewpoint to the teachers.

Low Cost:
Counseling services at school are provided at no cost to parents.

Convenience:
If your youngster receives counseling during school hours, you will not have to take time out of your schedule to transport her to appointments; and your youngster will not have to give up any of her free time after school.

SPECIAL DISADVANTAGES

Lack of Choice of Counselor:
Typically, you will have no choice about who will help your child. She will be seen by whatever person provides counseling services in the child's school.

Shorter Duration of Treatment:
Mental health services in schools tend to be short-term and problem-focused. When problems seem to be deep seated and when it appears that it will take a long time to remedy them, youngsters are typically referred to private therapists or to mental health clinics.

Greater Difficulty of Arranging
Meetings Between Parents and Counselor:
I feel that the major disadvantage of counseling in schools is the greater difficulty in scheduling regular meetings between a child's parents and the counselor. In almost all instances mutual cooperation between the counselor and the parents is a crucial ingredient in a successful treatment. Such coordination is more difficult to arrange in a school since one or both parents are often unable to attend meetings during school hours. Family meetings may also be indicated, but these are virtually impossible to arrange unless the counselor is able to meet with the family early in the mornings or in the evening.

Advantages and Disadvantages of Out-of-the-Home Care

For most parents confronted with the recommendation of inpatient or residential treatment, the chief question is whether or not such out-of-the-home care is absolutely necessary. Indeed, the major disadvantage of such treatment is that it is extremely disruptive to a child's and family's routines. On the other hand, inpatient or residential treatment is sometimes the best or the only way to help a youngster resolve what he or she is experiencing as overwhelming problems.

Typically, when parents are faced with the prospect of having to send their child away from home for psychiatric evaluation or treatment, they have little or no choice of therapeutic setting. This is because of the very limited number of such facilities around the nation. In fact, a major difficulty for many parents is finding *any* facility in their area which can provide such help.

There are important distinctions to be drawn between services provided in hospital settings and those provided at residential treatment centers. These distinctions, however, will be of importance to you only if your youngster is actually in need of out-of-the-home placement. Therefore this information will not be discussed here, but will be presented in detail in Chapter Fourteen.

Chapter 5

THE MAJOR MENTAL HEALTH PROFESSIONS

In addition to relatives, friends, and neighbors, there are a wide variety of people who can provide help for youngsters with problems. Many of them are not psychotherapists. Concerned teachers, for example, have always set aside time to try to talk with and advise their more troubled or troublesome students. Pediatricians and family physicians spend considerable time advising parents about youngsters' emotional difficulties. Priests, ministers, and rabbis are often consulted about problems in families. And attorneys sometimes are involved in trying to settle family disputes. Many of these professionals are gifted listeners and advice givers, and many parents and youngsters are helped sufficiently that they don't need to seek further assistance. However, in instances where youngsters' problems persist, it is often recommended that parents seek help from a "mental health professional."

A "mental health professional" is someone who has received formal training to prepare him or her to help people in emotional distress and who has received some form of social sanction to function in this capacity, typically in the form of state licensing or certification. The term "mental health professional" is generally reserved for psychiatrists, psychologists, psychiatric social workers, and psychiatric nurses.

There can be a tremendous amount of overlap in the services provided by psychiatrists, psychologists, psychiatric social workers, and psychiatric nurses. In practice, in fact, there often is no way to distinguish between them. For example, a psychiatrist and a psychologist trained in a particular school of treatment, e.g., transactional analysis, might provide far more similar treatment than would two psychiatrists trained in different theoretical schools. Indeed, some people feel that the "discipline" of a therapist is far less important than is the theoretical orientation, the general level of experience, or the overall skill and personality of the therapist in question. ("Discipline" is used to denote a person's training, either in psychiatry, psychology, psychiatric social work, or psychiatric nursing.)

Nonetheless, there are differences among these professionals in terms of their training and the process by which they are licensed or certified. In this chapter I will discuss these differences and the importance they may have in the kind of help provided for your child or family. Before beginning this discussion I'll try to clear up some of the confusion that parents have with the various titles used by people who provide mental health services.

A THERAPIST BY ANY OTHER NAME[1]

Mental health professionals may refer to themselves or be referred to as "therapists," "psychotherapists," "clinicians," "counselors," "analysts," or "shrinks." Although all these terms have entered into popular usage, they are not scientific; at best they are descriptive, and at worst they are vague and confusing.

The terms "therapist" and "psychotherapist" are usually used interchangeably. They are only descriptive—referring to people who provide psychotherapy. Beware that *anyone* who provides psychotherapeutic help, regardless of training, qualifications, or experience, can call him- or herself a psychotherapist. If you wanted to, you could advertise yourself as a therapist without fear of prosecution from any state or professional organization. The terms "child therapist" and "family therapist" are equally unprotected.

The term "clinician" is often used interchangeably with "therapist" and refers to anyone who is providing psychotherapeutic services, regardless of their training.

"Counselor" is another descriptive term, generally unprotected by law, and simply refers to someone who counsels someone else.* Some people distinguish between "psychotherapy," which they view as an in-depth attempt to understand the underlying causes of emotional distress, and "counseling," which is viewed as more of a supportive attempt to help people cope with problems. However, given the variety of techniques used to help children and families with problems, this distinction is often blurred or misleading.

There are certain kinds of "counselors" who do have specifically delineated roles. Vocational or career counselors at schools or in industry help people in making career choices and in trying to solve work-related problems. Anyone, however, with or without training in this area, can legally use these titles.

On the other hand, guidance counselors in schools must be certified to use the title "counselor." Certification requirements for guidance counselors vary from state to state.

"Analyst" is a shortened version of the term "psychoanalyst." Traditionally psychoanalysts have been psychiatrists (although some are psychologists, social workers, or educators) who, after completing all their other formal training, enter a psychoanalytic training program or institute to learn a highly specialized type of treatment, based on Freudian theory, called "psychoanalysis." More recently practitioners of other schools of therapy (Jungians, Sullivanians) have established their own institutes, and successful graduates of these institutes also refer to themselves as psychoanalysts. A formally accredited psychoanalyst, from whatever school of therapy, will have completed

* Some psychology departments offer advanced degrees in "counseling psychology," but graduates of these programs refer to themselves as psychologists.

many extra years of rigorous training to receive this credential. The term "psychoanalyst," however, is not protected by law; anyone can legally (although not ethically) refer to him- or herself by this title.

"Shrink" is a slang expression commonly used to refer to psychiatrists, although it can refer to any therapist. The word is an abbreviation of "headshrinker" and originated in the 1930s among people involved in the first wave of popularity of Freudian psychoanalysis. Initially half-humorous, half-derogatory, "shrink" has become widely accepted as an informal if slightly deprecatory word for many mental health professionals.

LICENSING AND CERTIFICATION— A CONFUSING AND CONTROVERSIAL ISSUE

In the sections which follow I will describe in some detail the training of the various mental health professionals and the various ways in which they are certified or licensed. The issue of the licensing and certification of mental health professionals is very complicated and equally controversial.

Complications arise for a number of reasons. First there is the matter of definition. The terms "licensing" and "certification," although sometimes used interchangeably, are not identical. Through "certification" the state (or some other organization) attests to the fact that an individual has certain skills, but it does not prohibit people without such a certificate from practicing in that occupation or profession. "Licensing," on the other hand, not only requires some demonstration of competence in a given field, but restricts practice in that field to people holding a license. Unlicensed practitioners are subject to a fine or jail sentence.[2] A second complication is that while licensing laws and regulations are written and administered by each state, certification requirements can be set either by the state or by various professional organizations. (For example, in some states there are certification requirements for psychologists. At the same time there is a national organization of psychologists which has certification procedures which are totally separate and different from the state laws.) Third, each discipline has its own licensing and/or certification procedures and they are not easily comparable. For example, physicians must be licensed by the state in which they live in order to practice medicine. However, there are no licensing laws for different kinds of physicians, and thus psychiatrists are not licensed. There is a certification procedure for psychiatrists, but it is under the supervision of a professional psychiatric organization, not under state regulation; and it is entirely voluntary. This is not comparable to the situation for psychologists, who in most states are licensed. In addition, the certification procedure for psychologists is quite different from that for psychiatrists, and only a small percentage of psychologists are certified. The licensing and certification procedures for psychiatric social workers and psychiatric nurses are quite different from each other and from those for psychiatrists and psychologists.

The controversy surrounding licensing and certification procedures centers around the question of whom such credentialing most benefits. Some authors have argued that licensing and certification are primarily designed to protect mental health professionals, by limiting competition from younger colleagues. Such authors go on to argue that licensing laws, as currently written, do little to protect the public from unethical or incompetent practitioners.[3]

From a parent's vantage point, this controversy can serve as a reminder that neither licensing nor certification should be taken as proof of a therapist's competence. They serve only to inform parents that a professional has satisfied some minimum requirements in his or her discipline.

TRAINING AND LICENSING REQUIREMENTS IN THE MAJOR MENTAL HEALTH PROFESSIONS

The difference in training and certification requirements among the four mental health disciplines—psychiatry, psychology, psychiatric social work, and psychiatric nursing—are outlined below. In each case a separate section concerns care for *children* as available from members of that profession.

Psychiatry

A psychiatrist is a medical doctor who specializes in the diagnosis and treatment of emotional disorders. In order to be licensed in any state as a physician, a person must have successfully completed four years of study in an accredited medical school, and must typically also have completed one year of postgraduate medical education and passed a licensing examination.* The four years of medical school education provide students with generalized training in all fields of medicine including some basic course work in psychiatry, while the first postgraduate year is spent providing general medical care for children and/or adults. (This first year of postgraduate training used to be called an "internship.")

It is important to note that any *licensed physician* can legally practice psychiatry without any specialized postgraduate training. However, the vast majority of practicing psychiatrists have completed what is called "residency training" in the speciality of psychiatry. The residency

* Licensing laws vary from state to state. If you are interested, you can check with your state's board of registration in medicine for their licensing requirements.

period involves four years of postgraduate training. During the first year a resident provides general medical care. The following three years are spent in intensive training in psychiatry. This full-time training involves supervised experience in an accredited psychiatric hospital or in a psychiatric department of a general hospital.

About fifty percent of those physicians who complete their residency in general psychiatry go on to earn certification by a national body called the American Board of Psychiatry and Neurology. To become "board-certified" a psychiatrist must be a licensed physician, have completed four years of residency in psychiatry, and pass a special series of examinations.

CHILD PSYCHIATRISTS

Psychiatry is the only mental health discipline which has a formally sanctioned and licensed subspecialty in child diagnosis and treatment. A "child psychiatrist" must complete five years of residency training, which must include one year of general medical practice, two years of supervised experience with adults, and two years of supervised experience with children. To be board-certified as a child psychiatrist, he or she must also have successfully passed special examinations in both general and child psychiatry.

Minimum Credentials

If you are considering consulting a child psychiatrist, and if you have any choice in the matter, I suggest that you see someone who has at least completed a residency in both general and child psychiatry. A further credential you may wish to look for is board certification in child psychiatry. However, many excellent child psychiatrists, especially the older ones, are not board-certified. This is true because it was not until recently that such certification was viewed as an important credential to obtain. Another credential that gives evidence of further specialized training is the successful completion of a postgraduate training program in child or family treatment. (The most lengthy and rigorous training institutes are those which prepare professionals to be psychoanalysts.)

Psychology

Psychology is a discipline which deals with the study of mental processes and behavior. It is important to note that many psychologists are not involved in providing psychotherapy. Such professionals as social psychologists, mathematical psychologists, or experimental psychologists are involved in research and teaching activities in universities, government, and industry. It is only in some subspecialties of this field, such as clinical psychology, counseling psychology, or school psychology that people are trained in the evaluation and treatment of emotional problems.

Clinical psychologists receive academic training in such areas as personality theory, abnormal psychology, and psychotherapy and have the equivalent of at least one year of full-time supervised therapy experience called an "internship."* They also are trained to administer intelligence and personality tests. After the successful completion of their academic studies, their internship training, and the writing of an academic or research paper called a "dissertation," clinical-psychology students earn a Ph.D. degree. It takes most students at least four years of postgraduate study to earn this degree.

Counseling and school psychologists receive academic training that is in many ways similar to that of clinical psychologists. School psychologists, as their name implies, receive training especially designed to prepare them to work in school systems. Programs in these fields are typically housed in schools or departments of education, and graduates receive Ed.D. (Doctorate in Education) degrees. Some psychologists earn a Psy.D. (Doctorate in Psychology) degree. This is a relatively new degree, offered at

* Requirements of clinical psychology programs vary and some expect their students to have the equivalent of two full years of supervised experience before graduation.

professional schools of psychology in which practical clinical experience is stressed to a somewhat greater degree than is research activity. Ph.D., Psy.D., and Ed.D. psychologists generally use the title "doctor" before their names, although they are not physicians.

Most states have licensing or registration requirements which restrict the use of the title "psychologist." To call oneself a psychologist a person generally has to have either a Ph.D., Psy.D., or Ed.D. degree from an accredited university; has to have completed at least two full years of supervised clinical experience; and has to have passed a special examination.* It is important to note that all psychologists, not just those interested in providing evaluation and treatment services, are eligible to be licensed. Therefore a professional who is involved in animal research and has no therapy experience can be a licensed psychologist. Legally such a person could represent him- or herself as a licensed psychologist who provides therapeutic services. However, this would be in violation of the code of ethics of the American Psychological Association, which requires its members to function only in their areas of competence.

In an attempt to help consumers identify licensed psychologists who are qualified to provide evaluation and treatment services, a special directory was compiled in 1975, and is updated each year. This *National Registry of Health Service Providers in Psychology* lists licensed or certified psychologists who have at least two years of supervised clinical experience, one of which is postdoctoral.

An additional credential received by some psychologists is the Diploma of the American Board of Professional

* Licensing and certification laws for psychologists are relatively recent. Psychologists without a doctorate who were practicing for a prescribed period of time before the laws took effect are licensed under what are called "grandfather provisions." These psychologists typically hold master's degrees in psychology.

Licensing and certification laws also vary from state to state. Some states require no special examination. Some require both written and oral tests. Many states require that applicants for licensing pass a special national written examination.

Psychology. One is eligible to apply for diplomate status after completing five years of clinical experience, four of which must be postdoctoral. The diploma is awarded to those applicants who pass a lengthy examination and give other evidence of their competency. Currently relatively few clinical psychologists apply for this diplomate status, even though they are eligible to do so.*

PSYCHOLOGISTS AS CHILD THERAPISTS

Some clinical psychology training programs offer their students special course work and training in the assessment and treatment of emotional problems in children. Professionals with such training and with supervised clinical experience in working with children, parents, and families sometimes refer to themselves as clinical child psychologists. (In some medical settings they are referred to as pediatric psychologists.)

However, unlike psychiatry, psychology as a profession has no formal standards or procedures to identify and certify properly trained child psychologists. Thus anyone who considers himself or herself qualified can use the title "clinical child psychologist."

Minimum Credentials

If you are considering consulting a clinical child psychologist, and if you have any choice in the matter, I suggest that you see someone who has at least:

1) Been certified or licensed in the state where you live, and
2) Received the equivalent of two full-time years of supervised training in working with children

If you wish to see someone with further credentials, you might seek someone who has successfully completed a

* Approximately ten percent of all licensed psychologists are diplomates.

post-graduate training program in child or family treatment.

Psychiatric Social Work

A professional social worker is a person who has earned an M.S.W.—a Masters in Social Work degree. Social-work training involves two years of graduate study, including two half-time years of supervised experience. A special emphasis of all social-work training is the understanding of psychological problems in a social and environmental context.

As is the case in psychology, not all social workers are therapists. Those who are refer to themselves as "psychiatric" or "clinical" social workers. Many of these psychiatric social workers practice in community agencies, schools, and hospitals, although an ever-increasing number are in private practice.

Many social workers of all types go on to earn certification from a national organization called the Academy of Certified Social Workers (ACSW). The requirements of ACSW certification are as follows:

1) Graduation from an accredited Master's program in social work
2) The equivalent of two full-time years of supervised social-work experience, and
3) The successful completion of a national qualifying examination

It is important to note that ACSW certification is not intended to insure competency as a psychotherapist. This credential is rather an attempt to certify the attainment of a certain level of knowledge and experience in the general field of social work.

Approximately twenty-five states have passed licensing

laws that regulate social-work practice.* As is the case with ACSW certification, this licensure process, in most states, is intended to apply to all social workers, not just to those who provide therapeutic services. The requirements for state licensure are generally the same as those for the ACSW certification.

In an attempt to help consumers identify those social workers who are qualified to provide evaluation and treatment services, the National Association of Social Workers (NASW) has compiled a directory called the *National Register of Clinical Social Workers.*** The requirements for inclusion in this register are similar to those for ACSW certification, except that the applicant must show evidence that his or her two years of supervised experience primarily involved therapeutic work.

SOCIAL WORKERS AS CHILD THERAPISTS

Like psychology, social work has no formal standards or procedures for identifying or certifying those of its members who are qualified to work with children. Furthermore, social-work training does not generally provide extensive training in the subspecialty of child evaluation and treatment. Therefore social workers interested in this specialization often seek post-graduate supervised training.

The exception to this general rule is in the area of *group therapy* with children, where social workers may be more experienced than their colleagues from other disciplines.

Minimum Credentials

If you are considering consulting a psychiatric social worker, and if you have any choice in the matter, I suggest that you see someone with at least the following credentials:

* Some state laws regulate the practice of psychiatric social work separately from other social-work practice.

** An organization called the National Federation of State Societies of Clinical Social Work also publishes a register of clinical social workers.

1) ACSW certification or state licensure
2) The equivalent of two full-time years of supervised experience in working with children

If you wish to see someone with further credentials, you might seek someone who has successfully completed a post-graduate training program in child or family treatment.

Psychiatric Nursing

The psychiatric nurse is an R.N. (Registered Nurse) who has received special training and experience in working with people in emotional distress. In general, to be licensed in a state as a registered nurse a person must have completed a two-, three-, or four-year undergraduate training program in an accredited school of nursing, and must have passed a state licensing examination.

Nurses who have completed a four-year nursing program are eligible for acceptance to postgraduate master's programs in what is called "psychiatric/mental health nursing." These master's programs, which lead to either an M.A. (Master of Arts), an M.S. (Master of Science), and M.N. (Master of Nursing), or an M.S.N. (Master of Science in Nursing), vary in length from one to two years and involve course work as well as supervised clinical experience.

There is no special state licensing of psychiatric nurses. Since 1977, however, the American Nurses Association (a national organization of professional nurses) has instituted a certification program for psychiatric nurses. Those nurses who plan to work for some percentage of time in private practice typically seek certification as psychiatric and mental health nursing specialists. The requirements for specialist certification are:

1) A master's degree in an accredited program in psychiatric/mental health nursing

2) Two years of supervised clinical experience, at least one of which must be postgraduate

3) The successful completion of a written examination, and

4) Documentation of competence as a clinician*

PSYCHIATRIC NURSES AS CHILD THERAPISTS

The profession of psychiatric nursing is moving toward a clearly and formally sanctioned subspecialty in child work. Currently applicants for national certification as specialists in the field request to be examined in either adult psychiatric nursing or child psychiatric nursing. Those interested in child psychiatric nursing must give evidence that most of their clinical experience has been in working with youngsters. Despite the fact that there is a special examination for nurses interested in child work, successful applicants do not receive formal certification in child psychiatric nursing as such. Their title is exactly the same as that of their colleagues in adult psychiatric nursing, namely, "psychiatric and mental health nursing specialists."

Because of the relatively short period of graduate training, some psychiatric nurses interested in the subspecialty of child work seek, like their colleagues in social work, postgraduate training in this field.

Minimum Credentials

If you are considering consulting a psychiatric nurse, and if you have any choice in the matter, I suggest that you find someone with at least the following credentials:

1) A Master's degree with an emphasis in psychiatric and mental health nursing

* The American Nurses Association also provides certification for psychiatric and mental health nursing "generalists." To be eligible for this certification, an individual must be a registered nurse with at least two years of relevant and clinical experience. Nurses with this certification typically work in organized mental health settings such as hospitals and mental health centers.

2) The equivalent of two full years of supervised clinical experience in working with children

If you wish further credentials, a postgraduate training program in child or family treatment would provide these.

WHY CHOOSE ONE DISCIPLINE OVER ANOTHER?

I believe that in many instances there is no reason to see, or not see, someone *primarily* on the basis of his or her discipline. Within each profession are many skilled, dedicated, and helpful people—as well as some who are unskilled, incompetent, or even destructive.*

However, if you prefer, for whatever reasons, to consult someone from one particular discipline, you should feel free to do so. Seeking psychotherapy for your child or your family can be a complicated and difficult undertaking, and anything (within reason) that will make you feel more comfortable with this process should be pursued.

In addition to your personal preferences there are some practical matters which may influence your decision as to which kind of professional to see.

* Each professional discipline has developed a code of ethics intended to govern the behavior of its members. If you have any questions or complaints about the ethical behavior or professional competence of your child's or family's therapist, contact the appropriate professional organization. For psychiatry this would be the state or local chapter of the American Psychiatric Association; for psychology it would be the American Psychological Association, which will put you in touch with your local psychological association; for social work, the state chapter of the National Association of Social Workers; for nursing, the Board of Registration of Nursing in your state.

Financial Considerations

In private practice* it is psychiatrists who tend to charge the highest fees. A minimum fee for most psychiatrists is forty or forty-five dollars per hour. In some parts of the country the minimum fee could be fifty or sixty dollars per hour. Psychologists' fees tend to be slightly lower, the minimum being thirty-five or forty dollars per hour. Psychiatric social workers and psychiatric nurses tend to have the lowest fees, a minimum being twenty-five or thirty dollars per hour. (Some therapists in private practice will lower their fees for people who cannot afford the regular rates; many will not.)

Insurance coverage also differs for psychiatrists, psychologists, social workers, and nurses in private practice. (Again, this issue does not arise at clinics, where the medical director typically signs all insurance forms.) In general, the fees of psychiatrists are covered by all government or private insurance policies that reimburse for mental health services. In some states licensed psychologists' fees are also covered. Charges for psychiatric social workers and nurses are currently the least likely to be reimbursed by insurance companies. The fees of psychologists, social workers, or nurses will usually be paid, however, if their services were performed under the supervision of a psychiatrist. Since insurance policies vary tremendously with regard to what and whom they cover, the best thing for you to do is to check with your insurance representative *before* committing yourself to a costly treatment.

One other thing to keep in mind is that, *in general,* psychotherapy is tax deductible as a medical expense regardless of whether it is provided by a physician or a nonphysician. I say "in general" because the Internal Rev-

* At publicly sponsored clinics, however, you are charged the same hourly fee, whatever it may be—regardless of whether you see a psychiatrist, a psychologist, a social worker, or a nurse.

enue Service reserves the right to review such deductions on a case-by-case basis.

Considerations Having to Do with Medications or Hospitalization

Psychiatrists, since they are physicians, are the only mental health professionals who can medicate a child or admit him to a hospital. If medication or hospitalization may be indicated for your child, you might wish to consult a psychiatrist rather than a professional from a nonmedical discipline. On the other hand, this is not a necessity since competent psychologists, social workers, and nurses establish close working relationships with at least one psychiatrist whom they consult when questions of medication or hospitalization arise.

A CLOSING NOTE

There are no "double-your-money-back" guarantees in the field of psychotherapy. And neither academic training, nor practical experience, nor state licensing can guarantee the effectiveness of any given therapist. The best-trained, best-thought-of clinician cannot be equally helpful to every single client. On the other hand, there are inept and even mentally unbalanced therapists who manage to help certain clients tremendously.

The reasonable thing for you to remember is that training and credentials can have some importance in the effectiveness of a therapist. All other things being equal, I would suggest that you seek help from someone who has had supervised training and experience in working with children and families, and who continues to see children as a regular part of his or her professional work. Other qualities to look for in a therapist will be discussed in Chapter Six.

Chapter 6

THE MAJOR SCHOOLS OF PSYCHOTHERAPY*

There has developed in this country a bewildering array of psychotherapies. It had been written that "groups, movements, and schools of [therapy] spring up like weeds."[1] It should come as a relief to already confused parents that much of this glut of new treatment technique was neither designed nor intended for use with children, parents, or families. Indeed, the major child-related treatment approaches are by now fairly well established. Even the relatively new field of family therapy has been in existence since the 1950s.

In this chapter I will introduce you to the four major schools of child and family treatment,** namely the psychoanalytic approaches, the behavioral approaches, the humanistic approaches, and the family systems approaches. In reading a description of these different schools, you may find one which seems suitable for your child or family, and thus may seek out a therapist who practices this kind of treatment. But before I detail these major schools, I'll address the question of the relative importance of the various therapeutic approaches to the outcome of any child's or family's treatment.

* The coauthor of this chapter is Helen Broskowski, Ph.D.
** Transactional Analysis (TA) and Gestalt therapy will be discussed briefly at the end of this chapter.

ARE SOME TREATMENT APPROACHES MORE HELPFUL THAN OTHERS?

You may wonder if there is any evidence that one treatment approach has proven generally more successful than any other in helping children and families resolve problems. The answer to this question is no. Indeed, none but the most fervent proponents of the different schools of therapy would claim such overall superiority for their methods.

It seems rather that a host of interrelated factors account for the relative success or failure of any given treatment. The theoretical approach of the therapist is one such factor, but of equal or perhaps greater importance are such factors as 1) the overall "quality" or competence of the therapist, 2) the match or "fit" between a given therapist and the child or family being helped, and 3) the relative motivation and capacity of a child or family to make difficult changes in their behaviors or attitudes.

It may be argued that the single most important factor in the relative helpfulness of any given therapy is the overall competence of the therapist. In his excellent book on psychotherapy entitled *A Complete Guide to Therapy,* Dr. Joel Kovel lends support to this notion when he writes, "It is not therapies as such that are [effective or] ineffective. They all have their limits—practical, theoretical, moral, and otherwise—but within their limits they are all designed to work if they are properly applied. And as all of them have to be applied by the person of the therapist, it follows that no matter what the form of treatment, for therapy to work at all the therapist must possess certain characteristics."[2] According to Kovel these characteristics include: 1) empathy—the capacity to sense what is going on psychologically within another person; 2) receptivity—the capacity to listen to the communications of others; 3) articulateness—the capacity to communicate clearly one's own thoughts and feelings; 4) a combination of flexibility and stability—the ability to change one's mind in the face of new information without losing one's identity or purpose; and 5) a capacity to maturely care about another's well-being. Mature caring is defined as the capacity to help a person grow and change for his or her own sake, not one's own. A therapist possessing these qualities will likely be helpful to a large proportion of his or her clients, regardless of that therapist's theoretical approach.

Of course, even the most skilled clinicians do not help all their clients. Thus it makes sense to expect that the "match" or "fit" between a client and therapist will also be an important factor in the outcome of any therapy. The ingredients that constitute a successful match are difficult to specify but may include some of the following:

1) The meshing or clashing of personalities between therapist and child or family: Just as in any other kind of relationship, some people, for whatever reasons, do or don't hit it off.

2) The specific kind of problem that a child or family brings to treatment: Some therapists find, over time, that they tend not to be helpful to children or families who experience certain kinds of difficulties; for example, delinquency or drug abuse. There are, however, clinicians who specialize in working with precisely these problems; just as there are therapists specializing in any number of other problems.

3) The capacity and motivation of a child or family to make use of treatment: It is not surprising that the most intelligent, well-motivated, and psychologically minded clients have traditionally been the easiest for therapists to help, while less motivated and less psychologically minded patients have often reaped the least benefits from treatment.

4) The fourth factor in a successful treament, and the one which will be addressed in this chapter, is the theoretical approach of the therapist: Experience has led some clinicians to believe that some kinds of psy-

chological problems and certain kinds of youngsters and families seem to benefit most from particular types of therapeutic intervention. Indeed the relatively newer treatment approaches, such as the behavior therapies and the family systems approaches, were designed especially to help those clients for whom the psychoanalytic and humanistic approaches proved relatively less effective.

In the sections which follow, I will not only describe and compare major schools of treatment, but I will also present any evidence that a particular treatment approach has proven especially helpful (or unhelpful) in dealing with specific kinds of emotional problems.

HOW COMPARABLE ARE THE DIFFERENT THERAPEUTIC APPROACHES?

Comparing different therapeutic approaches is similar in many ways to the proverbial difficulty in comparing apples and oranges. Each approach has its own theory of how personality develops and of the nature and causes of emotional difficulties. Each school of thought not only has its own view of how to help resolve emotional problems, but even of what constitutes a problem in the first place. As Kovel writes, "All therapists agree that they can help some people, but they don't have the same people in mind and they don't share the same view of what is wrong or what constitutes help. Not only do they speak at cross purposes, they don't really use the same language, even though many words are the same."[3] In the next sections I'll trv to bring some clarity to this confusion, but you should be aware of the fact that the field of psychotherapy is itself quite fragmented and confused.

One further note of caution is in order. When comparing and contrasting the major schools of therapy, you should be aware of the fact that there is often some disparity between what a therapist professes to do, and what he or she actually does when working with a client. There is much research evidence to suggest that as therapists become more experienced, they tend to become less wedded to a given treatment approach and become more willing to use whichever techniques may be helpful to a client. Therefore a psychoanalytically oriented therapist may sometimes employ behavioral techniques, or a family therapist may use psychoanalytic techniques. Nonetheless most therapists will identify themselves as working from one theoretical orientation and will tend to define treatment goals and employ treatment techniques which are compatible with this theoretical perspective.

AN OUTLINE FOR COMPARING THE MAJOR SCHOOLS OF THERAPY

As a way of helping you compare the different therapeutic approaches, I'll address the following questions under each school of thought.

1) What underlying assumptions are made about the causes of emotional disturbances?
2) When a youngster is brought for help, what are the evaluation procedures which are generally employed?
3) Which members of the family is the therapist most likely to focus on in resolving problems—the youngster brought for help, his or her parents, or the entire family unit?
4) What methods are typically used to try to bring about desired changes?
5) Which kinds of problems does each approach seem to be most (and least) helpful in resolving?

The Psychoanalytic Approaches

All psychoanalytically oriented treatments are based on the theories of Dr. Sigmund Freud. Freud was a physician who received his training in the late 1800s in Vienna. His original interest was neurology (the study of brain functioning and the treatment of diseases of the nervous system) but he subsequently became interested in treating emotionally troubled people; first through hypnosis and subsequently through his own methods, which he called "psychoanalysis."

DEFINITION OF TERMS

The term "psychoanalysis" refers to a variety of therapeutic techniques based on Freud's theory of personality development. Psychoanalysis involves frequent therapy appointments—four or five times a week—and the use of a couch, upon which the patient lies. The patient is instructed to follow one basic rule, namely to say everything which comes to mind (a task far more difficult than one would imagine). The psychoanalyst's role is to point out the countless ways that the patient resists this basic rule. The goal of this process is to help the patient become aware of the unconscious thoughts and feelings which underlie her psychological problems.

The term "psychoanalytically oriented psychotherapy" refers to a modified form of psychoanalysis, in which therapy appointments are less frequent—once or twice a week the patient sits in a chair facing the therapist, and the focus of the treatment is not only on uncovering unconscious thoughts and feelings, but also on a more direct resolution of the specific problems for which the patient has sought help.

Freud's psychoanalytic techniques were designed for use with adults, not with children or younger adolescents. In order to be helpful to these younger patients, psychoanalytic techniques had to undergo substantial modification. Such alterations in technique were pioneered and popularized by Anna Freud (Sigmund Freud's daughter). She originated a treatment referred to as "child psychoanalysis,"[4] which entails frequent appointments—four or five times a week, over the course of many years. However, instead of being told to say whatever comes to mind, a child is encouraged to express thoughts and feelings through play and drawing.

Because of the practical matters of time and expense, the techniques of child psychoanalysis were themselves modified so that a child could be seen less frequently—once or twice a week—over a somewhat shorter period of time—one to two years. The term "psychoanalytically oriented child psychotherapy" refers to this modified form of child psychoanalysis, and is by far the most commonly employed treatment technique used by therapists who adhere to Freudian principles.[5]

UNDERLYING ASSUMPTIONS

All psychoanalytically oriented therapies are based on a conflict theory of personality development. Freud believed that a child's needs (many of which are "unconscious" or out of the child's awareness) inevitably come into conflict with the demands of family and society. As a child matures, she is expected to learn behaviors which satisfy both her needs and the demands of the environment. Problem behaviors or "symptoms"* result when a youngster is unable to find an appropriate compromise between her desires and the demands of those around her. For example, a young child who wants attention is often faced with the reality that her mother has many other things to do.

* The word "symptom" is a medical term referring to a condition which indicates the existence of some underlying disease. A fever, running nose, etc., are considered to be symptoms of some infection, typically a cold or flu. In psychiatric parlance, symptoms refer to behaviors which signal the presence of some underlying emotional upset. (In this book I use the terms "symptom" and "problem behavior" synonymously.)

One solution to this conflict is for the girl to draw a picture "for her mother" and periodically show this to her in order to get some attention and affection. A less adaptive solution would be for the youngster to throw a temper tantrum because her mother wasn't spending enough time with her.

Psychoanalytic theorists and parents alike have asked the question of why some children are able to find appropriate solutions to conflict situations (e.g., drawing a picture to get attention) while others are not (e.g., throwing a temper tantrum). In the early days of psychoanalytic theorizing, the "cause" or "blame" for such behaviors was often laid on the shoulders of the mother. (For example, she was thought to be "rejecting" or "unconsciously hostile.") Current psychoanalytic thought holds that problem behaviors are the result of a complex interaction between a youngster and the environment. Perhaps the youngster by temperament has a very low capacity to tolerate frustration. Perhaps her mother is already overburdened by many other demands. Perhaps her father is not available to provide much support or relief to his wife. Thus psychoanalytic theory posits that the subtle interplay of any of a number of factors is typically what sets the stage for the development of problem behaviors.

EVALUATION PROCEDURES

Analytically oriented therapists tend to do rather lengthy evaluations before beginning any treatment. While a few therapists may be willing to begin therapy after one or two interviews, four or five evaluation sessions is more typical.

The therapist will usually want to begin the evaluation by interviewing a child's parents. During this first session parents will probably be asked a host of questions about their child's early development, including medical history and school history. A therapist may ask parents about their own childhoods, their courtship, and their marriage. All therapists will want to know about the specific problems that led parents to seek professional help. In addition, parents will be asked to sign releases of information so that their child's teacher and pediatrician can be contacted.

The next appointment or two will probably be with the child referred for help and the therapist. During these sessions the therapist will assess the child's psychological strengths and weaknesses, with a special focus on the youngster's capacity and motivation to make use of a therapeutic intervention. Personality testing (see Chapter Eight) may be used as part of the evaluation procedure.

The therapist may want to go to the child's school and observe her in that setting. Perhaps the entire family will be asked to participate in one interview. The evaluation period will conclude with the therapist summarizing her impressions and making a recommendation about what, if any, type of treatment is indicated.

FOCUS OF THE TREATMENT

The focus of treatment in psychoanalytic therapy is the child who was brought for help. This does not necessarily mean that only the child is seen for therapy, for oftentimes the therapist will also have sessions with a youngster's parents. It does mean that the emphasis of therapy is helping the child and her parents understand the nature and causes of her emotional difficulties.

Some analytically oriented therapists have sessions only with the child. These clinicians do not have much contact with the child's parents since such contact is believed to complicate the therapist's unique relationship with the child. Parents may have sessions with a different therapist who works closely with the child's therapist. This treatment structure is referred to as the "child-guidance model," since this was the traditional treatment model at child-guidance clinics.

Nowadays it has become more common for analytically oriented child therapists to have separate meetings with a youngster—typically once or twice a week—and with her parents—typically once every other week. At times a therapist will meet only with the parents, particularly when the troubled child is very young.

Individual therapy, as described above, is not the only

kind of treatment done by analytically oriented therapists. Some clinicians meet regularly with family members (family therapy) and some lead therapy groups for troubled youngsters (group therapy). However, whether the work of psychoanalytically oriented treatment is done through the parents, or in group or family therapy, the principal target of change is the child with the problem.

TREATMENT GOALS

The broad goal of all analytically oriented therapies is to help a child understand and resolve whatever conflicts there are in her life. The child's problem behaviors or symptoms are viewed as inappropriate solutions to unrecognized and unresolved conflicts, and with understanding, are expected to gradually subside or disappear.

Thus one of the basic tenets of all psychoanalytically oriented therapies has traditionally been that a child must first be helped to recognize and resolve underlying conflicts, before she can be expected to make significant changes in behavior. Since such understandings are difficult to achieve, it has been expected that such treatment will likely take a significant period of time, typically from one to three years or more. Furthermore it has been believed that if a youngster is pressured, by parents or a therapist, to give up a troublesome behavior or symptom, the result will simply be the youngster's development of a new set of symptoms or problem behaviors. This phenomenon is called "symptom substitution."

Some analytically oriented therapists now believe that symptoms can be alleviated without a youngster's understanding the conflicts underlying such behavior—and that once the original symptoms are removed, they are not typically replaced by other problem behaviors. These therapists therefore have as their goal the replacement of problematic behaviors by appropriate behaviors. Since underlying issues are not addressed, the treatment can take far less time.

TREATMENT METHODS

Psychoanalytic treatment methods will vary depending on the therapist's definition of the treatment goals.

If the therapist concentrates on changing behavior without first resolving underlying conflicts, the treatment methods will revolve around helping the child substitute appropriate behaviors for inappropriate ones. The therapist may make suggestions to both the child and the parents or encourage them to experiment with their own solutions. If the therapist feels that the child is not sufficiently verbal to talk about her problems, the treatment may focus exclusively on helping the parents find adaptive solutions for their youngster's difficulties.

Most analytically oriented therapists will concentrate, to some extent, on helping a child resolve her underlying conflicts. With this as a goal the therapist will be less likely to give suggestions and advice and more likely to interpret the possible meanings of problem behaviors.

Since the child's natural medium of expression is play, the therapist will typically provide a playroom setting. Many older children and adolescents are able to talk at length about their thoughts and feelings, and for such youngsters play activities are not necessary.

The therapist works on the premise that the more connections she can make between all the child says and does, the better she can understand the child's underlying (and often hidden) conflicts. The therapist tries to understand the symbolic meaning of the child's play and this understanding often clarifies the meaning and purpose of the child's symptoms. Then the therapist slowly and gradually helps the child understand the reasons for her inappropriate behaviors and shows the child how other behaviors can be substituted for the problematic ones. The therapist meets with the parents to help them understand the nature of the youngster's conflicts and to help them find ways of encouraging and reinforcing more adaptive behaviors.

An analytically oriented therapist considers her relationship with the child to be central to the treatment. The therapeutic relationship provides three key elements for such treatment. First, the therapist offers a relationship which is sufficiently nonjudgmental for the child to feel free to express herself. Second, over time the child begins to experience and to behave toward the therapist in ways similar to those in which the youngster behaves with her parents. When this happens, the child is said to be "transferring" feelings about her mother or father onto the therapist. Third and finally, the therapist encourages the child to try out new behaviors during the therapy sessions, as a way of preparing for their expression at home or in school.

Although psychoanalytic therapy has principally been an individually oriented treatment, it can also take place within a family or group context. In analytically oriented family therapy, the goal of the treatment is to help family members understand and resolve conflicts between them. In analytically oriented group therapies, children are helped to understand and resolve difficulties with each other. Groups for preschool- and elementary-school-aged children are typically "activity groups"; the therapist provides play activities in the form of games, crafts, sports, or trips. While the youngsters engage in these activities the therapist observes and comments on difficulties that each child has in getting along with her age-mates and offers suggestions on other ways in which the child may resolve conflicts. Therapy groups for adolescents may involve mostly verbal interchange in which the participants discuss difficulties in their lives.

PROBLEMS WHICH ARE MOST AND LEAST AMENABLE TO THE PSYCHOANALYTIC APPROACHES

Psychoanalytically oriented approaches, especially those which focus on the resolution of underlying conflicts, seem *best suited* to youngsters and families who are somewhat verbal, intelligent, and psychologically minded. The treatment is typically lengthy and children and parents alike must be willing to accept the fact that the therapy is not designed to lead to quick changes in behavior. Rather it aims toward more long-lasting changes in personality. Indeed, many analytically oriented therapists will advise parents, before beginning such treatment, that change will come slowly and that their child may even get "worse" before she gets "better."

Children who *adapt best* to this form of treatment are those who are able to acknowledge that they have some problems and who are sufficiently unhappy with their lives that they are willing to cooperate with the therapist in attempting to ferret out the underlying causes of their problems.

If parents or children are interested in very quick results, this form of therapy may not be indicated. The exception to this is short-term or time-limited treatments, which although based on psychoanalytic principles, are especially designed to lead to relatively rapid behavior change.

Analytically oriented individual psychotherapy has not been particularly successful in dealing with delinquent youth, or with adolescents who are heavily involved in drug or alcohol abuse. At times these youngsters can be engaged in analytically oriented group-therapies—especially if the other group members have similar problems, and if the therapist is someone who seems to be knowledgeable about their life-styles. Nonetheless, organizations such as Alcoholics Anonymous and specially designed drug-treatment programs seem to have more success with such youngsters.

Children with very severe forms of schizophrenia are also not generally suited for out-patient analytically oriented treatments. On the other hand such treatment may be successful if the child is placed in a psychiatric hospital or residential-treatment center so that the therapy is one part of an entire treatment program.[6]

Youngsters who are mentally retarded or seriously brain damaged are also typically unable to make use of analytically oriented therapies because they do not have the verbal and intellectual skills which such treatments generally require.

SUMMARY

In summary, psychoanalytic theory is principally a conflict theory of personality development and, traditionally, psychoanalytic therapy aims at the understanding and resolving of the inner conflicts which underlie problem behavior. Broadly defined problems and goals tend to make analytically oriented therapies long-term and open-ended. Parents and children alike must be willing to accept the fact that such treatment is generally not intended to lead to quick changes in behavior.

The Humanistic Approaches

I have chosen the label "humanistic" to refer to treatment approaches which might also be called nondirective, experiential, or client-centered. The term "client-centered" comes from the work of Carl Rogers, an American psychologist who pioneered this approach.[7] Although Rogerian treatment originated in this therapeutic work with adults, this approach has proven to be quite adaptable to work with children. Virginia Axline, a child psychiatrist, has been influential in popularizing the use of client-centered psychotherapy for troubled youngsters.[8]

UNDERLYING ASSUMPTIONS

Humanistic therapists believe, in Rogers's words, that "the innermost core of man's nature, the deepest layer of his personality, . . . is positive in nature—is basically socialized, forward-moving, rational and realistic."[9] These therapists believe that all children are born with the capacity to develop into loving, productive, and happy adults; to be "self-actualized." They maintain that maladjusted or problem behaviors develop because a given youngster, for whatever reasons, is not afforded the opportunity to develop his innate positive potential. Problem behaviors are viewed as an attempt by the child, albeit a maladaptive or distorted one, to realize his inner potential.

EVALUATION PROCEDURES

Since new learning takes place only in the present, experiential therapists will have comparatively little interest in collecting information about a child's past history. Nonetheless the therapist may meet for one evaluation session with parents to gather some information about the youngster's current functioning, and may wish to talk with a child's pediatrician or teacher. Typically the first session with the child is considered to be the beginning of the therapy.

FOCUS OF THE TREATMENT

Many humanistic therapists will see a child alone in individual therapy, usually on a once- or twice-a-week basis. Contact with the child's parents will be less frequent, the frequency often left to the wishes of the parent. Other family members may be included at the request of the child or parents.

The humanistic therapies also lend themselves very well to group and family treatment. Indeed, Dr. Axline feels that many children can progress faster in group therapy than they can in individual treatment.

TREATMENT GOALS

Humanistically oriented therapists will define problems in terms of those broad aspects of the child's environment that block his capacity to learn and grow in a positive direction. The therapists' goals therefore tend to be formulated very generally—to allow the client to express feeling and thought freely, and to discover his self-worth. Finally, these therapists share an underlying assumption that the child who values himself will choose to behave in ways that satisfy himself as well as significant others in his life.

TREATMENT METHODS

The humanistic therapies are purposely nondirective. The therapist's job is to provide a permissive, nondemanding environment where the child (or parents or family) can learn to freely express thoughts and feelings. The therapist will not make suggestions, give advice, or provide homework assignments. Rather it is the therapist's primary task to help the child experience and accept his own feelings. The therapist helps the child do this by communicating a feeling of "unconditional positive regard" for him. By this it is meant not that the therapist likes or agrees with all of the child's thoughts, feelings, or behaviors but rather that the therapist unconditionally respects the child's value as a human being.

As is the case in analytically oriented therapies, the humanistic therapist allows the child to communicate thoughts and feelings in whatever fashion is most comfortable. Thus humanistic therapists will provide the child with toys, games, drawing and craft materials that are appropriate to his age. Older children may choose simply to talk; but they will not be pressured to do so.

The permissiveness of humanistic therapies does not imply total freedom for the client. As in all therapies, a youngster will not be allowed to engage in an activity which would lead to harm to himself, to someone else, or to anyone's property.

Virginia Axline summarizes the humanistic approach as follows:

> . . . the therapeutic value of this kind of psychotherapy is based upon the child's experiencing himself as a capable, responsible person in a relationship that tries to communicate to him two basic truths: that no one ever really knows as much about any human being's inner world as does the individual himself; and that responsible freedom grows and develops from inside the person. The child must learn self-respect and a sense of dignity that grows out of his in-

creasing self-understanding before he can learn to respect the personalities and rights and differences of others.[10]

PARENT EFFECTIVENESS TRAINING (PET)

PET deserves separate attention as a humanistic counseling approach for parents. PET is unique among modern therapies in its emphasis on preventing problems before they occur. Indeed, PET was designed (by Thomas Gordon), not as a therapy, but rather as a technique to teach people how to be better parents. Of course, parents of children who have already developed problems may also benefit from the PET program.[11]

PET is based on the same underlying assumptions as are all humanistic therapies. Parents are taught to have positive regard for themselves and their children and are helped to become more empathetic listeners and more "genuine" (i.e., to develop a greater awareness of their own feelings and to learn how to communicate both positive and negative feelings in a nonjudgmental fashion). Another major focus of the program is to help parents develop skills in resolving family conflicts through discussion and negotiation rather than through the use of power.

PET methods are primarily educational. The program involves a series of lectures, usually over an eight-week period. In-class participation is encouraged with role-playing and group discussion. Assignments in reading, practice materials, and at-home activities are given. PET instructors are themselves former students—either parents or professionals—who have taken the course.

PROBLEMS WHICH ARE MOST AND LEAST AMENABLE TO THE HUMANISTIC APPROACHES

Humanistically oriented psychotherapy has been employed to treat a wide variety of clients, ranging from relatively normal adolescents struggling with issues of identity, to schizophrenic children struggling to gain a foothold on reality. The reason for the wide applicability of the humanistic approaches seems twofold: First, humanistically based treatments focus especially on problems of self-regard or self-esteem—difficulties which are present, to some extent, for all people. Second, humanistically based treatment is the most optimistic and inspirational of all the therapies; its proponents are committed to trying to help all people, regardless of the severity of their difficulties.

While it is true that humanistically oriented therapies can be used to help anyone, they seem to be most ideally suited to youngsters struggling with issues of self-esteem or to adolescents who are trying to "find themselves." Youngsters with drug- or alcohol-related problems may also be helped by the inspirational and caring aspects of this approach. Finally, this type of therapy can also be quite helpful to seriously disturbed children, for whom the support and attention of a caring therapist can be invaluable.

Since humanistically based treatment is open ended and nondirective, it may not be suitable for parents or children who need quick relief from pressing problems. It also does not seem like a particularly helpful treatment for severely or chronically conflicted families, since each family member does not need to realize his potential as much as he needs to live cooperatively with others.

SUMMARY

In summary, humanistically oriented therapy rests on a self-actualizing view of human nature. Evaluation procedures are relatively brief, since the focus of the treatment is on the client's present experience. The goals of treatment are broadly defined in terms of enhancing the client's self-esteem. Because of the emphasis on allowing a child to change or grow at his own pace, it will be difficult for a humanistically oriented therapist to provide parents with an accurate prediction of the length of any given treatment.

The Behavioral Approaches

The theoretical foundation of the behavioral approaches is primarily the pioneering work of Ivan Pavlov, a Russian physiologist, and B. F. Skinner, an American psychologist. Both Skinner and Pavlov were interested in specifying the conditions under which behaviors were learned and unlearned. The principles of learning which they detailed (and which have been elaborated and refined by subsequent researchers) form the basis of most behavioral treatment techniques.[12]

UNDERLYING ASSUMPTIONS

Underlying the behavioral approaches are two basic principles of learning. The first is called the "law of conditioned reflexes." Formulated by Pavlov,* this principle states that when a stimulus (called a "conditioned stimulus"; let's say a smile occurs *right before* another stimulus (called an "unconditioned stimulus"; let's say giving a child some food) then, over time, the conditioned stimulus will evoke the same response as did the unconditioned stimulus. So if giving a youngster some food typically led the child to feel contented, then, eventually, just smiling at the child ought to lead her to experience a similar kind of contentment.

The second principle is called the "law of effect." It was formulated by an American psychologist, Paul Thorndike, and elaborated by Skinner. This principle states that a stimulus (let's say a hug) occurring *just after* some behavior (for example, a child saying thank you), can increase

* In Pavlov's original experiments he rang a bell just before presenting a dog with food. The dog's mouth would water in response to the sight and smell of the food. After a period of time Pavlov could ring a bell—without presenting any food—and the dog would begin to salivate.

the frequency of that behavior. So if each time your youngster says thank you, you give him or her a hug, he or she is likely to say thank you more often. In this example your hug is referred to as "a positive reinforcer."

Behaviorists also talk about "negative reinforcement." When the *subtraction* of a stimulus *increases* the frequency of a behavior, that stimulus is a "negative reinforcer." Let's take an example of a youngster who compulsively bangs his head against a wall. As one method of getting the child to stop banging his head, a behavioral therapist may try to increase the frequency of that child's holding his head up straight (this method will work since a child cannot simultaneously hold his head up straight and bang it against a wall). Thus each time a child begins to bang his head, the therapist may hold the child's hair quite firmly, and then gradually loosen the grip. If the child's rate of holding his head up straight *increased* when the therapist loosened the grip, then the holding of the child's hair would be called a negative reinforcer.

Negative reinforcement should not be confused with punishment. When the stimulus which follows a behavior *decreases* the frequency of that behavior, then that stimulus is called a "punisher." For example, if a child was slapped on the wrist each time he banged his head, and if the child then began to bang his head less frequently, then slapping his wrists would be a punisher. In general, behaviorists don't like to use punishment, 1) since punishment tends to suppress behavior rather than change it and 2) because punishment has many potential side-effects—for example, making a child fearful or angry—and these adverse side-effects may, in and of themselves, create other problems for the child.

EVALUATION PROCEDURES

An evaluation conducted by a behaviorally oriented therapist is likely to be quite detailed, and can be as lengthy as that of a psychoanalytically oriented one; extending over a period of several weeks.

The therapist will probably begin the evaluation by meeting either with the parents alone or with the parents and child together. Other family members will typically not be included, unless they significantly contribute to the difficulties. During the initial sessions the therapist will ask about the child's development and about any significant family history. The purpose of this discussion will be to try to discover how the problem behavior was originally learned. As part of this process, parents may be asked to complete various checklists and questionnaires. Most important, the behavioral therapist will ask parents to begin to make careful, systematic records of their child's problem behaviors.

The next appointments will be either with the child alone or with the child and his parents. The therapist may want to observe the youngster at school or at home and will probably want to talk with teachers, guidance counselors, and the pediatrician. The evaluation will likely conclude with the therapist summarizing his impressions and making a recommendation about what, if any, type of treatment is indicated.

FOCUS OF THE TREATMENT

As is the case with psychoanalytically oriented therapies, the focus of behavioral treatments is the child who is evidencing problem behaviors. However, unlike analytic therapy, behavioral treatment may involve little actual therapeutic contact with the youngster. Rather, much of the time may be spent teaching the child's parents and teachers new ways of responding to a child's behaviors. Of course, when indicated, a behavioral therapist will meet with a child for individual sessions.

TREATMENT GOALS

It is an invariable rule of behavior therapy that goals be specific and measurable. For example, it is not sufficient to say that a child should "feel less anxious" or even that he "should stop throwing temper tantrums." Instead, parents and therapists need to state goals in such a way that it can easily be determined if these goals have been accomplished. For instance, a suitable goal might be that a child will ask to have his mother or father read or play with him once a day (an appropriate way to get attention) and will have no tantrums for a week (tantrums being an inappropriate way to seek attention). As part of the process of setting goals the child will be told of the consequences which will follow his behavior. For example, each day that he goes without throwing a tantrum, he earns a star, and six stars earn him a specified reward on the seventh day.

On the other hand, if the child's problems involve difficulties with certain feelings—for example, fearfulness—then the behaviorist will teach the child and his parents methods of reducing fearfulness and anxiety.

TREATMENT METHODS

Behavior therapy consists of more than the designing and monitoring of reinforcement systems (although this is one very common treatment technique). In general, reinforcement systems are used when a youngster is evidencing problem behaviors, while other techniques may be employed when the child is troubled by feelings of depression, fear, or anxiety.

Reinforcement Systems

A behavioral therapist will be quite active and directive in designing a reinforcement system for parents to carry out. Since it is believed that reinforcers are generally more helpful in modifying problem behaviors than are punishments, reinforcement systems are designed so that a child is rewarded for appropriate behaviors and not rewarded for inappropriate ones. Typically, parents and/or the child will be asked to keep careful track of the problem behaviors. When the youngster responds in a desired way (for example, talking about feeling angry, instead of throwing a tantrum) he earns a certain number of points or stars; if he does throw a tantrum, he either earns no points or he loses points. Points are often exchanged for rewards—

these can be in the form of toys or in the form of special treats, such as staying up to watch a special TV program or doing something special with a parent. At school a reward may be giving the child some free time to use as he would like.

It should be noted that some parents and educators have strong moral or philosophical reservations about such reinforcement systems. They believe that a child should not receive rewards for behaviors which are part of his day-to-day responsibilities. Parents may also believe that it is unfair to give special rewards to one child for doing what their other children do as a matter of course. In addition, parents may be concerned about how their other children will respond to one of their sibling's receiving such special treatment.

A behaviorist might answer such objections by reminding parents that, however subtly, they are always rewarding or punishing their children, if only by paying attention to their child on some occasions and ignoring him on others. In this light, behavioral techniques can be viewed as a way of helping parents become more consistent and constructive in the use of rewards and punishments.

My advice to parents is that if they have strong objections to reinforcement systems, they should not employ them. On the other hand, those parents whose primary objection is to the use of toys or other gifts as reinforcers, may feel comfortable rewarding their child in nonmaterial ways, such as taking him on a special outing.

Other Behavioral Techniques

Although I have focused much of the attention of this section on reinforcement, behaviorists employ a host of other techniques to help troubled youngsters. Indeed, when a child's difficulties have to do with feelings more than with bad behavior, behaviorists generally use any of a variety of relaxation or "desensitization" techniques.

Relaxation techniques involve teaching a youngster how to monitor and reduce anxiety. Desensitization techniques involve helping a child gradually approach objects or situations which he fears. In many instances relaxation and desensitization techniques are used in combination with one another.

PROBLEMS THAT ARE MOST AND LEAST AMENABLE TO THE BEHAVIORAL APPROACHES

Behavioral approaches seem best designed to help those problems which are readily observable and which both the child and parents would like changed; for example, phobias or bed-wetting. One instance in which behavioral techniques have proven to be especially helpful is with stuttering behavior. In such cases behavioral techniques, in combination with speech-therapy methods, have proven to be more successful in reducing stuttering than have any other methods.[13]

In addition, behavioral techniques have also been successfully applied to resolving problems like head-banging and self-mutilation among severely retarded, brain injured, or schizophrenic children. Other approaches have generally been found less effective in helping such children eliminate self-destructive behaviors.

Behavioral techniques are relatively less successful with children whose problems are embedded in a severely disorganized or disrupted family; for example, an adolescent whose running away from home is in reaction to an alcoholic and physically abusive father. Environmental manipulation—removing the youngster from the home, perhaps, or an attempt at family therapy—would seem more indicated in an instance of this kind. Behavioral approaches have generally not been widely applied to problems with childhood depression or to problems having to do with self-image, self-esteem, or "identity." Such difficulties seem more suited for psycho-analytic or humanistic approaches.

SUMMARY

In summary, behaviorally oriented therapies are based on principles of learning which have been applied to remedying emotional and behavioral difficulties. The often lengthy evaluation procedures are designed to arrive at a clear and measurable description of the problems which need to be addressed. Parents are ordinarily required to be very actively involved in the treatment, applying the therapist's suggestions in day-to-day situations. Since behavior therapy is problem focused, it can *sometimes* lead to relatively rapid resolution of behavioral difficulties.

The Family Systems Approaches

Only since the 1950s have large numbers of therapists dealt with the family itself as the focus of therapeutic intervention. Although analytic, behavioral, and humanistic therapists may meet with families on a regular basis, they generally do so as a way of supporting a child's treatment. Family systems therapists, on the other hand concentrate their attention on helping the entire family to change.

You should be aware of the fact that the term "family systems therapy" is not invariably used by practitioners of this approach. Such treatment may also be referred to as "structural family therapy," "strategic family therapy," or "Bowenian therapy" (named after Murray Bowen, an influential family therapist and theorist). Although there are differences in theory and technique between structural family therapy and Bowenian therapy, they are too technical to address here. For most parents' purposes the similarities between these types of therapy are substantial enough for them to be considered as basically the same treatment approach.[14]

UNDERLYING ASSUMPTIONS

The theory underlying family systems approaches is called "general systems theory." This theory is too complicated to explain in detail here. It will be helpful, however, for the reader to understand the following aspects of general systems theory since these underlie a family systems therapist's assumptions about the organization and functioning of *all* families.

First, all systems must, in order to survive, have an organization or structure which governs how and when various activities will take place. For example, in most families there are generally rules about who will prepare meals and when such meals will be served.

Second, all systems are composed of smaller units called "sub-systems." Each subsystem has its own special functions. For example, one subsystem is composed of the parents, whose task it is to insure that crucial family functions are carried out. Another subsystem is composed of all the children in a family. Other subsystems may be composed of all the males or all the females, or of all the older children. As you can see, each individual in a family may be considered to be a part of a number of separate subsystems; and in each subsystem that person will have a slightly different role or responsibility.

Third, all systems have "boundaries." A family's boundary defines who belongs to the family and who does not; boundaries also define how information is received and transmitted by family members. The boundaries of some families are relatively "closed," meaning that contact with anyone or anything outside of the family is severely restricted. For example, there are families who do not permit their children to attend school or to receive any medical care. On the other hand, there are families which are so "open" that they are barely identifiable as families; family members and nonfamily members can come and go so freely that it's hard to know who belongs to the family and who doesn't.

Fourth, all families must maintain some balance between periods of stability and periods of change. Such events as a child's going off to school or college, a mother's returning to work, or a divorce all require a family to make some basic adjustments in order to continue functioning smoothly.

There are many other aspects of general systems theory, but the above are the more important ones in terms of family therapy. Finally, it is important to note that it is a general assumption of all family therapists that a child's problem behavior (whatever else it may represent—and whatever may have originally "caused" it) has some adaptive aspect in terms of family functioning; in other words it is a solution of sorts to some family stress or conflict. For example, a youngster may develop serious problems at school in an attempt to help his parents stop fighting. After all, if the parents have to join together to help their child out of trouble, they will have less time and energy to attend to their own disputes.

EVALUATION PROCEDURES

An evaluation conducted by a family systems therapist is likely to be relatively rapid. Indeed, many family therapists make no formal distinction between evaluation and treatment, considering the first session to be the beginning of treatment.

The therapist will typically request that *all* family members attend the first session. She will be interested not only in hearing about everyone's perception of the problem, but also in having various family members re-create the problem situations right in her office. For example, a mother, father, and child may be asked to re-create a typical argument about the child's refusal to go to school in the morning. Although it is understood that people won't act exactly the way they do at home (everyone will be, in some ways, self-conscious), it is still felt that such re-enactments can provide a therapist with much more information than can verbal reports. Some therapists will schedule appointments in the family's home, so as to make things as lifelike as possible.

Some family therapists will be interested in accounts of a child's early development and of a family's past history. Others will discourage such discussion.

TREATMENT FOCUS

Family systems therapy is distinguishable from all other schools of treatment in that the focus of treatment is the family. This does not mean that the entire family will meet with the therapist at each appointment (although they may). It does mean that family systems therapists share the assumption that a youngster's problems are most readily solved by changing certain unhelpful patterns in his family's functioning.

TREATMENT GOALS

Family systems therapists ordinarily define the goals of therapy together with the family. Like behavior therapists, they define both problems and goals in clear, observable, and measurable terms. "Anxiety" or "low self-esteem" are not workable problems. Manifestations of anxiety, such as not going to school, *are* acceptable problems.

Family systems therapists will attempt to redefine or "reframe" the problems which concern a child's parents. For example, if the youngster is immature, a family therapist may suggest that the problem is for the family to help this youngster to act in a more age-appropriate fashion. This reframing of the problem changes its focus from "inside the child" ("He is immature") to "within the family" ("The family needs to help teach him more appropriate behaviors").

TREATMENT METHODS

Family systems therapists may differ widely in their treatment approaches. Some will ask the entire family to attend most or all of the sessions; others will want to meet primarily with a child's parents, or even with the youngster alone; still others will decide on a week-by-week basis with whom to meet.

In general the therapist will be quite active and directive. She will typically ask the family members to re-create their problems in the office, so that she may then make practical suggestions about how situations can be handled differently. However, unlike behavioral or even psychoanalytical therapies, these suggestions usually involve not what is said or done but who says it and when. For example, a behavioral therapist may give parents suggestions about setting up a reinforcement system as a way of eliminating a child's temper tantrums. A family therapist, on the other hand, may notice that the child's mother always tries to calm her child when he begins to throw a tantrum, while the father sits silently. After the mother'sefforts have failed to calm her child, she typically turns to her husband, who angrily sends the boy to his room. The family therapist will, perhaps, suggest that either the mother or the father must handle the situation from start to finish, and will instruct them to decide who is to be in charge of tantrums for that period. The other spouse will then be told to stay entirely uninvolved throughout the tantrums. The youngster will be instructed to throw as many tantrums as possible, so that his parents can practice this new technique. The thinking behind such "homework assignments" is generally that certain strategic changes in how the family typically deals with problem behaviors may well lead to a reduction, if not a total discontinuation, of those behaviors.

Family therapists (especially those influenced by Murray Bowen) may also focus a good deal of attention on the relationship between a child's parents and his grandparents. If the grandparents live a long way away, one or both parents may be instructed to return to their parents' home, in order to try to resolve long-standing issues. The assumption is that in order to make constructive changes in one's family, one must sometimes resolve problems with one's own parents.

Some family therapists borrow techniques from other schools of thought, especially the behaviorists, and thus may suggest that parents use reinforcement systems. Typically, however, the family therapist will assign one or another of the parents certain responsibilities for the implementation of such a system.

Family therapists may also employ techniques which are called "paradoxical"; meaning that they have the opposite effect from what one may expect. For example, a youngster who throws temper tantrums may be told to throw twice as many tantrums per week than usual, or parents who fight about child-rearing techniques may be encouraged to fight more often. Such tasks are, at times, quite helpful; since they can also backfire, they should only be attempted under the careful supervision of a therapist.

PROBLEMS WHICH SEEM MOST AND LEAST AMENABLE TO THE FAMILY SYSTEMS APPROACHES

Family systems therapists (as is the case with their humanistic and behavioral colleagues) believe that their methods can be applied to the entire range of behavioral and emotional difficulties of childhood and adolescence.

While this may be true, it seems that family systems approaches are best suited to those childhood problems in which parental conflict plays some role. And since most parents do periodically disagree about child rearing, family approaches will have wide applicability.

Family systems approaches, like behavioral approaches, are designed to be relatively short term and, as such, are well suited for those problems, such as school phobia or anorexia nervosa, in which the passage of time worsens rather than lessens the presenting difficulty. In addition, family therapists have reported excellent results in the treatment of psycho-physiological disorders.

Family systems therapy may not be indicated when a family is so disorganized or disrupted that it exists as a family in only the broadest sense of the word. In such cases each family member may be in need of individual attention. In addition, this type of treatment may not be suitable for older adolescents who want the individual support of a therapist to help them separate from their family. Psychoanalytic or humanistic therapy may be better suited for these adolescents.

SUMMARY

In summary, family systems therapies are based on general systems theory; a model of how all living systems function. Evaluation tends to be brief and aims at a clear definition of the problem behaviors to be addressed. It is generally assumed that in order for a child to make changes in his behavior, that youngster's family will need to make changes in the way it functions. As is the case with the behavioral approaches, family systems therapy can, at times, lead to relatively rapid resolution of certain kinds of problems.

Other Treatment Approaches

Transactional analysis (TA) and Gestalt therapy are two treatment approaches which deserve separate attention. I will mention them only briefly, because they are primarily adult-oriented therapies. However, some TA and Gestalt therapists do work with children, adolescents, or families. In addition, both treatment approaches are suitable for parents who are seeking help in connection with their child's problems.

TRANSACTIONAL ANALYSIS

The late Eric Berne, originator of transactional analysis, was a psychoanalyst by both training and practice much of his professional life. In the 1950s he began to rethink his view of personality and in 1964 published *Games People Play*.[15] This and other best-selling TA books that followed, including Thomas A. Harris's *I'm OK—You're OK*,[16] have had great popularity among the public. Although TA derives from psychoanalytic theory, a significant aspect of TA is that it provides a comprehensible tool for change for anyone who wishes to read and apply its principles to everyday life.

TA theory rests on the premise that observable human behavior consists of three states: Child, Parent, and Adult. In the Child state we behave much as we did when we were young children. This Child part of our personality allows us to enjoy ourselves and have fun. Our Parent is a kind of carbon copy of how we *perceived* our parents to be, and is generally viewed as a reservoir of values and "correct" behavior. The Adult state is developed gradually as we mature and allows us to accurately perceive reality, make decisions, and evaluate the appropriateness of our Child and Parent behaviors. We get in trouble when one aspect of our personality dominates, when the Child or Parent intrudes excessively on the Adult state, or when we have trouble shifting as needed from one state to another. The state we are in determines the role we play with others and so the kinds of interactions or *transactions* we have with others.

As in psychoanalysis there is a strong emphasis in TA on the importance of developmental history in the formation of personality. Similarly there is in TA an implication of conflict among the three behavior states in the troubled person. Nevertheless, TA theory optimistically believes in our ability to consciously control our behavior and to actualize our human potential if we so choose (and in this regard is similar to the humanistic approaches).

As in psychoanalytic therapy the focus of treatment in TA is the individual client. In contrast to psychoanalytic therapy, however, the basic emphasis in TA is on the *inter*personal (transactional) behavior rather than the *intra*personal or inner conflict. Thus TA has evolved primarily as a group therapy, although some TA therapists do treat individuals, couples, and families.

GESTALT THERAPY

The originator of Gestalt therapy was Frederick "Fritz" Perls, who was trained as a psychoanalyst. Although Gestalt treatment has its roots in psychoanalytic theory, Perls's treatment approach has many similarities to the humanistically oriented therapies.

Perls felt, as do all humanistic therapists, that the human being should function as an integrated whole—not as an organism split into mind and body, thought and feeling. He believed that most of us have overdeveloped minds and underdeveloped feelings. In order to function as a whole person and to actualize our potential, we need to remove the blocks within ourselves that prevent total awareness and we need to mobilize our energies to get what we need from our environment. Gestalt therapy deemphasizes talk, thought, and intellectual understanding, while focusing on feelings, especially deep-seated feelings.

Gestalt therapists have developed a host of techniques and exercises, including psychodrama, art, and role-playing. Sometimes called "games" these exercises assist the client in developing awareness and expressing feelings. Thus, in contrast to humanistic therapists, Gestalt therapists are quite active and directive.

SUMMARY

In summary, TA and Gestalt therapy are two kinds of treatment which have similarities to both the psychoanalytic and the humanistically oriented approaches. They are suitable for parents who are seeking help in connection with their children's problems, although some therapists employ these methods directly with child or adolescent clients.

Similarities Among All the Approaches

Although I have focused in this chapter on detailing the differences anong the major child-oriented therapies, all such treatments share some practical similarities.

First and foremost, all therapists, regardless of their theoretical orientation, recognize the crucial importance of parental cooperation for the success of any treatment. Indeed, most therapists will not even attempt to help a child without the full cooperation of that youngster's parents. Some therapists (especially those employing behavioral or family systems techniques) work primarily with and through the parents. But even those therapists who do work with children directly generally insist on ongoing contact with a child's parents.

Second, therapists from each approach may employ

their techniques in a variety of treatment "modalities." In other words, they may work directly with children (in individual or group therapy), with a child's parents (in parent counseling or marital therapy), or with an entire family (in family therapy). Even though some theoretical approaches do lend themselves to one modality rather than another (for example, family systems approaches are obviously most suited to family therapy), a therapist from any approach may choose to employ any of the above-mentioned modalities, or some combination of them. Typically the choice of the therapeutic modality will depend on 1) the specific problems of any given child (for example, a youngster whose primary problem involves an inability to make or get along with friends may be referred to group therapy; if, on the other hand, a youngster has trouble getting along with his or her parents, individual or family treatment may be recommended); and 2) the expertise of a given therapist (for example, some individually oriented child-therapists have little training or experience with group or family treatment, while some family therapists have little training or experience in individually oriented child-therapy).

Finally, experienced therapists from each school of thought recognize the limitations of their theories and methods, and caution parents that they can never *guarantee* a successful outcome. I would caution parents to be skeptical of anyone who would make any claims to the contrary.

Chapter 7

THE USE OF DRUGS IN THE PSYCHOTHERAPEUTIC TREATMENT OF CHILDREN*

Medications have been used for centuries to help youngsters with emotional or behavioral difficulties. It was not until the 1930s, however, that significant research was begun on the physical and psychological effects of certain drugs in childhood. At present, although much research has been done, there are still wide gaps in our understanding of how and when to use medications. In this section I will provide you with some general information about the use of medications for children, including a discussion of which drugs have been used to aid in the treatment of which emotional disorders.

GENERAL GUIDELINES

Most child psychiatrists advocate that drug therapy be used only in conjunction with other kinds of therapeutic assistance—such as individual or family therapy, parent counseling, or special schooling.[1] Only in special instances should medications alone be considered a sufficient treatment for a troubled child.

Another accepted guideline is that medication should be used only after a thorough psychiatric and medical evaluation is completed. (Of course, in time of emergency this may not be possible.) In addition, all drug treatment should be combined with careful medical follow-up. A physician should monitor the effectiveness of the medication and watch for the possible development of adverse

* The coauthor of this chapter is Mitchell Wangh, M.D.

side-effects. This monitoring should take place approximately every few months, or more often if indicated.

Psychiatrists have found that parents' and children's attitudes about any medication will play an important role in how it is used and in how effective it can be. If parents have a strong belief that a given drug will not be helpful, or if they feel that it may even be harmful, it is unlikely that it will be taken regularly or given a fair trial. At the other extreme, if a medication is expected magically to solve all of a youngster's behavioral difficulties, parents are bound to be disappointed, even if the drug does provide some benefit.

Finally, I am aware that some parents are opposed to giving any medications to their youngsters, in all but the most extreme of circumstances. These parents may be worried about the possible short- and long-term side-effects of the drugs or about the possibility that the medications may unnaturally alter their children's behavior. While I am quite sympathetic to these parents' concerns, it must also be noted that for some youngsters, medications can provide significant relief from severe psychological distress.

The question of the relative advantages and disadvantages of medications is not one that should be answered in the abstract. It is an oversimplification to say that "medication X or Y should always be used with children with these difficulties," or conversely, that "all medications do more harm than good." Parents need to decide on the use of a given medication based on its advantages and disadvantages for their youngster. Parents should request and expect their physician to be helpful and sympathetic to them in making this decision.

THE USES OF VARIOUS MEDICATIONS IN THE TREATMENT OF SPECIFIC DISORDERS

Hyperactivity

Of all the behavior disorders of childhood, hyperactivity is the one for which medications are most commonly prescribed. As was detailed in Chapter Three,* hyperactive children generally have three related areas of difficulty, as follows: 1) Excessive movement which is purposeless and non-goal directed, 2) An inability to concentrate or maintain attention, and 3) A difficulty in social interaction—characterized by impulsive, domineering, and attention-seeking behaviors.

GENERAL CONSIDERATIONS

Many physicians believe that a diagnosis of hyperactivity is not, in and of itself, a sufficient reason to prescribe medications.** They advocate the use of drugs for hyperactivity only under the following circumstances:

> 1) If a child's distractibility and short attention-span adversely affect his school performance (which is, admittedly, often the case)
>
> 2) If a child's social difficulties are sufficiently severe that he has major problems with peers, and if other attempts to remedy these problems have proven unsuccessful
>
> 3) If a child's motor restlessness presents major problems for his parents, and if attempts to help parents cope with these problems have failed

Medications for hyperactivity, as is the case with all other drugs, can have negative side-effects, and should therefore be used only when necessary. You and your physician will need to discuss the advantages and disadvantages of drug therapy, if your child is diagnosed as hy-

* The reader may find it helpful to read this section in conjunction with the section on hyperactivity in Chapter Three.

** Some physicians advocate a more liberal use of drug therapy for hyperactivity. One such physician, Dr. Marcel Kinsbourne, in an article written especially for parents of hyperactive children, expressed the belief that the only way to "find out whether a stimulant should or should not be prescribed for a particular . . . hyperactive . . . child . . . is . . . by trying the drug to see if it is effective."[2]

peractive. Bear in mind that medications are employed to treat the symptoms of hyperactivity, not the "hyperactivity" itself. Therefore, if other methods can be found to alleviate these symptoms, they should be employed, before beginning a course of drug treatment.

MEDICATIONS USED WITH HYPERACTIVE CHILDREN

Many different kinds of drugs have been used to try to help hyperactive youngsters, but to date the most effective are those drugs which are classified as stimulants. The stimulants most commonly used are dextroamphetamine (Dexedrine) and methylphenidate (Ritalin). The choice of one or the other of these drugs is likely to depend on the preference of your youngster's physician. (Following a trial period on one or the other of these drugs, a physician may decide to try switching to the other medication.)

Stimulants are used neither to "stimulate" nor to "quiet" hyperactive children. Rather, their purpose is to help youngsters focus attention. The reasons that stimulants are effective in doing this are not completely understood.

It should be noted that almost all physicians believe that it is wise to be conservative about the continued use of these or any other medications. Such drugs, they argue, should only be continued beyond a trial period of a week or two if they prove to provide significant and undeniable benefits. Medications should not be continued if they provide only marginal or dubious results.

As do most medications, Ritalin and Dexedrine sometimes produce adverse side effects. Two of the more commonly experienced side effects are appetite suppression and sleep disturbances. These may be mitigated by a readjustment of the amount of medication that a youngster takes, or of the time of day she takes it. Other reported side effects include irritability, headaches, and stomachaches.

Some research seems to indicate that use of amphetamines in children over a period of years may lead to some slowing of physical growth. These findings are only tentative and have yet to be confirmed. Nonetheless, many pediatricians prefer, whenever possible, that youngsters *not* take medication over weekends or school vacations, so as to reduce the possibility of this or other side effects. In addition, since the need for medications for hyperactivity often lessens with age, many pediatricians also advise that a youngster start each new school year without medication. Of course, drug therapy will be reinstituted if indicated.

Some parents fear that their youngsters may become addicted to the drugs they take, especially if they continue to take them over the course of many years. Research evidence indicates that this simply has not happened.

Another common parental fear is that stimulants will subdue or suppress their youngsters' natural spontaneity and turn them into "zombies" or "robots." However, it is believed that the way these drugs work is not by suppressing behavior but rather by helping a youngster focus his or her attention on given tasks. This increased ability to maintain concentration and attention is believed to reduce the motor restlessness characteristic of hyperactive children. If a youngster is very listless and lacking in energy after beginning stimulant medication, it is possible that the dosage of the drugs should be altered, not necessarily canceled altogether.

Other medications, including antipsychotic drugs and antidepressants (these drugs will be discussed later in this chapter) have been experimented with to see if they might prove helpful with hyperactive youngsters. The antipsychotic medications have not been found to be effective, while recent research seems to indicate that antidepressants may prove helpful for some hyperactive children.

As detailed in Chapter Three, some physicians and writers on medical subjects have recently proposed dietary regulation as a way of treating hyperactivity without medications. The most famous dietary prescription is that of Dr. Ben Feingold who argues that artificial food flavorings and colorings, may, in certain children, cause the symptoms associated with hyperactivity. If you are interested in attempting a trial period of dietary regulation, I suggest you discuss this with your pediatrician and then try an additive-free diet to see if it proves effective.

Psychosis/Schizophrenia

There is no evidence that any medications (or any other treatment, for that matter) will result in *dramatic* changes or improvements in children or adolescents who have a long history of severe emotional and developmental disturbances. Nonetheless, some drugs have proved helpful in reducing certain *symptoms* associated with childhood psychosis or schizophrenia, including agitation, assaultiveness, hallucinations, disorientation, confusion, and self-mutilation. These same medications have proven to be of even greater help to adolescents who develop acute psychotic symptoms.

Medications used to treat these children are generally referred to as "antipsychotic agents" or "major tranquilizers." The more commonly used drugs are chlorpromazine (Thorazine), trifluoperazine (Stelazine), thioridazine (Mellaril) and haloperidol (Haldol). Which of these antipsychotic drugs will be prescribed depends partly on the preference of the physician and partly on the symptoms that most affect the youngster. Some of these drugs are more sedating than other and are used for children who are especially agitated.

Antipsychotic drugs are very powerful, and can produce undesirable side-effects. These include neuromuscular disorders such as stiffness and tremors, sleepiness, listlessness, and allergic reactions. It is quite important that youngsters on antipsychotic medications be monitored frequently for the possible development of these side effects. In addition, parents should have a full discussion with the prescribing physician about the possible side effects of these and all other medications before the youngster begins to take such drugs.

Depression

Depression in childhood is a very poorly defined syndrome. Although various medications called "antidepressants" have been proven to alleviate depression in adults, these same drugs have not been proven effective for children.

In general, psychiatrists in this country believe primarily in using psychotherapy and environmental change to deal with depression in childhood. Nonetheless, antidepressants are sometimes recommended by a youngster's psychiatrist or pediatrician. Those most commonly used are called "tricyclic antidepressants" and include imipramine (Tofranil) and amitriptyline (Elavil). Another group of antidepressant drugs called "monoamine oxidase inhibitors" (MAO inhibitors) are used only rarely with children.*

If used at all, antidepressant medications should always be considered as merely one part of an overall treatment program which will include psychotherapy for the child, his parents, and/or his family.

The side effects of these drugs can include neuromuscular disorders, allergic reactions, insomnia, blurred vision, jaundice, and dryness of the mouth.

Lithium salts, which are used to treat manic-depressive illness in adults, are not approved in this country for use with children under twelve.** It is not even clear that

* The reason that MAO inhibitors are so rarely used is that these drugs, in combination with compounds found in many foods, can lead to very serious side-effects. People on these MAO inhibitors must, therefore, follow a very strict diet, and it is felt that it is almost impossible to get children to be faithful to such a severe dietary regimen.

** Lithium is a very powerful and potentially dangerous drug. This is because the amount of lithium in the bloodstream which is necessary to provide therapeutic benefits is very close to the amount of lithium which can be harmful or even lethal. Therefore, adolescents and adults who take this drug must be given regular blood tests.

manic-depressive disorders occur in children before puberty.

Anxiety Reactions

As is the case with the depressive reactions, medications to aid youngsters who suffer from severe anxiety are generally used only in conjunction with other forms of treatment, such as individual or family therapy or parent counseling. Anti-anxiety medications offer only short-term and symptomatic relief, and it is often feared that their use may lead a youngster to become psychologically dependent on them, rather than help her cope in any lasting way with her worries. On the other hand, the use of these agents to relieve acute periods of intense anxiety is considered appropriate, as long as the youngster receives subsequent help in understanding the causes of his emotional distress.

The drugs most commonly used to treat anxiety (when it is not associated with psychotic disturbances) are referred to as the minor tranquilizers. The two most common minor tranquilizers are chlordiazepoxide (Librium) and diazepam (Valium). In general, the use of either of these drugs is preferable to the use of barbiturates because of some of the potential side-effects of the barbiturates.

Sleep Disorders

Most youngsters go through periods of time when they have difficulty going to sleep. Even if difficulty in sleeping becomes prolonged or chronic, drug therapy should never

---

You should be aware of the fact that some researchers are investigating the use of lithium for the treatment of hyperactivity. However, compared to the potential benefits of this drug, its potential hazards seem so great that it should not be used to treat hyperactive (or any other) young children.

be considered until other remedies have been tried, including environmental changes or some form of therapy.

An exception to this general rule can be made for children whose sleep difficulties have been brought about by some traumatic event, such as a hospitalization or the death of a parent. In such instances drugs such as chloral hydrate or diphenhydramine (Benadryl) may be indicated.

Other Syndromes

Drug treatment has been attempted to help youngsters who evidence a wide range of behavioral difficulties. In general, with any of these difficulties, it is felt that medications should be used only as adjuncts to other forms of therapeutic intervention.

ENURESIS

Some psychiatrists and physicians advocate the use of tricyclic antidepressants, especially imipramine (Tofranil), for youngsters who have not responded to any other method of controlling their bedwetting. Again, such drug therapy should not be instituted until all other reasonable therapies have been tried and found unsuccessful. It is not understood why these anti-depressants should be helpful in the treatment of enuresis, but they sometimes are.

SCHOOL REFUSAL/SCHOOL PHOBIA

School phobia is considered to be an emotional and behavioral problem which needs to be handled with one or another form of psychotherapy. Usually, drug therapy is not considered an appropriate treatment. Some children, however, evidence no improvement with psychotherapy of any kind. For these children the disadvantages of missing school for long periods are so great that some psychiatrists and pediatricians advocate trying drug treatment. The drugs typically used are either minor tranquilizers (to try to reduce the anxiety believed to be at the root of school phobia) or tricyclic antidepressants (whose salutary effects, when they occur, are not well understood).

ANOREXIA NERVOSA

In some cases a psychiatrist may prescribe either an antipsychotic or an antidepressant agent to a client who evidences symptoms of anorexia nervosa. The purpose of medication is to reduce the confusion of thinking or the depression that sometimes accompanies this disorder.

TICS

Common tics are not treated with medications. However, one particular kind of tic, called Gilles de la Tourette's syndrome, is found to respond well to drug therapy. Indeed, this is one of the few childhood disturbances in which chemotherapy is considered to be the treatment of choice. The drug that is used is the major tranquilizer haloperidol (Haldol).

Summary

In summary, I would like to reemphasize that drug therapy with children is almost always used as an adjunct to other therapeutic interventions. Such medications should only be prescribed after a thorough psychiatric and medical evaluation is completed. Finally, physicians should regularly monitor drug therapy in order to assess its effectiveness and to watch for the development of adverse side effects.

Chapter 8

PSYCHOLOGICAL TESTING

As I mentioned earlier, many therapists, before they begin any treatment, will first conduct a thorough evaluation. The purpose of such an evaluation is to assess the nature and severity of a child's problems in order to determine what, if any, treatment is indicated. In addition (as I'll detail in Chapter Thirteen), school personnel also conduct evaluations in order to assess youngsters' academic and school-related behavior problems. During the course of either an educational or a psychiatric evaluation, it may be determined that psychological testing is indicated.*

In this chapter I will clarify the nature and purposes of psychological tests. Because so many parents are confused or frightened by them, special attention will be paid to clearing up some common misconceptions.

GENERAL USE OF PSYCHOLOGICAL TESTS

Psychological tests, when properly used, are simply one way of gathering information about some aspect of a

* Readers interested in a more comprehensive coverage of psychological tests are referred to Stanley D. Klein, *Psychological Testing of Children: A Consumer's Guide* (Boston: The Exceptional Parent Press, 1977).

child's functioning. If information is needed about a youngster's intellectual functioning, intelligence tests will be administered; if there are questions about a child's emotional functioning, personality tests will be used. Be aware, too, that since emotional, intellectual, and academic functioning are closely interrelated in every child, many psychologists believe in administering what are called "test batteries." A test battery is a group of tests each of which is designed to measure a different aspect of a child's functioning. For example, a test battery might include an intelligence test, one or more personality tests, and a test to measure basic academic skills. (See below for a description of each of these kinds of tests.)

I'd like to emphasize that psychological tests should always constitute only one part of a complete evaluation. Other aspects of an evaluation may include interviews with the child and with his parents or family. In addition, an evaluator may observe a youngster at home or at school, talk with the child's teachers and pediatrician, or request that the youngster be seen by one or more medical or educational specialists.

If psychological tests were used without obtaining other relevant information, an evaluator could be significantly mistaken about a child's functioning. For example, a little girl preoccupied by her parents' divorce might not be able to pay attention while being administered an intelligence test. If the examiner were not aware of this youngster's preoccupation, the child could be misdiagnosed as a slow learner. Or a child with an undiagnosed hearing problem could be mislabeled as "learning disabled."

SOME IMPERFECTIONS OF PSYCHOLOGICAL TESTS

Psychological tests are designed to gather information in a structured, standardized fashion. To "standardize" a test means to establish scoring procedures and norms that can be used to compare one child to another. Tests are standardized by being given to a carefully selected group of youngsters. These children are supposed to be representative of all children in the population.

However, many tests are standardized using youngsters who have no obvious emotional, intellectual, or physical handicaps. Thus a learning-disabled, physically handicapped, or emotionally disturbed youngster is likely to score "below average" on such a standardized test, because he is being compared to children without any handicaps. For example, on an intelligence test an emotionally troubled or hearing-impaired youngster may receive a very low score, although he has average or above-average intelligence. This highlights one reason that all test scores need to be interpreted in the context of a child's entire functioning.

Another thing to keep in mind about all psychological tests is that they are designed to obtain "samples of behavior that are representative of the individual's usual behavior."[1] For example, an intelligence test may consist of one hundred to two hundred questions. A youngster's answers to these questions are supposed to be representative of his overall intellectual functioning. However, it doesn't always work this way for a given child. Intelligence tests in particular have been criticized because they depend heavily on a child's verbal skills and on his exposure to certain kinds of information. For example youngsters raised by non-English-speaking parents may have had significantly different experiences from other youngsters and therefore may do poorly on standardized tests. Their low test scores reflect the fact that the tests do not measure their particular cognitive skills and abilities.

Intelligence Tests

Typically, intellectual functioning is measured through the administration of an intelligence test. (These tests are also commonly referred to as "IQ tests," IQ being an abbreviation for Intelligence Quotient.)

There are many different kinds of intelligence tests.

Some are administered individually and some in groups. The individually administered test affords a psychologist the opportunity to observe firsthand how a child thinks and solves problems and thus provides a breadth and depth of information which cannot be obtained from a group test. For most psychological assessments, therefore, an individually administered intelligence test should be considered a necessity. This testing should be conducted by a psychologist certified to perform such work.

It seems relatively straightforward that, as their name implies, these tests are designed to measure a person's intelligence. However, the matter is complicated by the fact that "intelligence"* is not an easy term to define. Experts in the field disagree about its specific components; and it follows that they also disagree about how to measure it.

Different kinds of intelligence tests are administered to youngsters of different ages. The tests that parents are most likely to hear about are those used with school-aged children. The most commonly used of such tests are the Wechsler Intelligence Test for Children—Revised, usually referred to as the WISC-R, given to youngsters aged six to fifteen; and the Wechsler Adult Intelligence Scale, referred to as the WAIS, given to individuals aged sixteen and up. Preschool-aged children may be given either the Wechsler Preschool and Primary Scale of Intelligence (the WPPSI) or the Stanford-Binet Intelligence Scale.

There are also tests designed to measure the intellectual functioning of infants. Some of these include the Catell Infant Intelligence Scale, the Bayley Scale of Infant Development, and the Griffiths Mental Development Scale. There are also tests designed especially for use with children with specific disabilities. The Nebraska Test of Learning Aptitude for Young Deaf Children and the Interim Hayes-Binet Intelligence Test are two such instruments. Finally, some tests are designed in such a way that they require little use of language. These include the Leiter

* One helpful definition is that "intelligence refers to the capability of a person to learn from experience and, consequently, to solve problems in day-to-day life."[2]

International Performance Scale, the Columbia Maturity Scale, and the Ravens Progressive Matrices.

A DESCRIPTION OF THE WECHSLER TESTS

Excluding children under age five, the most commonly used intelligence tests are those constructed by Dr. David Wechsler. Each of the Wechsler tests (the WPPSI, the WISC-R, and the WAIS) is divided into two parts or "scales." In the 'Verbal Scale" the child is asked to respond verbally to a wide variety of questions, such as "Name three Presidents of the United States" or "How many dimes are there in a dollar?" In the "Performance Scale" the youngster is asked to solve problems non-verbally; for example, by putting together a puzzle or by pointing to the missing part of a picture.

Scoring

The Verbal and Performance Scales are each composed of five parts or "subtests." (There is an optional sixth subtest for each scale.) A youngster receives a separate score on each of these ten subtests. The scores of the five verbal subtests are combined to arrive at a Verbal IQ score; likewise the scores of the five performance subtests are computed to yield a Performance IQ score. Finally, the Verbal and the Performance scores are added together to yield a "Full Scale IQ." This is the one score which is often reported to parents.

MISCONCEPTIONS AND MISUNDERSTANDINGS ABOUT INTELLIGENCE TESTING

There is both much disagreement and much misunderstanding about what intelligence tests actually measure and how to use the information they provide. A few helpful things to understand about these tests are the following:

1) A youngster's IQ score is simply one way that psychologists have of summarizing a child's *functioning* on a test designed to measure intelligence. The IQ

score is *not* a measure of a youngster's "native intelligence" or "intellectual potential." Rather, it is a measure of a child's performance on a particular test. How that child's test performance is related to his or her "intellectual potential" is often a very difficult and complicated question to answer.

This point is dramatized by the case of a ten-year-old boy, David, whom I was asked to evaluate before he was placed in a class for retarded children. On previous intelligence tests David had scored in the low 60s. (Scores ranging from 90 to 110 are considered average. Scores in the 60s are well below average.)

On the IQ test which I administered to him, David again scored about 60. When I asked him to draw me a picture of himself, however, David gave me some clues about why his test performance was so poor. Instead of drawing a picture of himself, he drew a monster who he said was going to hurt him. He grew quite frightened as he drew this picture and needed me to reassure him that the monster was only in his imagination and was not really going to hurt him. David's behavior during this picture-drawing task (as well as on other personality tests) indicated that the reason his IQ score was low was that his mind was constantly preoccupied with nightmarish worries and fears. David's emotional problems were so severe that they interfered dramatically with his intellectual functioning. Obviously he needed a program for emotionally troubled youngsters, not one for retarded children.

The example of David is a dramatic one, but I use it to underline the point that a low IQ score can be related to many factors other than a limited intellectual potential.

2) A youngster's IQ score is *not* a permanent, unchangeable figure. On the contrary, it is assumed that if a child were to take two comparable intelligence tests in a short period of time (and even if she were able to concentrate exactly the same on both

tests and had exactly the same motivation on both days) her IQ score should vary by as much as ten points.

But, of course, motivation, ability to concentrate, and many other factors do vary from day to day and even from hour to hour, so that on different occasions a youngster's IQ score might vary by much more than ten points.

In summary, IQ scores in particular, and intelligence tests in general, can provide important information to trained professionals who use them in the context of all the other information they have about a youngster's emotional and social functioning. In isolation an IQ score has, at best, very limited meaning; at worst it can be quite misleading.

Personality Tests

"Personality tests" are designed to help a psychologist understand how and what a youngster thinks about himself and others.

Such tests can often provide an understanding of a child's thoughts and feelings that cannot be obtained from an interview alone. However, the tests are not magical, and there are many instances in which they shed no additional light on what's troubling a given child.

A DESCRIPTION OF PERSONALITY TESTS

Personality tests are designed to elicit a youngster's thoughts and feelings about different emotional issues. For example, rather than asking a child to say how he feels about himself (a question which most would find difficult to answer) the test may ask the child to make up a story about a picture of a boy looking in the mirror. It is the assumption of all such tests that the stories a child tells are in some way an indication of his feelings and thoughts. In one instance a twelve-year-old boy was referred to me for testing because he was always being picked on by his classmates. When shown the picture of a boy standing in front of a mirror he said, "This is a picture of a boy who's looking in the mirror wondering if he's funny looking. Everybody always teases him, and he can't figure out why. So he went to the mirror to see if something's wrong with the way he looks." It's obvious that this story reflects the youngster's attempts to understand why he's being picked on. Of course, most stories are not so transparent, so that a psychologist will need to make use of all of a child's stories, as well as other test materials, in order to try to understand what is going on in his or her mind.

Some of the most commonly used picture-story tests are the TAT (Thematic Apperception Test); the CAT (Children's Apperception Test); the TED (Tasks of Emotional Development); and the Blacky Pictures.

Some psychologists are also qualified to administer the Rorschach test, a method in which individuals are asked to describe what various inkblots look like. Although it is more complicated to score and administer than are the other personality tests, the Rorschach test is based on exactly the same principle as the picture-story tests: that in responding to ambiguous stimuli an individual will provide information about his thoughts and feelings.

Children are also asked to draw pictures of themselves and of their families (Draw-a-Person Test) or to complete sentences such as "What I hate most about school is——" (Sentence Completion Test).

PERSONALITY TESTS ARE NOT MAGIC

Sometimes parents or children are frightened by personality tests. They fear that the psychologist will somehow be able to "read their minds" or uncover some awful truth about them. In reality personality tests are only one method which can be used to try to understand how a person pictures himself and the world.

It's important for parents to remember that there are no absolute "findings" of a personality test. A psychologist attempts, through a youngster's responses, to understand how he is feeling and what he is thinking. It would be accurate for a psychologist to report, for example, that Johnny seems to be quite angry and is having trouble knowing how to handle his feelings. On the other hand a statement such as "Johnny is basically a hostile child" may give parents or educators the misleading impression that this youngster is intrinsically aggressive. Perhaps Johnny is angry because his parents abandoned him when he was three and he has been shuttled from foster home to foster home over the course of the past three years. Or perhaps his anger is mostly a result of frustration caused by his inability to do schoolwork, which in turn is caused by a learning disability. In summary: As with all other techniques, personality tests used in isolation cannot be expected to provide a well-rounded picture of a youngster's functioning.

Tests to Determine the Presence of Learning Disabilities

As was discussed in Chapter Three, many different problems are included under the heading "learning disabilities." In essence, learning-disabled (LD) children evidence a "discrepancy between the school performance expected of them on the basis of their potential and the performance they actually produce."[3] It follows, therefore, that learning-disabilities (LD) testing would be indicated when a youngster's actual school performance is far below what would be expected on the basis of his tested intellectual performance.*

* Such testing may not be necessary for those youngsters whose academic difficuities are *clearly* related to emotional factors and not to learning disability. I stress the word "clearly," because it is often quite difficult to distinguish between academic problems caused primarily by emotional factors and those caused primarily by learning problems. In addition, emotional difficulties and learning problems often go hand in hand.

Unlike the area of intelligence testing, where a relatively few tests are used nationwide, many different tests are used to determine the presence and nature of learning disabilities. In some ways all LD tests are similar in that they are designed to pinpoint the reasons why a child isn't learning in accordance with his potential.

There is general agreement that in order to be able to learn, an individual must be able to:

1) Accurately take in information, whether visually, aurally (by hearing), or tactilely
2) Store or retain this information for later use (a function referred to as memory)
3) Make sense of this information (a function often referred to as "information processing")
4) Express what he has learned, usually through speech or writing

Learning-disabilities tests, therefore, attempt to assess a youngster's functioning in one or more of these areas.

A DESCRIPTION OF LEARNING-DISABILITIES TESTS

The Illinois Test of Psycholinguistic Abilities (ITPA) is perhaps the best known of the tests for learning disabilities. It is divided into twelve subtests, some of which test auditory (or "verbal") information processing, and others which test visual information processing. The subtests are further subdivided: Some test receptive skill (i.e., how well the child understands incoming auditory or visual information); some test associative skill (i.e., how well the child can relate two pieces of auditory or visual information); and some test expressive skill (i.e., how well the child can express information either verbally or with his hands). There are also subtests which test auditory versus visual memory. Each subtest yields an age equivalent and a "scaled score," and by comparing the child's scores on various subtests one can sometimes see a pattern of relative strengths and weaknesses in his information-processing skills.

There are a few other tests which also attempt to compare a child's relative information-processing strengths and weaknesses. The Slingerland Screening Tests for Identifying Children with Specific Learning Disabilities and the Detroit Test of Learning Aptitude are two such tests. In addition, the Wechsler tests (WPPSI, WISC-R, and WAIS) can also be used to check a child's relative information-processing strengths and weaknesses.

There are other instruments which are designed to test only specific types of information processing. Auditory-perception tests are designed to assess how well a child can recognize, hear the differences between, remember, and blend individual sounds. Such tests include the Wepman Auditory Discrimination Test and the Goldman-Fristoe-Woodcock Auditory Skills Test Battery.

There is also a wide variety of tests designed to test visual information processing. Some of these are the Bender Visual-Motor Gestalt Test; the Developmental Test of Visual Motor Integration; the Marianne Frostig Developmental Test of Visual Perception; and the Motor Free Test of Visual Perception.

Finally, there are numerous tests which assess language function. Some of these are the Northwest Syntax Screening; the Spencer Memory for Sentences; and the Experimental Test of Comprehension and Linguistic Structure. These tests of language function are usually administered by a speech-and-language function pathologist, while other tests of information processing may be administered by school psychologists or by specialists in learning disabilities.

WEAKNESSES OF LEARNING-DISABILITIES TESTS

Learning disabilities are, by definition, apparent discrepancies between a child's intellectual potential and his academic achievement. Yet most of the tests designed to pinpoint learning disabilities look only at the underlying information-processing skills; they do not analyze the child's academic skills as such. A child may perform below average on a given learning-disability test or may show some information processing deficit, and yet may be performing quite adequately in school. Therefore tests for learning disabilities must be viewed in conjunction with a child's intellectual level and his academic-skill level.

Another problem with tests of learning disability is that they often do not measure the skills they say they are measuring. If, for instance, a child is asked to repeat a series of digits such as four, seven, nine, three, this is often called a task of "auditory memory." If the child says, "seven, nine, four, three," he gets the task "wrong" but is it really his memory which was at fault? It may also be that the child is anxious, or has not understood that the numbers were to be repeated in correct sequence. Just because a task purports to measure a specific information-processing ability, a comparatively low score should not necessarily be taken as certain evidence that the child has a deficit in that ability. One must analyze the task and the many factors that could have contributed to the child's poor performance.

Frequently two tests of information processing both purport to measure the same ability and yet a child may do poorly on one and well on the other. In all likelihood this is because the two tests actually measure different abilities. One example of this might be two tests which ostensibly measure a child's ability to notice a visual detail in a larger picture. (This is sometimes called "visual closure.") One test may ask the child to note a detail missing from a picture, such as eyelashes missing from a woman's face. Another test may show a child a picture of a fork, and ask the child to find all of the forks hidden in a complex picture of a kitchen. These tasks both require "visual closure" but are influenced by other factors as well, and a child may do well on one and poorly on another. The best way to avoid misdiagnosing a learning disability on the basis of one test is to administer a variety (or "battery") of tests. If an information-processing deficit exists, it should be evident in consistently lower scores on all subtests involving that ability.

In summary, if a child shows a deficit on all tests which involve a specific ability, and if his academic skills also reflect this same deficit, and if school performance is lower than one might expect on the basis of intellectual potential, then and only then is it reasonable to assert that that child has a learning disability.

Tests for Basic Academic Skills

The purpose of these tests is to give a general sense of a youngster's current level of proficiency in the basic academic skills, namely reading, arithmetic, and language arts (spelling, punctuation, and sentence structure). These skills are typically evaluated through the administration of "standardized achievement tests."* Such tests are often given to every child in a school, not just to those with academic problems. Some of the more commonly used achievement tests include the Stanford Achievement Tests, the California Achievement Tests, the Iowa Tests of Basic Skills, The Metropolitan Achievement Tests, and the Science Research Associates (SRA) Achievement Series. If a psychologist or educator wished to administer an achievement test in a one-to-one situation, she would probably use the Wide Range Achievement Test (WRAT).

SCORING

The results of these tests are usually reported in either "grade-level equivalents" or "percentile ranks." For example, Joan (who is in the third grade) could be reported as

* Any test designed to measure what a child has learned is an "achievement test." (Thus, all classroom tests are achievement tests). "Standardized achievement tests" are those which are given to many children as a way of comparing a great number of youngsters' functioning in specified academic areas.

earning a grade-level equivalent of 4.0, or as being in the 90th percentile of her classmates in reading.

As is the case with any test where the results of a child's functioning are summarized in one score, parents must be careful to understand exactly what the score means.

A "grade-level equivalent" is the average score of all children in a given grade who took the test. Therefore a grade-level equivalent of 3.0 on the Iowa Tests is the average score of all third graders *in the nation* who took the Iowa Tests.

Scores reported as grade-level equivalents can be misleading for a number of reasons. First, since a grade-level equivalent is an average, it follows that half the children who take the test will automatically score below that average, and half will score above it. Scoring below the national average on an achievement test is, therefore, not in and of itself an indication that a youngster is experiencing any academic or learning problems. Second, grade-level equivalents compare a youngster with a nationwide sample of children. In some communities, scoring exactly at "grade level" may place a child near the top of her class; in other communities, being at "grade-level" will mean that a youngster is functioning far below most of her classmates. Finally, because of the way that standardized achievement tests are constructed, a change in just a few of a child's answers can lead to a noticeable difference in her grade-level equivalent. This in turn can lead to an incorrect assumption about how much that youngster does or doesn't know.

Some of these disadvantages can be overcome if scores are reported in the form of percentile ranks. These scores indicate where a child stands compared to others in her grade. For example, a percentile score of 90 means that Joan scored as well as or better than ninety percent of her classmates, while ten percent did better than she did. Percentile scores can be reported in relationship to all children who took the test nationwide, or in relationship to a local group of children. The latter scores are more helpful in assessing a child's performance in a given school.

Summary

In summary, psychological tests can be used to provide educators and mental health professionals with important information about a youngster's intellectual, academic, and psychological strengths and weaknesses. Care must be taken, however, to interpret the results and scores from such tests in the context of a child's overall functioning. When used in isolation, test results can lead parents, educators, and mental health professionals alike to misleading or incorrect conclusions about a youngster's capacities.

This chapter on psychological testing concludes Part I (or the "handbook" section) of this book. In the preceding eight chapters I have attempted to provide parents with all the basic information that they might need when seeking help for their child or family. In Part II (the "guide" section), I take parents through the step-by-step process of obtaining help in a wide variety of mental health settings.

Part Two

A STEP-BY-STEP GUIDE TO GETTING HELP

Chapter 9

OBTAINING HELP FROM A THERAPIST IN PRIVATE PRACTICE

Psychotherapy from a private therapist is the most expensive kind of outpatient treatment you can obtain. Fees for such service typically range from a low of forty dollars per hour to a high of seventy-five dollars per hour or more. Since therapy appointments are usually scheduled at least once a week, sometimes over the course of a year or more, committing yourself to this kind of help represents a substantial investment of time and money.

As was discussed in Chapter Four, children and families can receive less expensive therapy from mental health clinics. Nevertheless, many parents prefer to seek help privately. By doing this they can afford themselves a greater opportunity to work with the therapist of their choice in the kind of treatment they prefer. However, all too many parents forego these potential advantages by taking their child or family to a therapist about whom they know very little.

The process of making a careful choice of therapist does not need to be very complicated or costly. It does, however, require an investment of time and a willingness to ask questions. Throughout this process you should remember that you are a consumer about to spend a significant amount of money to purchase a professional's time and knowledge.

A FIVE-STEP PROCEDURE FOR CHOOSING A THERAPIST

I recommend that parents use the following simple, five-step process when shopping for a therapist:

1) Consider the criteria that are important to you in your selection of a therapist.
2) Compile a list of therapists who satisfy your criteria.
3) Telephone people from your list and ask them some questions. Their answers will help you decide which one or ones you'd like to meet.
4) Meet with one or more therapists. The purpose of this initial appointment will be to help you decide if a given professional is likely to be helpful to your child or family. Provided you have the time, you may want to meet with more than one therapist. This will afford you the opportunity to compare a few different styles and techniques.
5) Choose a therapist.

Why Shop for a Therapist?

You may feel that you simply don't know how to judge whether a therapist is going to be helpful or not. Why, then, should you bother to shop around at all?

My answer to this objection is that each step that I've outlined is designed to help make the task of evaluating a therapist less formidable. By compiling a list of well-respected therapists you can feel confident that whoever you ultimately choose from this group will be competent and professional. By asking a few basic questions on the phone, you can narrow your list to those people whose fees you can afford and who have appointment times available that are convenient for you. By having one or more face-to-face meetings, you can decide which therapist you feel most comfortable with. It is often possible in just one meeting with a therapist to judge how confident you are in her ability. Your confidence is especially important, because in the course of your child's or family's treatment the therapist will need your cooperation and trust.

A good example of the importance of such trust is illustrated by the following case:

> A widow brought her son to me because he was threatening to burn down their house. Indeed, on a few occasions he had been caught setting fires. This youngster, Sam, announced to me during our first meeting that he was bored and didn't want to see me anymore. I told him that his mother and I had (as he knew) talked at length and had decided that it was quite important for him to have these meetings. I reminded him of some of the problems that were bothering him, and he reluctantly agreed to return. However, during the next few weeks he talked less and less, and when he did say something it was to complain about having to see me. One day, an hour before his appointment, he ran away from his house and hid in some nearby woods. When his mother finally found him, he threatened to run away again and never to return home if she made him continue to come to my office. Eventually she persuaded him to come to his appointment, but she shared with me her concern about whether we should allow him to stop. I told her that, even though Sam might continue to try to run away before his appointments and might even increase his fire-setting behavior, it was important that she continue to bring him. I reminded her of our earlier discussions in which she had talked about her frequent feeling that it was he, not she, who was running their house and how she wanted this to change. I reminded her of my warning that there might be times in the treatment when Sam would

> seem to be getting worse rather than better. She thought about what I said and agreed to continue to bring him. Eventually, when I was able to understand why Sam so desperately wanted to stop seeing me and was able to talk about this with him he began to come to his appointments willingly. As he began to talk with me about the things that were upsetting him, his fire-setting and running away gradually stopped. A few months later his treatment was successfully concluded.

Looking back on this case, it is clear that Sam's mother had to trust in my judgment. There was no way for me to prove to her that it was best for Sam to continue to see me; I couldn't even guarantee that I could help him. Indeed, all the evidence indicated that Sam had been feeling worse and acting up more since his sessions with me started. Had Sam's mother harbored any doubts about my competence, she would probably have decided to stop bringing him. It was because she and I had built a trusting relationship up to that point that she was willing to see things through.

You too, should be prepared for some rocky times in any therapy. In fact, it is often necessary in treating children to encourage them to vent their hostility toward the therapist. After a session your youngster may tell you that he hates the therapist or that he just sat around and did nothing. You can see, therefore, how important it is for you to choose someone whom you genuinely trust and respect from the beginning. You'll need to draw on this reservoir of good feelings when the expected storms in treatment arise. (This is not to suggest that once you have started with someone, you should continue with that person even if you are continually dissatisfied. A discussion of what to do in such a case can be found in Chapter Twelve.)

Step One—
Considering Your Criteria

Shopping for a therapist, like shopping for any major purchase, is best done in an organized way.

Before you draw up a list of possible professionals, you should have some ideas about what criteria are especially important to you.

Some of the things you might want to consider are the following:

1) Fee: Since private practitioners' fees vary considerably, this may be an important consideration.

2) Geographical location: Some people prefer to take their children to see someone very close to their home for the sake of convenience. Others, who are afraid of running into a neighbor in the waiting room, prefer to see someone whose office is outside their immediate area.

3) Sex: Do you prefer a male or female therapist, or is this unimportant?

4) Age: Some parents seek younger therapists to work with their adolescent youngsters, believing that their children will feel more comfortable with someone closer to their own age; other parents seek a much older person who might be viewed by their child in the neutral light of a grandmother or grandfather.

5) Race or religion: Some people prefer to see someone of their own race or religion, believing that such a therapist will more easily relate to the child and the family, and vice versa.

6) Theoretical orientation: As outlined in Chapter Six, a therapist may use any one of a wide range of techniques in working with a client. To some people it is very important to find a clinician whose theoreti-

cal orientation makes sense to them. The following case illustrates this consideration.

> Billy Bonds was very disruptive at home and at school, constantly defying his teachers and his parents. After an evaluation the Bonds accepted my recommendation that they might benefit from parent counseling. As our talks progressed, it became clear to me that Billy's defiance usually followed occasions when he felt bossed around by his older brothers or by his father. I suggested that the whole family come in for family therapy so that we might see exactly how Billy's disruptive behavior was triggered. Mr. Bonds disagreed with this suggestion. He wanted me to give him some practical suggestions as to what to say or do when Billy was disrespectful. I made some suggestions, but Mr. Bonds found them either too vague or too impractical to carry out. I took this occasion to talk with Mr. Bonds about whether he felt I was being helpful to his family. After some discussion of other kinds of treatment techniques, the Bonds decided that they would like to try behavioral therapy techniques. Since I do not specialize in this kind of work, I asked a colleague who is a behaviorist to join the Bonds and myself. This colleague helped the Bonds design a reinforcement schedule to help their son control his troublesome behavior.

7) Discipline: Some professionals in each of the major mental health disciplines (psychology, psychiatry, psychiatric social work, and psychiatric nursing) are specially trained to work with children, parents, and families. If you prefer to work with someone from one particular discipline, for whatever reason, you should feel free to do so. (See Chapter Five for a complete discussion of the four major disciplines.)

Step Two—
Drawing Up a List

Having considered these suggested criteria for choosing a therapist, you should note which of these (or of others that you've come up with) are important to you. With your criteria in mind you can now make a list of possible therapists.

There is no *one* foolproof way to find out about qualified therapists in your area. Rather, there are a number of good methods, and each has its advantages and disadvantages. You may thus want to use a combination of methods.

SOURCES OF NAMES OF THERAPISTS

One of the easiest ways to obtain names of therapists is to ask friends, neighbors, coworkers, or relatives who themselves have had their children or families in treatment. There are some obvious advantages to this approach. First, it's convenient. You can talk to a friend or relative for as long as you need to ask as many questions as you want. You also have the advantage of knowing the person well enough to be able to evaluate the recommendations they give you. In addition, if your friend's child or family has been seeing a therapist for a while, you can make your own judgments about how helpful their therapist has been. On the other hand, current or former clients do not always report accurately on the way a particular clinician works; and even if they did, you would probably experience the person differently.

A second very common way of getting names of therapists is from your family physician or pediatrician. The advantage of this method is that your physician not only has known your child and family for a long time, but might have, in the course of her work, referred other children to psychotherapists. In principle, your physician is in an excellent position to find you a clinician whose skills and experience are well suited to your family's particular problems. I say "in principle," because some physicians refer to a relatively small number of therapists. Ideally your physician should have made detailed inquiries into the work of the therapists to whom she refers; but you should not *assume* that this is the case. I'd recommend simply that you apply the same standards when you consider your doctor's referral as you do when you consider others'.

(Also keep in mind that there are some physicians who hold strong negative feelings about all forms of psychotherapy. If you ask your youngster's pediatrician for the names of therapists, there's a chance that you may be told not to bother with such hogwash. You can listen to the doctor's viewpoint but you should feel free to make your own decisions about psychotherapy.)

Asking your child's school social worker, psychologist, or guidance counselor for referral suggestions can have some unique advantages. These professionals may have a good deal of contact with your youngster and thus have a good understanding of his problems and needs. However, they, too, sometimes refer to only a few people, whom they may not know very well. When you are given a name, be sure to ask how well the person making the referral knows the therapist she is recommending. Keep in mind, too, that a referral from a guidance counselor or physician whom you trust and respect does not automatically insure that you will trust and respect the person to whom she refers you.

A fourth method of obtaining names involves calling your local mental health center or child guidance clinic. If you do not know the name or telephone number of your local facility, you can obtain it by calling your state department of mental health, your local board of health, or the local Mental Health Association. Many mental health centers and child guidance clinics maintain extensive lists of local practitioners, including information on fees and areas of specialization.

There are two major disadvantages to this method. The

first is that it is relatively impersonal. The person you reach on the phone will have a very limited understanding of your child's or family's difficulties; it may therefore be hard for her to match you with a particularly appropriate therapist. Second, many clinics have a policy of making referrals on a rotating basis, so that all approved therapists will get referrals in turn. From your point of view, this means that essentially you will be getting a random referral—the next name or two names on the clinic's list. I suggest that you ask the clinic how referrals are made. If you're lucky, you'll be told that therapists are recommended based on your description of your child's problems.

Another place to call is the child psychiatry or child psychology department of a large teaching hospital (one that is affiliated with a medical school). The advantage of this method is that you may be given names of people who are on the staff of the hospital and therefore are actively involved in the teaching of child psychiatry or psychology. The disadvantages are similar to those of calling a mental health center—it is an impersonal method, and you can't know, unless you ask, whether the referral is tailored to your description of your child's problems or is made according to some rotating system.

You could also call the local professional societies for psychiatrists, psychologists, or social workers. Here again, though, you should be aware that these organizations tend to dispense names on a rotating basis.

Some people look for therapists by consulting national directories of psychologists, psychiatrists, psychiatric social workers, or psychiatric nurses. Although these directories are useful for checking the credentials of professionals whose names you have already been given, they are a very haphazard way of finding names in the first place, and I don't recommend that you use them for that purpose.

The preceding suggestions are not intended to be exhaustive. If you discover other ways of learning about qualified therapists in your area, use them. Be sure, though, to think through the possible disadvantages of any method and take them into account.

After compiling your list, try to rank-order the names,

putting the therapists who seem most desirable at the top of your list and working your way down. One way of rank-ordering is to put at the top of the list those people whose names you have heard from a number of different sources. Once you've done this rank-ordering, you're ready for the next step. But first, a word of caution is necessary.

DON'T LET YOUR FINGERS DO THE WALKING

One source of therapists' names that unfortunately is used by many people is the Yellow Pages. People are often embarrassed to talk to anyone about an emotional problem in their family, so they turn to the Yellow Pages and pick a name at random.

There are important disadvantages to this method. First, anyone can call the telephone company and ask to be listed under "Psychologists," "Physicians and Surgeons," "Social Workers," or "Nurses." In many states, but not all, there are laws prohibiting the use of these titles without proper credentials; but the telephone company does not check on people before listing them. Misrepresentation may be rare in actual practice, but it is one risk you take by using the telephone listings. A second disadvantage is that many of the finest professionals in all disciplines do not list themselves in the Yellow Pages. In general, looking in the Yellow Pages is such a totally haphazard way of selecting a therapist that, unless you have no other recourse, I strongly discourage its use.

Step Three—
Making Some Initial Calls

The next step in choosing a therapist is to make some phone calls. Be prepared to reach an answering service or a receptionist. If the receptionist tries to arrange an appointment for you, *do not accept it*. Instead, say that you are interested in talking briefly, by phone, with Dr. X about the possibility of her seeing your youngster. When the therapist returns your call, she may again offer you an appointment. I suggest that you ask if she can first spare a few minutes on the telephone so that you can ask a few questions. I suggest this because, after receiving answers to your questions, you may find you do not want to make an appointment with that particular person.

If the therapist won't spare the few minutes to talk, either then or at some appointed time, this ought to give you an idea of how busy, uninterested, or unavailable she will generally be. On the other hand, keep in mind that therapists often leave themselves only ten minutes between appointments, so they may not have much more than a few minutes to talk.

WHAT TO ASK ON THE PHONE

Here are samples of questions you might ask:

1) *"What is your fee?"*

If the fee is totally out of your range, you can ask if the therapist offers reduced rates. If not (unless your insurance will cover or defray the costs), you needn't talk any further.

2) *"Do you have time now, or in the immediate future, to do an* evaluation *of my child's or my family's problems to see if treatment is indicated?"*

The purpose of an evaluation is to delineate carefully what problems, if any, exist and the extent of their severity. The therapist can then decide whether treatment is necessary and, if so, what kind of therapy would be most likely to help. (As I discussed in Chapter Six, not all therapists have a formal evaluation period. Some like to begin treatment immediately and gather necessary information as they go along.)

3) *"Will you have time to treat my child or family if it is determined that therapy is indicated?"*

This question is very important. Some therapists will do an extensive evaluation, recommend therapy, and *then* inform you that they have no time to do the treatment, but that they'd be happy to refer you to a colleague. Most people find this very upsetting. They reasonably feel that, after investing so much time and energy and building some rapport with one person, they do not want to have to "start all over again."

If the therapist has time to do an evaluation but not to do treatment, tell her that you have other people to call, but will get back in touch if you need further help. This is perfectly acceptable practice, and it leaves the door open to you in the future. Most important, it keeps you and your child from becoming attached to one person, only to have to switch abruptly to someone else.

If the therapist's fees are affordable, and if she can do not only the evaluation but also the treatment, then you can set up the initial appointment.

SOME POTENTIAL COMPLICATIONS

There are a couple of other things you should be prepared for when making these initial calls. One is that the first few people you call—the people at the top of your list—may not have time to do an evaluation and/or treatment. It is easy to get discouraged at this stage and to think that you'll only get to see "second rate" therapists. Try to keep in mind that your rank-ordering was done, of necessity, on the basis of very sketchy information. It gave you a way to proceed, but it didn't necessarily guarantee that the best therapists were at the top of your list and the worst were at the bottom. Don't forget that everyone on your list should be someone who comes highly recommended. Also, don't assume that someone who has no available time is therefore very qualified or, conversely, that anyone with time is probably undesirable. Therapists' schedules vary, and some very well-thought-of and exceedingly competent people may have time to see you.

The second thing to be prepared for is that, if you call someone who doesn't have time, she will probably offer you the name of a colleague who does. These recommendations are necessarily made on the basis of very little information about your child. You might be receiving the name of a person who would work marvelously with your youngster. But it is equally likely that you're being referred to someone who is just starting a practice and who is known to have free time. You needn't disregard these referrals; just be careful to be as discriminating in evaluating them as you have been with all the others.

CALLING A PRIVATE CLINIC

You may find when you start making calls, that you have been given the name of a therapist who is either a partner or an employee in a private mental health clinic. This may or may not present added complications for you, depending on the policies of that clinic. What you will want to know is whether you will be able to work with the specific therapist to whom you were referred, or whether you will be assigned to someone of the clinic's choosing.

To obtain this information I suggest you telephone the person to whom you were referred and ask the following questions:

1) Do you *personally* have time to evaluate my child or family?

2) If, after the evaluation is complete, you feel that treatment is indicated, will you *personally* have time to provide this help?

3) After treatment has begun, will you feel free to transfer my child's or family's treatment to one of your colleagues or employees?

If you are fortunate you will be told that the therapist will be able personally to provide any appropriate help and that she will continue such treatment as long as it seems advisable. However, if the therapist tells you that she has no time personally, but will be happy to refer you to a well-respected associate, I suggest you contact another therapist from your list.

Step Four—
The Initial Appointment

Therapists have such widely differing styles, and approach the initial appointment in so many different ways, that it would be impossible for anyone to tell you exactly what to expect. There are a few general things, however, that you may do well to be prepared for.

WHAT TO EXPECT

First, as detailed in Chapter Six, some therapists consider the first session to be primarily for evaluation, while some see it as the beginning of treatment. Those who see it as evaluative will want to collect enough information to determine what, if any, treatment might be most helpful. These therapists will spend much time during the first appointment asking questions. On the other hand, those who see the first meeting as the beginning of treatment will not only gather information but also begin to step in and make comments or suggestions.

Second, therapists vary as to which members of the family they wish to see for the first appointment. Some will want to talk with the parents, without the youngster; some will want to see the parents and youngster together; and some will want to see the entire family, even though the parents are concerned about only one of their children. Usually, with youngsters under twelve or thirteen, therapists will not ask to see the child first. If the therapist should want to see your child first, you might ask if it would be possible for you and your spouse to have the first appointment. Explain that you want to make sure the therapist is someone with whom you'll be able to work comfortably. In the case of teenagers, therapists sometimes ask to see the youngster first. This is done out of respect for the adolescent's growing need to feel autonomous and independent from his parents. Starting therapy with an adolescent presents so many unique complications that it will be discussed separately, later in this chapter.

If the therapist meets with you alone, she will probably ask about your child's early development, including the pregnancy and birth, the child's feeding and sleeping patterns, speech and motor development, toilet training, medical history, school history, and relationships with peers, siblings, parents, and other adults. A therapist may also ask you and your spouse for a brief summary of your own childhoods, your courtship, and your marriage, and inquire how your other children are doing. Most important, all therapists will want to know about the specific problems that led you to seek professional help and why you sought help at this particular time.

If the therapist meets with the entire family, the focus of the first session will probably be very different. Rather than ask questions about your child's difficulty, the therapist will want to observe how that child and the other children actually get along in the family. Indeed, the therapist may discourage talking about any one youngster's problems, and instead ask you all to re-create the difficulties right in the office where she can see things firsthand. Even in the first session the therapist may attempt to suggest to you ways of handling problems differently from the way you usually do.

More often than not people come away from a first appointment with many unanswered questions. To avoid this frustration, request ten minutes at the end of your session for a question-and-answer period. You might even want to bring some written questions with you.

WHAT TO ASK

The following are some questions that may be important to you:

Questions about the Evaluation

1) What questions are you trying to answer during this evaluation?

2) Will you want to see us again? Our whole family? When will you want to see our youngster?

3) At the end of the evaluation, will you meet with us and share your findings and recommendations?

4) Whom will you want to talk with about our child's school or medical history?

Questions about Treatment
(if the therapist has begun to treat you)

1) What kind of treatment do you have in mind?

2) Do you have an idea how long the treatment will take?

Questions about Theoretical Orientation

1) What school(s) of therapy were you trained in? Is this the kind of treatment you do now?

2) Can you explain to me, in language that I can understand, what this means in terms of your working with my child or family?

Questions about Qualifications

1) Are you a psychologist, a psychiatrist, a psychiatric social worker, or a psychiatric nurse?

2) What is your highest degree? Where and when did you receive it? (See Chapter Five for an explanation of the typical credentials of the various disciplines.)

3) How much training and experience have you had in working with children, parents, and families?

4) Are you licensed or certified to practice in this state? (See Chapter Five for a discussion of licensing regulations.)

Financial Questions

1) How much do you charge per session? How long is a session?

2) Is there any flexibility in your fee? What would happen if, at some future time, we were unable to afford this fee?

3) What are your arrangements for collecting your fees?

4) What are your arrangements for canceled appointments? (Some therapists require twenty-four-hour notice, or you are subject to being charged. You are not charged if your hour is filled by someone else.)

5) Are you eligible to collect third-party payments (insurance, Medicare, Medicaid)? Will our insurance, Medicare, or Medicaid cover all or part of your fee? Do you collect directly from them, or do you require that we pay and get reimbursement?

Practical Questions

1) What are your usual office hours? What regular times could you offer us if we were to ask you to continue this evaluation or treatment?

2) If we have a question or concern, can we feel free to call you between appointments? Do you charge for time that you spend on the phone?

3) How can we contact you in case of emergency? For example, do you have a telephone answering service, or can we call you at home?

Evaluation of the Therapy

1) What do *you* typically do if you don't think things are working out?

2) What happens if *we* feel things aren't going well?

Step Five—
Choosing a Therapist

After your initial appointment with a therapist you are faced with a choice: whether or not to entrust your child's or your family's care to that person. While there can obviously be no fast rules for making your choice, here are some things that you might want to consider.

A CHECKLIST

1) Did you feel that the therapist was giving you her undivided attention? (Or did she interrupt to talk on the telephone or to read her mail?)

2) Did you feel that the therapist understood the problems your child or family was facing?

3) Did you feel that the therapist was compassionate and sympathetic, and genuinely cared that your child or family was in distress?

4) Did the therapist give you a feeling of confidence that she could help you with your problems?

5) Was the therapist willing to answer your questions, or to explain why it would be unhelpful or impossible to answer them?

6) Did the therapist clearly explain what would take place in the first session? For the rest of the evaluation or treatment? (Or did she talk over your head, or use psychiatric/psychological jargon?)

7) Did the comments and suggestions the therapist made appear reasonable and sensitive to your needs?

8) Was the therapist willing to talk openly about fees, missed appointments, and so on?

9) Did the therapist seem concerned about your financial situation?

10) How did you feel after the appointment? How did your spouse feel? (It is important to note that feeling upset or nervous after a first appointment is

not necessarily bad. It is sometimes necessary for a therapist to confront you with information that is not pleasant. For example, I periodically talk to parents who are very skeptical of their child's or family's need for help. Perhaps they were referred by the school and only agreed to come to see me under some pressure. In some instances these parents hope I will "take their side" and tell them that everything sounds okay to me. I will, of course, say this if I believe it is true. However, it is sometimes my responsibility to tell such parents that from their reports, or the school's, it sounds as if their youngster might be having some troubles, and that they should at least let someone do a complete evaluation. Understandably these parents may be angry or upset when they leave this first session.)

11) Did the therapist treat both you and your spouse with equal respect? (Or did you feel that she took sides?)

MAKING YOUR CHOICE

You're not going to learn everything about a therapist in one visit, just as she won't learn everything about you and your child. But you probably will have some impressions about what working with her will be like. These impressions, together with the answers to the questions you asked on the phone and at the initial appointment, will be the information you will use to make your decision about whom to see. If you are still undecided after a first interview, you can, of course, request a second appointment.

Choosing a Therapist with or for an Adolescent

Shopping for a therapist with or for an adolescent presents its own special difficulties for parents. Many adolescents demand or expect a large voice in choosing the therapist they will see. Others have strong objections to seeing anyone. Parents and therapists must address these issues with great sensitivity if they hope to be successful in engaging an adolescent in treatment.

Before beginning the process of shopping for a therapist for your adolescent, you should decide how much of your concern you want to share openly with your child. The entire therapy process will get off to a better start if you can begin by sitting down with your youngster and talking frankly about the possibility of his getting help. If the child is interested in such help, you can then offer to find out about therapists. The procedure for finding the right professional will be quite similar to that already described, the major difference being that you will involve your son or daughter in the choice of the therapist. This can be arranged by including the youngster in the initial appointment or by having two initial appointments—one for you and your spouse and one for your adolescent.

If you feel that you cannot discuss your concerns openly, or if, after such a discussion, your child refuses to accept help, you are in a tricky situation. Treatment of adolescents is difficult, if not impossible, to start or maintain if they want no part of it. Depending on the nature and severity of your child's problems, some therapists may be willing to attempt coercive treatment (therapy that the adolescent neither requests nor agrees to); but such work does not progress unless and until the youngster begins to develop some motivation of his own for working on the problems.

If your youngster is unwilling to get help, or if you don't want to discuss the matter with him, you can still call a therapist and explain your concerns. Some therapists may set up an appointment with you; others may first try to talk with your child and attempt to get him to come in for at least one session. If it is impossible to get your youngster to keep even one appointment, many therapists will offer to work with you in parent counseling. The goal of this work is for parents to learn how to guide their youngster toward more appropriate behavior. Sometimes an adolescent who refuses to be seen alone (since this implies that he is *the* problem in the family) is willing to be seen as long as all other family members also participate. In such cases family therapy becomes the best vehicle for effecting desirable changes in a youngster's behavior or attitude.

A REMINDER

Keep in mind that your careful search for a therapist has been designed to increase the likelihood of successful treatment; but it cannot guarantee such a result. Throughout the course of your child's or family's therapy, you should periodically be evaluating its effectiveness. A discussion of how to make this evaluation, including how to raise any concerns you may have with your therapist, can be found in Chapter Twelve.

Chapter 10

OBTAINING HELP IN A CLINIC SETTING

Some people prefer, for financial or other reasons, to seek help at a publicly sponsored mental health clinic. As was discussed in Chapter Four, it is the responsibility of these agencies to offer mental health services to area residents regardless of their ability to pay. Fees for services are on a sliding scale ranging from a high of thirty or forty dollars per hour, down to a nominal one dollar per week for many hours of service. Some clinics actually offer help at no cost. In addition, some people pay nothing because their fees are taken care of by Medicare or Medicaid. Without these clinics, many parents could not afford the cost of psychotherapeutic services.

It is important not to confuse relatively inexpensive treatment with low-quality care. It is possible to receive the same service at such clinics as from private practitioners—or better. Indeed, there are many reasons (apart from cost) why you may prefer to take your child to a clinic rather than to a private therapist. As detailed in Chapter Four some of the special advantages of clinics are: 1) geographical convenience—in some regions, clinics are the most convenient, if not the only practical place to go for help; 2) variety of available services—clinics generally can provide a wider variety of therapeutic services than can be obtained from an individual therapist; 3) the possibility of specialized services—because clinics assist large numbers of families, they can create programs for special client populations; 4) the existence of emergency facilities—clinics typically have more extensive and accessible emergency facilities than can be provided by any private practitioner.

On the other hand, there are some special difficulties which you may encounter when seeking help at a publicly sponsored clinic. As detailed in Chapter Four, these include: 1) waiting lists—you may have to wait longer than you'd like before receiving help; 2) type and length of treatment—you may not have a choice of the kind or duration of treatment provided to your child or family; 3) lack of choice of a therapist—you may have little or no choice as to which therapist will see your child or family.

A FOUR-STEP PROCEDURE FOR CHOOSING A PUBLICLY SPONSORED CLINIC

To minimize or counteract any or all of these potential difficulties, I recommend that you use the following four-step process when seeking help from a publicly sponsored clinic.

1) Locate the mental health clinc(s) in your geographic area.

2) Telephone the clinic(s) and ask some questions. The answers to these questions will help you decide if any given agency can help your child or family.

3) Request the kind of service you'd prefer and/or the particular therapist you'd like to see.

4) Have your child's or family's problems evaluated in the clinic that seems best suited to meet youı needs.

Step One—
Locating Your Local Clinic(s)

There are a number of ways for you to locate your local mental health clinic(s). As discussed in Chapter Four, one of the best places to call in order to obtain information about publicly sponsored clinics in your area is your local or state branch of the Mental Health Association. (The easiest way to locate your local MHA is by looking under "Mental Health Association" in the White Pages of your telephone directory.) You could also call your town, city, or county health department, your state department of mental health, or a local chapter of the United Way or Community Chest. Other resources would be your child's pediatrician, guidance counselor, or school psychologist.

As I've warned in earlier chapters, trying to locate your appropriate mental health facility by looking in the telephone directory is a poor way to begin. The Yellow Pages do have listings under "Mental Health Services"; but if you live near any large urban area there may be scores or even hundreds of listings under this heading. These listings will include private therapists and private clinics, as well as publicly sponsored ones. Without calling them and asking some questions, it will be very difficult to distinguish between private and public clinics.

If you live in a rural or sparsely populated suburban area it is likely that there will only be one publicly sponsored clinic which serves your geographic region. However, if you live in or near a large city it is likely that you will have more than one such clinic from which to choose. For example, residents of the Boston area can choose among their local mental health center, a number of community-sponsored child guidance clinics, and the outpatient departments of a number of teaching hospitals.

Step Two—
Calling One or More Clinics

The second step in the process of choosing a clinic is to make one or more telephone calls. Your purpose in calling is to find out if a given clinic will be able to help your child or family.

WHAT TO EXPECT WHEN YOU CALL

Some people are frustrated by their first call to a clinic. They expect to receive some immediate assistance and instead get what they perceive to be a runaround. You can avoid this disappointment by understanding how clinics typically respond to requests for help.

Many clinics make implicit or explicit distinctions between three stages of providing assistance: 1) intake; 2) evaluation; and 3) treatment.

The first, or intake, stage usually takes place on the phone, although this can be done in person. Both for you and for the clinic, this stage has several purposes. First, to determine if the clinic you've called can be of help to you. If not, you'll be referred to a more appropriate agency. Second, to determine if your child's or family's problems have reached crisis proportions. If so, an attempt will be made to provide you with immediate support. Third, to exchange any necessary practical information, such as your name, address, phone number, and who referred you for help; and what the clinic's fee will be, based on your financial situation. Fourth, to determine what kind of evaluation is indicated and which staff member(s) might best conduct this evaluation.

Some clinics distinguish only between intake and treatment. The intake stage at these agencies combines information gathering with the actual evaluation of your child's or family's problems. The intake process at such an agency may be relatively rapid, primarily because the clinic has a relatively narrow range of treatment options to offer you.

The second stage at most clinics is called evaluation. The purpose of this stage is to carefully delineate the nature and severity of the problems, in order to determine what, if any, kind of treatment will be most beneficial. An evaluation might involve anywhere from one to perhaps six visits over a time ranging from a few weeks to three months. It is not until after the evaluation is completed that the third stage, the actual treatment, begins.

Thus, you should keep in mind that in calling a clinic you have started a process which is designed to lead to your getting help. The actual treatment that you're seeking may not begin till months later. Ideally, you will find some help and support in the evaluation process itself, since it offers you the opportunity to share your concerns with a professional; the evaluation may, in fact, reassure you that your child does not need therapeutic help.

WHAT TO ASK ON THE PHONE

When you first call a clinic the receptionist will probably transfer your call to an "intake worker." The intake worker will ask you a number of questions about your child's or family's problems, and about the kind of help that you are seeking. I advise you to take the opportunity of this initial telephone conversation to ask some questions of your own.

1) *How will my fee be determined?*

If you have reached a publicly sponsored clinic you should expect to hear that fees are set on a sliding scale, based on a person's ability to pay. If you are told that the fee is thirty to forty dollars per hour *regardless of your income,* you have reached a private clinic.

2) *How long will it take before my child or family can be evaluated?*

Depending on whether or not the clinic has a waiting list, the evaluation might proceed immediately or you might have to wait for a substantial period of time.

3) *If it's determined that my child or family needs therapy, how long might we have to wait before such treatment will actually begin?*

At some clinics you will be seen shortly after you call for help and will be given a thorough evaluation. However, after the evaluation phase is completed, you may have to wait many months before the actual treatment is available. There are even some clinics where you may be told that treatment is totally unavailable. After investing so much time and energy in an evaluation, this can be terribly frustrating. Thus this third question is an important one to ask at the outset.

By asking the three questions detailed above, you should be able to get a sense of 1) whether you can afford a given clinic's services; and 2) how long you'll have to wait for an evaluation and/or treatment. If the fees are too high or the waiting period too long, you should call other agencies. If there are no other available facilities, assert yourself: Ask if the clinic, because of your special needs, can make any exceptions for your youngster. On the other hand, if the fees are affordable and the waiting period not too long, you may have located a clinic that can be of help to you, and you should proceed to step three.

Step Three—
Requesting a Particular Therapist
and/or Kind of Treatment

If you have any preferences for a particular kind of treatment (such as individual, group, or family) or for a particular therapist (whom you've heard good things about) you should express them *during the intake process.*

REQUESTING A PARTICULAR CLINICIAN

Some parents will have more confidence in a therapist whom they've helped to select than in someone who is simply assigned to them. If you are likely to feel this way, you should make an effort to have some say as to whom your child or family will see.

You might want your child to be evaluated by a particular kind of therapist; for example, a woman rather than a man, or an older person rather than a younger one. You may prefer someone from a particular theoretical orientation; for example a behaviorist. (See Chapter Six for a discussion of the different theoretical schools.) Or you may wish to see someone from a given professional discipline. (See Chapter Five for a discussion of the major mental health disciplines.) If any of these considerations are important to you, you should express them to the intake worker. It is important to realize that a clinic may not be able or willing to honor your preferences. However, it will do no harm to make such requests and they may well have some effect on which therapist is assigned to work with your child or family.

Rather than requesting a professional with certain characteristics or qualifications, you may wish to ask to see a particular therapist about whom you've heard good things. Keep in mind that most clinics will not *offer* you the opportunity to select your own therapist. You will need to make a special point of asking for a particular person.

You will probably be told that this is not how the clinic usually functions and that there can be no guarantee that you will see whom you wish. Nonetheless, many clinics will at least attempt to honor your request. You can greatly increase the likelihood of your being seen by a person of your choice if 1) you are willing to wait until that person has free time; or 2) you specify more than one person whom you'd like to see.

A conversation you might have with an intake worker could sound like this:

PARENT: I wanted to ask if my son could be evaluated by Mrs. Smith. I've heard she specializes in working with youngsters like him.

INTAKE WORKER: I'm afraid that we can't make such special arrangements. We have many people who call us and we can't assign staff on the basis of client preference. It's possible that Mrs. Smith will be able to see your son, but I can't give you any guarantees.

PARENT: I understand your clinic's position. But since I don't feel that the situation is a crisis, I'd be willing to wait for a few months to see if Mrs. Smith would, over the course of this period, have time to do this evaluation. Would it be all right if I waited?

Frankly, there's no way to predict whether any given clinic will honor this request, or whether your waiting will enable you to see whom you wish. However, if you have the luxury of being able to wait, and if you do very much want to see a particular therapist, you will increase the likelihood of that happening if you follow my suggested course of action.

An important distinction: A therapist in private practice, in many instances, will be able to provide any necessary treatment after evaluating your child or family; but this is not necessarily the case at clinics. After a clinic evaluation is completed, and if treatment is recommended, you could be told that someone else will be providing the therapy. Many people find this disconcerting. If they have built up some trust in one person, they don't want to have to "start all over again" with someone new. If you find yourself in this position, I recommend that you discuss your feelings openly and ask whether the person who did your evaluation can continue as your therapist. Again, you can increase the possibility of this happening if you wait until his schedule clears.

REQUESTING A SPECIFIC KIND OF HELP

Most parents do not know what specific kind of help will be best suited to their youngster; they will want to leave this decision in the hands of professionals. Some parents, however, do have specific kinds of treatment in mind. For example, they may have been told by their school guidance counselor that their son's problems with friends could be helped by group therapy; or they may have already tried family therapy without success and decided that their youngster needs to be seen individually.

Keep in mind that requesting a particular kind of service does not guarantee that you'll receive it. One of the purposes of an evaluation, after all, is to determine what kind of treatment will be helpful. Although an evaluator should take your concerns and preferences into consideration when making a recommendation, he should also weigh other factors before making a decision. This issue is illustrated by the following example:

> Mrs. Lewis's ten-year-old son, Tim, was constantly being picked on by his schoolmates—who knew that he wouldn't fight back if teased. Tim's school guidance counselor had tried talking to Tim and to the boys who were teasing him but this wasn't successful. Finally the guidance counselor had suggested to Mrs. Lewis that Tim be placed in one of the therapy groups conducted at the mental health clinic where I work. Mrs. Lewis called the clinic and I was assigned to do the evaluation.
>
> During the course of the evaluation it became clear that Mr. Lewis had practically no contact with his son. I told Mr. Lewis and his wife that Tim's problems with his peers could be substantially improved if Mr. Lewis could teach his son how to defend himself verbally or physically, and if he could tutor him in some athletics, so that Tim would have some skills that his friends could admire.
>
> Mr. Lewis felt that these suggestions were reasonable and began to spend more time with his son. I scheduled some appointments with Mr. Lewis and Tim to see how they were progressing, and kept in touch with the school to see if the bullying was diminishing. I told the Lewises that if this plan didn't

have results I'd look into a group-therapy program for their son.

Happily, Tim responded very well to his father's tutelage. He did have to get into a few fights with his worst tormentors (and Mrs. Lewis did have to bite her tongue so as not to chastise him for getting into these scrapes). But the bullying did gradually subside. Mr. Lewis, realizing that he had an important role to play in his son's development, continued to spend more time with him; and Mrs. Lewis, freed from her worries about Tim, was able to spend more time with their five-year-old daughter.

I give this example to illustrate that the treatment that is first suggested or that you may first have in mind for your child is not necessarily the only therapy that will help. In this example I used a family-oriented treatment rather than the group therapy that was originally requested. If my attempts had not been successful I would have then followed the guidance counselor's suggestion of a group.

In summary, if you prefer a specific kind of treatment, by all means request it at the outset. But be flexible enough to realize that other forms of therapy may be equally or more helpful.

Step Four—
The Evaluation Process

As I've explained, the purpose of an evaluation at a clinic is twofold: 1) to specify the nature of a child's or family's problems; and 2) to determine what, if any, kind of treatment will be most beneficial.

Clinicians have such widely differing approaches to evaluation that it's impossible for anyone to tell you exactly what to expect in your individual case. There are a few general things, however, that you should know.

HOW LONG AN EVALUATION MAY TAKE

The length of an evaluation can vary widely. This will usually depend on 1) the orientation of the evaluating therapist—for example, some family therapists will begin treatment without any formal evaluation period, while some individually oriented child therapists will conduct lengthy evaluations (See Chapter Six); and 2) the nature of your child's or family's problems; for instance, if the presenting complaint was that a youngster was talking about suicide, a therapist may want to conduct an especially lengthy evaluation. An extended evaluation does not necessarily indicate that your child's problems are especially serious. It may simply indicate that the evaluator is having difficulty sorting out what kind of treatment will be most effective.

WHO WILL BE INTERVIEWED

An evaluation typically involves a number of appointments. On one occasion you and your spouse may be seen, while on another visit the evaluator may wish to talk with just your child. It is possible that you will be asked to bring in your entire family, even grandparents, if they are living in or near your home. A psychologist might be called in to do personality testing, or a psychiatrist might be asked to determine a youngster's need for medication.

WHAT TO ASK THE EVALUATOR

You have the right to know the results of your family's or youngster's evaluation. You should expect that at the end of the evaluation period the therapist will allot some time for the purpose of summarizing his findings and explaining his recommendations. You should be given time to ask questions and to share your reactions.

Some questions that you may want to ask are:

1) Why do you think that individual (or group or family) therapy will be the most helpful treatment?

2) Will you be providing the treatment or will someone else?

3) (If the answer is someone else, and you'd prefer to remain with the person who did the evaluation:) Is there some way that you could provide the treatment so that we don't have to switch to someone new?

4) Do you have any idea how long the treatment will take?

Receiving Help From a Trainee

A substantial percentage of clients who seek help at clinics are assigned to trainees for evaluation or for treatment, or both. You may object to this, wishing to place your child only in the hands of a very experienced therapist.

While this is understandable, you should be aware that there are some unique advantages in receiving help from a trainee. First, the evaluative and therapeutic work of each student is supervised by a professional on the clinic's staff. Under the supervision system, the intern will discuss in detail his clinical work and will receive advice or suggestions from the supervisor. Thus the progress of any child's or family's therapy will be continuously monitored by two people: the therapist-in-training and a more experienced clinician.

Second, most trainees are extremely committed to becoming effective help-providers. They are usually quite aware of their inexperience, and work with extra diligence to provide excellent care.

On the other hand, there are disadvantages to working with a trainee. First and most obvious, trainees will be relatively less experienced in psychotherapy than will senior members of the staff. Second, because trainees typically work at any given clinic for only one year, it will be difficult for you to obtain any information on their skills from former clients or from other professionals, and if your child's or family's treatment needs to continue beyond a year you will have to transfer to another therapist.

If, after reading this discussion, you have a definite wish either to see or not to see a trainee, you should state this at the time of intake. As always though, be aware that the clinic may be unable to honor your request.

A CLOSING NOTE

All your careful preparations in selecting a clinic, kind of treatment, or particular therapist cannot guarantee that your child's or family's therapy will be successful. Psychotherapy is a complicated process and you should not hesitate to monitor its effectiveness continuously as you go along. In Chapter Twelve, I will discuss the topic of how to evaluate therapy.

Chapter 11

THE GROUND RULES OF PSYCHOTHERAPY

Psychotherapy, whether provided by a private practitioner or in a clinic setting, involves a more or less structured series of contacts between a client and a therapist. Parents typically understand that they (or their child or family) are expected to attend their regularly scheduled appointments, to cooperate with their therapist's attempts to help them, and to pay for these sessions. They trust that in return, their therapist will employ his or her knowledge and expertise to help them resolve their problems.

Aside from these very general understandings, parents often begin treatment with little clarity about exactly what they should expect from a therapist and what will be expected from them. This lack of clarity can set the stage for subsequent misunderstandings and disappointments. To minimize the possibility that this will happen to you, I suggest that, at the outset of your treatment, you and your therapist discuss and agree to (as much as is possible) the goals, methods, and arrangements of therapy. It may be that such discussion will actually help your child's or family's therapy progress more smoothly, as well as prevent or reduce subsequent difficulties.

TREATMENT GOALS

It should be obvious that you and your therapist will need to agree about the goals of treatment. All too often parents feel that the results they expect from therapy have been clearly defined despite the fact that they have never discussed this matter in any detail.

Take the example of the Blakes and the Johnsons. Both of these couples have six-year-old sons who are uncooperative at home and disruptive at school. Although the Blakes and the Johnsons both want a therapist to help their sons behave more appropriately, they have very different expectations of therapy. Mr. and Mrs. Blake want a therapist to focus specifically and directly on helping David change his behavior. Their hope is that treatment will proceed rapidly and will end when David begins to behave better. The Johnsons, on the other hand, are not concerned about Tom's disruptive behaviors per se. Rather they assume that such behaviors reflect the fact that Tom is basically an unhappy child. They want a therapist to help them and their son understand the sources of this discontent. They expect that it may take quite a long time before Tom or they will be able to understand fully the nature or causes of his distress, and they are prepared for the fact that his problem behaviors may well continue, or even worsen, until this takes place.

As you can see from this example, the Blakes and the Johnsons differ greatly in their expectations of treatment, despite the fact that they have sought therapeutic help for exactly the same behavioral difficulties. Thus a relatively detailed exploration of your goals for treatment is indicated, even if you think that your expectations are self-evident.

TREATMENT METHODS

It will be impossible for any therapist to specify in advance all the techniques that she may employ. Nonetheless, your therapist should be able to provide you with some information about how treatment will proceed. For example, will she be meeting primarily with your youngster, and talking with you only infrequently? Or will she expect that most of the treatment will involve meetings with you, interspersed with only occasional sessions with your child? Will you be given very specific instructions to carry out at home, or general guidelines to be applied as you see fit? (See Chapter Six for a discussion of some of the treatment methods employed by different therapists.)

TREATMENT DETAILS

In addition to agreeing on treatment goals and methods, you will also need to have some idea about the following treatment details.

Frequency of Appointments

At the very outset of treatment you will need to agree upon the frequency of sessions. Will your child or family be seen once or twice a week, or even more frequently? If the presenting problems (that is, the problems that led you to seek help in the first place) begin to resolve, will you be able to schedule appointments less frequently?

Although the frequency of appointments may vary depending on the nature of your problems and the theoretical orientation of your therapist, many clinicians believe that once-a-week sessions represent the minimal frequency necessary for treatment to be effective.

Length of Sessions

Most therapists, even if they don't state this explicitly, allot a fixed amount of time per therapy appointment. The traditional length of time is fifty minutes. (Family therapists may allot sixty to ninety minutes per session.) The purpose of the "fifty-minute hour" is simply to allow the therapist ten minutes between appointments to answer telephone calls, write some notes, go to the bathroom, or just take a short break. Some therapists have "forty-five-minute hours" while others see clients for a full sixty minutes. Typically, when a therapist says that he or she charges forty dollars per hour, this means forty dollars per session, regardless whether the session lasts for forty-five, fifty, or sixty minutes.

Financial Details

During your first telephone contact with a therapist, or, at the latest, by the end of the first evaluation session, you should have reached some agreement about the cost of treatment. However, there are many other financial details which ought to be discussed early in the therapy. For example, does your therapist expect to be paid after each appointment, or weekly, or monthly? If you have insurance, will she wait to be reimbursed by your insurance company (which can sometimes take months)? Or will she expect to be paid directly by you, and leave it to you to be reimbursed by your insurance company?

One area of conflict between therapists and clients is the issue of payment for missed or canceled appointments. Most therapists will expect you to give them twenty-four hours' notice when canceling an appointment. If you do not (or cannot) give such notice, you are "subject to being charged" for that session. Some clinicians apply this rule rigidly, others loosely. Almost all therapists will charge you for a session which you simply forgot. But what if your youngster gets sick a few hours before his appointment, or if your car breaks down on the way to your session? Some therapists will charge you in these instances. Others will not.

You may feel that a therapist's charging you under such circumstances is unfair and arbitrary. Why should you be penalized for circumstances over which you have no control? Therapists who do charge in such instances argue that unlike physicians, dentists, or lawyers, who can often use the time provided by missed or canceled appointments to see other clients, they reserve an entire hour for each client and typically cannot use that time to see anyone else.

Duration of Treatment

It is usually quite difficult for a therapist to tell you exactly how long treatment will need to continue. Nonetheless, this is an issue which should be addressed in a general way, since your own timetable may be appreciably different from the therapist's. For example, if you are planning to move out of the area in eight months' time, and your therapist expects no appreciable results in less than eight months, you may wish to postpone treatment until after you move.

As part of this general topic, you and your therapist may wish to agree to some periodic review of therapy, say at three-month to six-month intervals, so that you can assess your child's or family's progress (or lack thereof).

Many parents assume that the severity of their youngster's or family's problems will determine the length of the treatment; the more serious problems take more time to resolve than the less serious ones. However, there are many factors other than the severity of problems which may influence the duration of any particular therapy. Perhaps the most important of these is the goals that parents and therapists establish for the treatment. For example, a family with many long-standing, unresolved difficulties may decide that they wish a therapist's help in handling only one circumscribed problem; let's say their son's failing out of high school. Perhaps these parents have already been unsuccessful in using therapy to repair their own failing marriage, so they do not wish to address this more fundamental problem in treatment. It may be possible for a therapist to help this family handle the problem of their son's academic failure without addressing their marital issues, and for this to be done in a relatively short period of time. Conversely, a comparatively well-functioning family may wish to address a wide array of nagging problems and their therapy may continue over a long period of time.

Continuity of Treatment

Most parents assume that a therapist will be available to provide treatment to their child or family for as long as such help is necessary. In reality this is often not the case.

At clinics much of the treatment is provided by students or interns who typically stay in that agency for one academic year. At some clinics, too, there may be a relatively high staff turnover, with many therapists staying only a year or two before moving on to other jobs or more lucrative private practice.

While the private therapist is more likely to be able to provide treatment over an extended period of time, a private therapist also may move out of your area or accept a position which could affect her ability to continue your treatment.

Therapists should, as a matter of course, let you know if they will be available to you for only a limited period of time. However, a therapist may not think to tell you, unless you ask.

Special Circumstances

Therapists vary widely in their policies and procedures as to talking with you at other than regularly scheduled appointment times. Some will encourage you to call them between appointments; others will expect that, except in an emergency, you will wait to talk with them until your next scheduled appointment. (You should, as a matter of course, have a telephone number where you could contact your therapist in case of emergency. Many therapists have either a telephone answering service or an automatic answering machine, which provide their clients with a way of contacting them around the clock.)

Confidentiality

Professional ethics require that a therapist not release any information about her contacts with a client without prior written permission.

The exceptions to this policy involve situations in which your child, your family, or someone else may be in imminent danger. For example, if your adolescent son has a gun and talks of his plans to "get back" at his girl friend's father, a therapist, depending on the circumstances, may feel it necessary to call you, or the intended victim, or the police. The therapist may or may not inform the client of her intention to do this; or may do so although expressly told not to. (In some states a therapist is required to do so, by law.) In cases of child abuse or neglect, a therapist may reveal confidential information to appropriate agencies without her client's permission. (Again this may be required by law in some states.)

Other exceptions to the general policy of confidentiality involve court proceedings in which a therapist is subpoenaed to testify. Whether a therapist can be ordered to provide information about you against your wishes is a complicated question, depending on a number of factors. In general, all clients do have some rights to have information they gave to a therapist kept confidential, even from a judge.

At times therapists make audio or video recordings of their clients' sessions. These are often used by a therapist as a memory aid or as a way of assessing progress. As a matter of course you should be asked if you have any objections to this, and your therapist should not put any pressure on you to agree to such tapings. These recordings cannot ethically be shared with anyone else without your prior written permission. It is also unethical for any therapist to make any recordings without first asking your permission.

Intrafamilial Confidentiality

Another type of confidentiality involves how much information provided by one family member will be shared with other members of the family. This issue most typically arises when a youngster is being seen in individual therapy, while his parents have separate sessions with the therapist. In general, therapists try to maintain a delicate balance in this situation; on the one hand letting a youngster know that he can say things which will not be told to his parents, while, on the other hand, respecting the fact that parents need to be kept advised of their youngster's concerns.

Contact with Other Professionals

You should expect a therapist to ask your written permission to contact any other professionals who care for your child, such as a pediatrician, a family physician, or any appropriate school personnel.

You may feel uncomfortable about a therapist talking to anyone about your child's or family's difficulties. If so, you should discuss your feelings in order to reach an understanding about what information, if any, your therapist will disclose.

Some parents prefer that a therapist have absolutely no contact with other professionals. If this is your preference, you can expect a therapist to question you about your reasons and, perhaps, try to change your mind (since such contacts are often in a youngster's best interests). However, you have the right to refuse the therapist this permission, and she must respect your wishes.

A WRITTEN CONTRACT

Some therapists and clients begin therapy with a written contract which carefully spells out the goals of treatment and procedures for assessing whether those goals have been met.

The Health Research Group, a public interest, consumer-oriented organization, strongly recommends that clients enter into a written contract with their therapist. The following sample contract is paraphrased from a book written by this group, entitled *Through the Mental Health Maze: A Consumer's Guide to Finding a Psychotherapist.* This book is primarily written for adults who are looking for therapeutic help for themselves. It can be purchased from the Health Research Group, 2000 P Street N.W., Washington, D.C. 20036.[2]

> We, Mr. and Mrs. Smith, agree that our son, Thomas, will meet with Dr. Hamilton each Tuesday afternoon from January 1, 1979, until June 30, 1979, from 4:00 to 4:50 P.M. During these six months Dr. Hamilton and our son will direct their efforts to two goals:

1) Helping Thomas control his temper so that he no longer yells or hits every time that he is frustrated, and

2) Helping Thomas concentrate on his schoolwork so that he raises his grades from the C's and D's he is currently receiving to the A's and B's of which we believe he's capable.

We also agree to meet with Dr. Hamilton every other week during the same six-month period on Wednesday afternoon from 5:00 to 5:50 P.M. We will direct our mutual efforts toward two goals:

1) Understanding why Thomas reacts so aggressively to frustration, and

2) Learning ways to respond less angrily to Thomas's outbursts.

We agree to pay $40.00 per hour for Dr. Hamilton's time and for the use of his resources, training, and experience as a psychotherapist. If we are not satisfied with the progress made on the goals here set forth we may cancel any and all subsequent appointments for these sessions, provided that we give Dr. Hamilton three days' warning of our intention to cancel. In that event we are not required to pay for sessions not met. However, in the event that we miss a session without forewarning, we are financially responsible for the missed session. The one exception to this arrangement being unforseen and unavoidable accident or illness.

At the end of the six months Dr. Hamilton and we agree to renegotiate this contract. We include the possibility that the stated goals will have changed during this period. We understand that this agreement does not guarantee that we will have attained the goals; however it does constitute an offer on our part to pay Dr. Hamilton for access to his resources as a psychotherapist, and his agreement to apply all his resources as a psychotherapist in good faith. We further stipu-

> late that this agreement become part of our son's medical record, and that that record be accessible to us at will, but to no other party without our written permission. The therapist will respect our and our son's right to maintain the confidentiality of any information communicated to him during the course of therapy. In particular, the therapist will not publish, communicate, or otherwise disclose, without our written permission, any such information, which, if disclosed, would injure us in any way.

Since most therapists don't typically enter into written contracts with their clients, don't be surprised if yours is skeptical of the need for such an arrangement. (The use of written contracts is most compatible with the behavioral and family-systems approaches. On the other hand, it may be far more difficult for a humanistic or psychoanalytically oriented therapist to outline such a specific blueprint for change. (See Chapter Six.) Whatever the theoretical orientation of your therapist, if you feel that a written contract is worthwhile, you should request such a document. You should expect that your therapist will either accommodate your request or explain why she feels that such an arrangement would be unnecessary or unhelpful. You may feel, on the other hand, that a verbal agreement, as long as it is detailed and explicit, will meet your needs as well as a written one.

Chapter 12

EVALUATING THERAPY

Evaluating your child's or family's treatment should not be a problem if things are progressing well. If, after a month or two, your child's temper tantrums are less frequent or if there is less fighting in your family, you are most likely to feel pleased and eager to continue therapy.

In many instances, however, positive results do not occur quickly or are not so clear cut. For example, you may feel that your youngster is somewhat less tense but his bedwetting may be getting worse rather than better. Or perhaps family sessions have made it easier for you and your daughter to communicate, but they seem also to have led to increased tensions between you and your husband.

Or it may be that things have actually gotten worse since treatment started. Perhaps your youngster is refusing to see his therapist and promising to behave only if you let him stop his sessions. Perhaps you feel that your therapist is stirring up, rather than settling, family tensions; for example, by encouraging your previously cooperative teenager to complain about her curfew, or your wife to push harder about her wish to have a part-time job.

Parents who begin to have doubts or dissatisfactions about treatment often find themselves with many unanswered questions:

1) Are they being too impatient with the lack of clear progress in treatment? Or, on the contrary, are

they wasting their time by continuing something which is just not going to help?

2) Is their discontent reasonable, or are they really only upset because the therapy is forcing them to face unpleasant characteristics of their children, themselves, or each other?

3) Is their dissatisfaction serious enough for them to stop treatment; and if they do so, has all their time, energy, and money been wasted?

Any parent who has struggled with these issues knows how difficult and complicated they are to resolve. In this chapter I will provide you with some guidelines about evaluating psychotherapy and some suggestions about what to do if you have significant and continuing dissatisfactions with your child's or family's treatment.

THE DIFFICULITIES OF EVALUATING ONGOING THERAPY

It is often very difficult for a parent to evaluate the effectiveness of an ongoing therapy. Some of the reasons for this are the following:

Ambiguous Goals

Some parents seek therapy for the children or family with only an ambiguous and vague sense of what they hope to gain from such help. For example, parents may feel that they need "to understand their child better" or "to improve family communications." These aims, while commendable, are sufficiently vague that it could be difficult for the parents to judge whether treatment is significantly helpful. You may be able to meet this difficulty if you try to define specific goals at the outset of treatment and to set up a timetable for when these goals should be met.

Uncertainty About How Long to Wait for Improvement

Most people enter therapy with the awareness that change will not necessarily come quickly and that things may even get worse before they get better. This leaves them with little sense of how to distinguish a treatment which is not getting anywhere from one which is on the verge of stimulating much-needed changes.

Doubt About Whether to Trust Negative Feelings

It is rare that a therapy goes totally smoothly; problems, concerns, and discoutent can and do arise in the most helpful of treatments. However, such feelings are also common when therapy actually is proving unhelpful, for any of a number of reasons. It is because negative feelings can arise when therapy is working, as well as when it is not, that it can be especially difficult for parents to evaluate its effectiveness.

In general, doubts and dissatisfactions about therapy can arise for any or all of the following reasons:

1) Treatment is providing little or no help or a therapist is inconsiderate, critical, or insensitive.
2) After some progress or gains have been made, a child or family slips back into old ways of behaving.
3) The treatment stimulates parents or their children to face upsetting feelings or conflicts.

Most parents can accept negative feelings about therapy, provided that they arise only periodically and that they are counterbalanced by feelings that the therapy is proving helpful in some ways. However, when negative feelings arise continuously or when they arise before the treatment has produced any positive results, parents are faced with the difficult decision whether to continue or stop the therapy.

A further complication is that although you and your spouse may feel that the therapist is sensitive and likely to be of help, your child may be expressing strong feelings about disliking the therapist and wanting to stop the sessions. Since negative feelings on your or your spouse's part need to be handled differently from negative feelings on your child's part, these issues will be addressed in separate sections later in this chapter.

Why Evaluate Therapy at All?

Some parents feel, since it can be so difficult to evaluate an ongoing treatment, and since they have placed their child or family in the hands of a professional, that they should be able to depend on the professional to tell them whether or not things are progressing as expected. Although this attitude is understandable, it is not realistic.

First, it assumes that your therapist is quickly able to recognize difficulties in your child's or family's treatment, and is willing to address these problems with you as they arise. The flaw in this assumption is that if your therapist is not able to do this, you or your child may remain in an unhelpful treatment for long periods of time.

Second, some therapists may assume, if you are not raising any dissatisfactions about therapy, that you are reasonably satisfied with the results. A therapist may have no way of knowing that you are discontented unless you share your feelings openly.

Finally, by placing the total burden of evaluation on your therapist's shoulders, you are transferring the responsibility for your child's or family's welfare from your hands, where it belongs, to those of a therapist, who cannot and should not assume such total responsibility. In summary, the task of evaluating your child's or family's treatment, even though it can be difficult, is one which you should be ready to share with the therapist.

PARENTAL DISSATISFACTION WITH THERAPY

I suggest the following three-step procedure if you or your spouse is feeling some serious dissatisfaction with your child's, your family's, or your own treatment:

How to Approach the Problem

Step One— Talk over Your Feelings with Each Other

If you or your spouse have serious doubts about the therapy, you would do well to spend some time together discussing your feelings. By talking together you may not necessarily arrive at a decision about what to do, but you can often clarify the nature of your doubts.

By prepared for the fact that it is usually rare for two parents to experience their own, their child's, or their family's treatment in exactly the same way. More than likely, one parent will have more strongly negative feelings than the other. The purpose of your conversation is not for one spouse to convince the other of anything, but to enable you to understand each other's feelings, so that you can then discuss them with your therapist.

Of course, sometimes both parents do share similar negative feelings about the therapy, and this will often convince them that they should stop the treatment.

Step Two— Discuss Your Feelings with Your Therapist

Expressing doubts or dissatisfactions to a therapist is not an easy thing for most parents to do. They may be fearful that their comments will hurt the therapist's feelings, or lead him to attack them in return. Some parents may also fear that any discussion of their negative feelings will jeopardize their child's relationship with the therapist and thus do more harm than good.

Your discomfort or apprehensiveness about talking openly about your concerns needs to be balanced by the realization that if you do not feel comfortable enough with the therapist to talk about such feelings, eventually you will probably become so dissatisfied that you will stop treatment altogether. Also keep in mind that a competent therapist will be eager to discuss your reactions to the therapy. Since most clients feel at least some periodic discontent over the course of a treatment, it will come as no shock to your therapist that you too are experiencing some negative feelings.

It is the therapist's responsibility to help you sort out whether your feelings are the result of mistakes, misunderstandings, or insensitivity on his part, or whether they are due to your having been brought face to face with some painful conflicts in your relationship with your child or in your marriage.

For a therapist to acknowledge that he was mistaken in the advice given to you or in the way that the therapy has been conducted, should not necessarily be taken as an indication that the therapist is inept or incompetent. (Of course, this may be the conclusion you reach, and you may wish to stop treatment with that person.) Rather, such an acknowledgment on the therapist's part may lead to very productive changes in the treatment.

Bear in mind also that a therapist who suggests that your complaints stem mainly from your own difficulties, is not necessarily trying to defend himself or to attack you. It is sometimes the case that feelings of dissatisfaction are primarily in reaction to anxiety stirred by confronting difficult family problems. If your therapist can help you face these feelings and resolve them, he will be providing a great service to you and your family.

Of course, discussing your negative feelings does not always lead to a clear understanding of their source. Perhaps such feelings are caused by a combination of the therapist's insensitivity and your own defensiveness. Perhaps the reasons for your feelings are so complicated that it will take a long time to understand them. Perhaps you don't yet feel comfortable enough to discuss all your concerns openly, or perhaps your therapist is having trouble accepting or acknowledging your legitimate complaints.

If you explore your discontent with your therapist and still feel unclear about whether or not to continue treatment, you may wish to seek another opinion about what you should do.

Step Three—
Get Another Opinion

Seeking another professional opinion about your child's or family's treatment is a reasonable step to take, if your discussions with your therapist have not clarified the reasons for your dissatisfaction or have left you undecided about whether to continue the treatment. Seeking another opinion (often called a "consultation") is an accepted practice and you should expect your therapist to support your decision to do this.

You should be just as careful in choosing a consultant as you were when you first chose a therapist. Finding a consultant, however, should be far easier, since you are only asking someone to provide you with an hour or two of their time. Ideally, a consultant should be a well-respected and well-established clinician who does not personally know your therapist. Sometimes consultants will want to talk with your therapist before or after they talk with you; sometimes they will feel that this is unnecessary or unhelpful.

It is the consultant's job to help you sort out your own feelings about your child's or family's therapy or therapist. It is *not* her job to judge or evaluate your therapist's overall competence. Even though consultants are paid to be impartial and unbiased, not all are capable of this. Some are all too eager to find fault with their colleagues, while some will tend to assume that all your dissatisfactions are due to your own defensiveness. Some may be influenced by the fact that your therapist is or is not an M.D., or by your therapist's theoretical orientation. A consultant who is a family therapist may believe that individual therapy is almost never helpful, while a therapist who works with children individually may not approve of family-oriented treatment. Thus it is especially important, in looking for a consultant, to try to locate someone whom you feel will be an impartial and unbiased sounding board.

Of course, after your discussions with your therapist (and a consultant) you will have to make up your own mind. The following guidelines are offered to help you distinguish an unhelpful treatment from one which may be stimulating you to face unpleasant feelings or conflicts. (Bear in mind that these are only general guidelines and should not be used to take the place of discussions with your therapist.)

Indications that the Therapy is Unhelpful

Some examples of real sources of incompatibility between you and your therapist are the following:

VALUE CONFLICTS

Some therapists and clients have widely differing views on how to raise children. If your therapist believes that children should never be spanked and you feel strongly that such punishment is at times effective, you and your therapist may not be able to work together productively.

OVERINVOLVEMENT

A therapist's job is to help you and your spouse resolve difficulties in your family or to help you, your spouse, and your child resolve your youngster's problems. It is not the job of the therapist to take over child rearing for you.

If a therapist treats you as if you were incompetent parents, he has lost the capacity to be helpful to you. On the other hand, it is the responsibility of a therapist to help you be more effective and understanding parents, and this may lead him to make suggestions about alternate ways for you to handle certain situations. Advice and criticism is not necessarily an indication that your therapist is questioning your adequacy as parents. The tone and manner of your therapist is crucial in this area. Do you generally feel that the therapist is pointing out areas that you yourself know need correcting? Or do you feel constantly attacked and belittled?

UNPROFESSIONAL CONDUCT

A therapist enters into an implicit agreement with his clients to behave in a professional manner. This means that he will *not* constantly keep you waiting for long periods of time for your appointments, or allow your time to be interrupted while he answers the phone or reads the mail, or change or cancel your appointments at the last minute, or constantly talk about his own problems.

You may probably wish to overlook occasional instances of such behavior (though you should feel free to speak up if such behavior ever does occur). On the other hand, if those occurrences are more the rule than the exception you have a legitimate reason to think seriously about stopping treatment.

UNETHICAL BEHAVIOR

Certain behaviors of a therapist are not only unprofessional but also unethical. In such instances, not only should you stop treatment, but you should report your therapist to the appropriate professional or legal body so as to protect other children and parents from similar abuses. (See Chapter Five.)

Unethical behavior includes any sexual contact or advances, any physical assault or threat of violence, or any release of information about your child or family without your prior written approval. (The few exceptions to your rights to confidentiality are discussed in Chapter Eleven.)

TAKING SIDES

A therapist's role is to help family members resolve differences in ways that they all find satisfactory. A therapist should be an impartial agent of change. If you find your therapist continually taking sides, either with or against you, you should take this as an indication that he may be losing the capacity to be helpful.

The situation is somewhat complicated when a therapist is seeing your child regularly on an individual basis, and meeting with you only infrequently. The therapist may then see it as his role to be an advocate for your child. This can be helpful and appropriate, as long as the therapist is respectful of your feelings and of your role as the youngster's parents.

GENERALLY UNHELPFUL TREATMENT

If nothing else, therapy should leave you with the feeling that you are gaining a better understanding of your child's, your own, or your family's problems, and that you are receiving some assistance in resolving these difficulties. If you leave session after session feeling less and less optimistic about your problems, or if, after a reasonable period of time, you feel no closer to solving them than when you started, it may be that the treatment is not helping.

THERAPIST'S UNWILLINGNESS TO DISCUSS YOUR COMPLAINTS

If your therapist is unwilling to discuss your feelings of dissatisfaction or is actually antagonistic to you when you mention them, this may well confirm that your discontent is well founded.

NEGATIVE FEELINGS IN THE CONTEXT OF A HELPFUL TREATMENT

The following situations are examples of times when negative feelings may be stirred in reaction to upsetting but necessary experiences, in the course of a basically constructive treatment.

1) You begin to feel that it's time to stop treatment, although your child is showing signs of changing her behavior: At times when youngsters begin to progress in therapy, their parents begin to feel competitive with their child's therapist. They may wonder why their youngster can talk with a comparative stranger and not with them. Or they may contrast the helpfulness of the therapist with what they perceive as their own relative inadequacy. The emergence of such feelings is *not* a good reason to stop treatment. On the contrary, these feelings, embarrassing though they may be, should be raised and explored with your child's therapist.

2) You suddenly decide that the therapy is too expensive or too much of an inconvenience, although, in reality, up until now you have been able to afford both the expense and the time that therapeutic help entails: These feelings are likely to be an indication of some other discomfort or discontent, and should be discussed with the therapist, not acted on by precipitously ending treatment.

3) You begin to feel that the therapist is "creating" problems in your family by pointing out conflicts and issues which you prefer not to discuss: Although there can be instances where a therapist does create problems, for example, by fostering competition between himself and you, or by taking sides in family disputes, a therapist does not create difficulties by bringing painful issues to your attention. If you feel

that some problems are too painful to discuss at a given point in time, say this. A therapist should be sympathetic to your request, though he may not always agree with your feeling that an avoidance of these topics is necessary.

4) Your child or family has been in treatment before, and you find yourself experiencing the same discontents in your present therapy that you encountered in previous ones. When you face recurrent difficulties with different therapists, it is usually a sign that the problem is at least partly your own. In such instances it is wise to try to resolve the sources of your dissatisfaction within yourself, rather than assume that your therapist is at fault. If such a resolution is not easy to reach, this would be an appropriate time to seek another professional opinion.

I've been discussing the issues you as parents face when you evaluate therapy. I have outlined ways to deal with your doubts and ways to distinguish legitimate causes for complaint from necessary though uncomfortable experiences. Yet a major element in evaluating therapy is your child's own reaction. It can be hard for you to sort out her valid objections from invalid ones. The following discussion may help you keep some complaints in perspective—while allowing you to know when a therapy is genuinely unhelpful.

YOUNGSTERS' COMPLAINTS ABOUT THERAPY

It is quite common for children either to express discontent about their therapist or to state that they wish to stop their sessions altogether. This is not surprising, since the decision to seek help is almost never made by the child; typically he isn't even consulted before such assistance is obtained. In addition, most youngsters do not believe that their difficulties at home or in school are caused by their own behaviors. Rather, they see their problems as being caused by forces out of their control. As a result they cannot imagine how talking to anyone, especially a relative stranger, can make them feel better.

Many children go to their first therapy appointments without any sense that they may be required to commit themselves to a long-term, ongoing process. Many go to please their parents or because they feel they have no other choice. Some are curious to meet this doctor who is somehow going to help them just by talking. When it turns out that the therapist has no magic cures to make them feel better, many children decide that the therapist is unhelpful and wasting their time.

If parents were to take all their children's negative comments about therapy as indicators that treatment should be terminated, then only the most compliant or fearful of children would remain in therapy for any period of time.

On the other hand, a child's constant, bitter resistance to seeing his therapist poses a problem for parents. How can they decide whether their youngster's protests are legitimate or not?

Further complicating the picture is the fact that since individual therapy with children is often a fairly long-term process, lasting anywhere from six or eight months to a number of years, progress may be hard to discern at the outset of treatment, and parents may find themselves less and less inclined to go through the hassle of taking their protesting child to the sessions.

If you find yourself feeling this way, you should discuss it with your child's therapist. Almost all therapists agree that a child's therapy cannot be successful without the confidence and support of the child's parents. Your youngster's therapist should be able to explain to you why your child is experiencing negative feelings about the treatment, and should be willing to offer you some suggestions about what to say or do when your child resists going to his appointments. You will need to be relatively convinced of the advantages of continuing treatment, because if you yourselves are unsure about its benefits, there is little reason to expect your child to feel any differently.

Nonetheless, it will not always be easy to decide if your child's treatment is progressing well. The following information may help you in making this judgment.

Legitimate Difficulties with Treatment

There may be a real reason to consider stopping treatment with a therapist when:

1) Your child reports any sexual overtures or acts, or any threats or acts of physical violence: You should immediately discuss this with the therapist.

2) Your child has been in treatment for a relatively long period of time, say eight to ten months, and neither you nor school personnel have noticed any signs of progress.

3) You yourself have serious doubts about the value of the therapy to your child or your family.

4) You feel that your child's therapist is insensitive, excessively critical, or hostile to your youngster.

Signs of Resistance to a Potentially Helpful Treatment

It may be that your child's complaints merely reflect the necessary unpleasantness of dealing with difficult issues when:

1) Your child's behavior is clearly showing signs of improvement, yet he is still protesting that the therapy is unhelpful.

2) The complaints about therapy either begin or grow markedly stronger after major changes in your

child's life; for example, the birth of a sibling or a divorce or death.

3) The complaints occur from the very outset of therapy, well before any progress or lack thereof can be reasonably measured.

4) A youngster's complaints about his therapist are markedly similar to his chronic complaints about teachers or parents.

5) A youngster's refusal to go to therapy appointments follows a pattern of refusals to do other things which are required of him.

A CLOSING NOTE

Evaluating your child's or family's treatment is an important part of the process of therapy in a private or clinic setting. I hope that this chapter will have helped you to see it as a constructive step rather than a bewildering problem.

Chapter 13

OBTAINING HELP THROUGH YOUR CHILD'S SCHOOL

The primary purpose of public schools is to provide high-quality education for their students. In the past it has not been considered the responsibility of the schools to provide therapy for students with emotional problems. Many students, however, are unable to learn because of emotional difficulties, and school systems have been asked to provide guidance for these youngsters.

In response to this need, some schools have furnished extensive mental health services; others have provided virtually no such help. Indeed, over the years many youngsters have been excluded from public schools because of emotional or behavioral problems, and the parents of these children have had to obtain for their youngsters as good an education as they could afford. Other youngsters with physical handicaps or learning disabilities have met with equal difficulty in obtaining the special help they need within the public-school framework.

In response to this situation, Congress passed a law (Public Law 94-142) called the Education for All Handicapped Children Act. Its purpose is to insure that each handicapped child* receives a free, appropriate public education.

* Handicapped children are defined as "mentally retarded, hard of hearing, deaf, speech-impaired, visually handicapped, seriously emotionally disturbed, orthopedically impaired or otherwise health-impaired, or children with specific learning disabilities, who by reason thereof require special education and related services."

Although the focus of this chapter will be on services provided to children enrolled in their local public school, it is important to note that even if your child is enrolled in private school, he or she is eligible, by law, to receive the same special educational services as children enrolled in public schools. The school system in the city or town where you live is responsible for providing and funding these serivces. This is the case even if your child has never been enrolled in public school.

PL 94-142 came into effect in September 1978. Its importance is that parents now have a legal right to expect that a youngster will receive certain diagnostic and treatment services if his or her handicaps interfere with learning.*

In this chapter I will explain what you can do if your child is having academic, social, or behavioral problems at school. (Unlike the other chapters in this section, which focus exclusively on emotional difficulties, this chapter will also address itself to academic problems. The distinction between behavioral and learning problems is in itself artificial, since these difficulties often go hand in hand.)

STEPS FOR GETTING HELP

The following two-step procedure is offered as an outline of what to do if you learn that your child is having significant difficulties at school.

1) Request a meeting with your youngster's teacher. At this meeting ask for a detailed description of your child's difficulties and for a summary of the teacher's attempts to remedy them. One of the pur-

*For further information about Public Law 94-142, you can write to either the Council for Exceptional Children, 1920 Association Drive, Reston, Virginia 22091, or to Closer Look Information Center, Box 1492, Washington, D.C. 20012.

poses of this meeting will be to design a plan to help resolve your child's problems.

2) If the problems persist, request that the school's diagnostic team conduct a formal evaluation in order to understand more fully the nature, severity, and causes of your youngster's difficulties. According to the provisions of Public Law 94-142, every public school must be able to carry out this kind of assessment. At the end of this procedure the school is required to hold a meeting to review the results of the evaluation and, if special needs are found, to write an educational plan specifically designed to meet those needs.

Step One—
Meeting With Your Child's Teacher

If you know or suspect that your youngster is having difficulties at school, you should prepare yourself *before* you meet with her teacher. Your goals for such a conference should be twofold: 1) to exchange as much information as possible, in order 2) to decide what steps should be taken next.

You will, therefore, want the teacher to detail the exact nature of your child's difficulties. If the problems are primarily social, ask the teacher for specific examples so that you can get a clear picture of your child's behavior. For your part, detail how your child behaves in similar situations at home. If the problems are primarily academic, ask the teacher to show you examples of your child's work, and, for comparison, examples of work of youngsters who are functioning at a more appropriate level. Ask the teacher to specify what he has already done to try to solve the problems, whether social or academic. Then you and the teacher can decide which of the following steps would be taken next:

1) Possibly you will feel that because the problems

are not very serious, or because they might go away of their own accord, no further action is necessary. In this case the teacher can monitor your child's progress and report back to you. It's usually a good idea, at this conference, to schedule a follow-up meeting for one or two months later, when you can review your youngster's progress. The case of Nancy Marks suggests how this might work:

Nancy was a five-year-old who had a great deal of difficulty when she started kindergarten. She would scream violently when her mother left her off at school, sometimes clinging to her mother's skirt as if her life depended on it. After her mother was gone, Nancy would continue crying for ten to fifteen minutes and then, for the rest of the school day, would remain withdrawn and teary-eyed. At the school conference, Mr. and Mrs. Marks noted that Nancy had always been a fearful child and had protested bitterly when they had first tried to leave her with a babysitter; but they added that, over time, Nancy had grown more comfortable with strangers. The Markses had expected that Nancy would have a difficult time adjusting to school, but they were concerned because they had imagined that after six weeks she would have begun to show some signs of settling into a school routine.

Mrs. Cahill, Nancy's teacher, said that there were some subtle signs of improvement; notably that Nancy was beginning to make some friends at school and was participating more in class activities. Since Nancy had just begun to show some signs of improvement, and since she had always been slow to adjust to new situations, the Markses and Mrs. Cahill decided that the most reasonable course of action was simply to monitor Nancy's progress to see if she would continue to grow more comfortable at school.

2) A second possibility is to agree to some rela-

tively simple program which you and the teacher can put into effect.

An example would be for the teacher to give your child stars or points for certain behaviors: staying in her seat for a whole reading period, perhaps, or completing a homework assignment. You can arrange with your youngster that a certain number of stars will earn her a treat such as a trip to the movies or some other special outing. Sometimes such interventions are all that's necessary to help a youngster get back on track.* (It is then expected that the child's new-found success and your continued praise will be rewards in and of themselves, and that eventually the point system can be discontinued.)

To return to the previous example, if Nancy's behavior hadn't improved over time, it might have been decided at a follow-up conference that she would earn a star for each day she was able to go to class without protesting. Five stars would earn her some specified reward.

Reward systems such as the one outlined above are by no means the only relatively simple plans that can be tried. For example, it might have been decided that rather than Mrs. Marks walking Nancy to class each day, a teacher's aide could meet them at the car and take Nancy to her classroom. Or perhaps Mr. Marks, rather than his wife, could take Nancy to school in the mornings. In many cases such changes in routine are enough to solve the immediate problem.

However, if monitoring of a child's behavior or a relatively simple plan are not indicated, or if they have been

* Such reward systems are not quite as simple as they appear. Among other things, one must be careful to select a reward which is appealing enough to motivate a youngster to try to change his or her behavior. It is also important to spell out clearly exactly what behaviors will be rewarded. (See the section on behavior therapy in Chapter Six for a further discussion of reward systems.)

tried without success, then other measures become necessary. At this stage you can either request a formal evaluation (Step Two) or you can continue meeting with appropriate school personnel on a less formal basis. If you have a good relationship with your school's guidance counselor, principal, or other specialists, you may want to continue informally. This approach will save both you and the school some of the adminstrative bother which is inherent in formal evaluations. On the other hand, if you don't know the school personnel well, or if you feel that your child's problems warrant an "in-depth" look, you should request a formal evaluation.

CONTINUING INFORMALLY

The next informal step might be to have a conference with your child's teacher and guidance counselor and the school's principal in order to generate new approaches for helping your youngster resolve her problems.

For example, if Nancy's crying only worsened when her father took her to school, and if she totally refused to walk to class with the teacher's aide, and if a reward system accomplished nothing, then other measures could be tried. Perhaps the school's guidance counselor might observe that the more that Nancy cried, the longer it took Mrs. Marks to leave her daughter's side. He might then instruct Mrs. Marks to leave the class as soon as Nancy was in the room, regardless of how bitterly her daughter protested. Since this would not be an easy thing for Mrs. Marks to do, the counselor would have to be available to support her in following through on this plan consistently.

In this example the counselor would have to meet with Mrs. Marks frequently and perhaps over a long period of time. At some schools such help is unheard of, while at other places it is typical. If you cannot obtain such assistance, or you have tried various plans and they have proven unsuccessful, then the school will need to perform a formal evaluation.

Step Two—
A Formal Evaluation

This evaluation must be conducted according to the regulations spelled out by your local school system in compliance with the Education for All Handicapped Children Act.

Most simply, the purpose of this evaluation is to try to identify and understand the nature and causes of a child's problems so as to be able to provide her with any necessary special educational services.

WHAT GOES INTO A FORMAL EVALUATION

The formal evaluation should be designed to spell out your child's strengths, as well as her weaknesses, both academically and socially. It should always include at least the following three basic elements:

1) A medical examination, including a report of any significant medical history: The purpose of this is to rule out the possibility that physical problems are causing or contributing to your child's difficulties at school. Tests of vision and hearing are included under this heading.

2) A developmental and family history: This is usually obtained by the school social worker, counselor, or nurse. It may provide some clues about the cause and nature of a child's problems.

3) An up-to-date summary of your youngster's school functioning and previous school history: This should include a review of the attempts already made to remedy her difficulties.

In addition, a formal evaluation often includes one or more of the following components (exactly which components are necessary will depend on the nature of the problem):

4) An assessment of current intellectual functioning.
5) An assessment of emotional/psychological functioning.
6) An assessment to determine if a youngster has any specific learning disabilities.
7) An assessment of basic academic skills.

Often, as part of these last four assessments, your youngster will be administered any of a number of different kinds of psychological tests. Such tests, often misunderstood or overemphasized, are simply one technique which may be used to gain a better understanding of your child's functioning. For a full description and discussion of psychological testing see Chapter Eight.

SPECIAL ASSESSMENTS

As part of an overall evaluation, it may be judged useful to have specialists (from either within or outside the school) conduct specialized observations or testing. A description of some of these specialists follows.

Physical Therapist

This is a specialist who evaluates and works to improve a child's motor skills. Physical therapy is particularly useful for children whose school performance is affected by physical handicaps such as cerebral palsy, muscular disease, or loss or absence of limbs.

Occupational Therapist

This is a specialist who evaluates how specific perceptual or motor deficiencies interfere with daily living skills and designs activities to either remedy or compensate for these deficiencies.

Neuropsychologist

This is a psychologist who specializes in the study of how the brain and nervous system affect behavior. By studying a child's performance on a variety of problem-solving tasks, the neuropsychologist attempts to diagnose specific brain dysfunctions, and to deduce how these may affect academic functioning.

Neurologist

A neurologist is a physician who specializes in the study of the brain and nervous system. Since they are only a limited number of techniques for looking directly at the brain,* a neurologist looks for external symptoms of possible brain dysfunction, such as problems with reflexes, motor skills, attention span.

Since neurologists are concerned about brain activity they also must consider a child's intellectual or cognitive functioning. Therefore a neurologist will frequently also do a brief survey of a child's intellectual and academic development.

Audiologist

This hearing specialist is trained to examine the ways which children respond to a wide variety of sound stimuli. A special emphasis of an audiological examination should be to determine if a youngster is experiencing any difficulties in hearing or understanding speech.

Otolaryngologist

This physician specializes in diseases of the ear, nose, and throat. The goal of an otolaryngological exam will be to

* The direct means of studying the brain which a neurologist may use include: 1) The electroencephalogram (EEG), which measures the electrical activity of the brain but which is generally useful only in diagnosing seizure disorders such as epilepsy, and 2) The Computerized Axial Tomography (or CAT) scan, which is a method of detecting any growths or "scars" in the brain.

determine if disease or other physical factors have reduced the efficiency with which a child hears sounds.

Optometrist

An optometrist is a vision specialist who is trained to examine the ways in which children respond to visual stimulation.* An optometric examination should determine if a youngster is experiencing any difficulties in visually taking in or processing school-related materials. Some optometrists prescribe various exercises which are designed to improve a child's visual-motor functioning. However, there is significant controversy about whether such exercises actually help a youngster's functioning in school.

Ophthalmologist

This is a physician who specializes in diseases of the eye. The emphasis of an ophthalmological exam will be to determine if disease or any other physical problem is impairing a child's vision.

Parents and school personnel alike are often confused about the different roles which medical specialists (neurologists, ophthalmologists, and otolaryngologists) versus nonmedical specialists (neuropsychologists, optometrists, and audiologists) should play in providing assessments of vision, hearing, and brain functioning. These decisions can be difficult ones even for experts to make, and you should consult carefully with your child's pediatrician or appropriate school personnel before trying to determine who is to examine what. Some things to keep in mind are that the medical specialists are especially trained to diagnose and treat physical illness or disease; so they should be consulted if there is any question of your child having a medical difficulty. Conversely, since physicians are trained to look for organic difficulties and not educational deficits, not all of them are helpful in aiding parents and educators in designing appropriate educational programs. If learning

* Not all optometrists are trained in this kind of examination. Those who are generally refer to themselves as "developmental optometrists."

problems, not medical ones, seem clearly to be the cause of your child's academic difficulties, you might first consult with a nonmedical specialist. If this person suspects any physical problems, he can then refer you to an appropriate physician.

THE INDIVIDUALIZED EDUCATIONAL PLAN

After all the assessments are completed, a meeting will be held to review all the findings. If it is determined that a youngster has special educational needs, then it is the school's responsibility to write an "Individualized Educational Plan." This IEP is a detailed description of your child's current educational functioning, including her strengths and weaknesses and a statement of the specific educational and/or counseling services that the school will provide to help remedy any of the child's difficulties. It must also include a statement of when these special services will start to be provided and for how long they're expected to be necessary, and a plan for monitoring the child's progress. The law states that "school personnel, parents, and, whenever appropriate, the child, must participate in developing the educational plan."

The IEP will be drawn up at a meeting attended by appropriate school personnel, outside experts if needed, and you and your spouse. The first part of the meeting will be devoted to a summary of all the relevant assessments. The second part of the meeting will be devoted to the actual designing of the educational plan.

Some parents, because they are not familiar with educational terminology, or for other reasons, feel intimidated by large school meetings. I have attended such conferences at which parents have sat silently for hours, while plans were drawn up for their child's education. The parents have sometimes commented to me after the meeting that they totally disagreed with the school's plans, but that they were too embarrassed to say this in front of everyone.

If you are likely to feel uncomfortable at such a meeting, there are a number of things you might do. One is to bring a friend or relative to provide you with emotional support. Or you might wish to go to the meeting accompanied by a professional educator or psychologist who would serve as your consultant. Another idea is to request a small, informal conference with appropriate school personnel, that can be held before the larger, more formal meeting. During this small conference you can review the assessments and ask questions.

You might wish to come to either the smaller or the larger meeting with some questions already prepared, such as the following:

1) Can you summarize the kind of assessments or tests that were done on my child?
2) What did these tests or assessments show?
3) What does this mean in terms of my child's education?
4) Will my youngster need special help in order to reach his or her academic potential?
5) Exactly what kind of help will be provided? By whom?

Finally, keep in mind that it's not necessary for you to give your final approval of the educational plan at the end of the formal meeting. Rather, if you have any doubts or questions about the assessments or the Individualized Educational Plan, I advise that you take a summary of the reports and the plan home with you to look over. You can then consult with your friends, relatives, or a professional. In some communities there are organizations of concerned parents and professionals who may be of help to you with such matters.*

It is important to note that under the provisions of the

* For information about such organizations, write to Closer Look Information Center, Box 1492, Washington, D.C. 20012.

new federal law, if you do not agree with the results of the school's assessments, you have the right to an independent evaluation, paid for by the schools. If, on the other hand, you are not satisfied with the Individualized Educational Plan, you need only to notify the school that you are rejecting it. Then either the school can modify the plan so as to make it acceptable to you, or the school's representatives can appear with you at a meeting where an attempt will be made to mediate your differences. If the mediation attempt is unsuccessful, an impartial hearing will then be held, in order to arbitrate the dispute. If the ruling at the hearing is not in your favor, you can appeal it by bringing suit against the school system in civil court.

While most parents will not want or need to go through this complicated and time-consuming process, it is important for you to know that you have the legal right to a number of appeals, if you are dissatisfied with the assessments carried out or with the educational plan designed for your child.

MENTAL HEALTH SERVICES IN SCHOOLS

If it is determined that some or all of your youngster's problems at school are caused by emotional difficulties, it is the school's responsibility to provide special services to help resolve these difficulties. But bear in mind that according to the law it is the school's responsibility to provide such special help *only* when emotional difficulties are interfering with a child's functioning in school. Most public school systems take the position that it is not their responsibility to provide special services for youngsters whose emotional difficulties are primarily manifested at home. School personnel may recommend therapeutic help for such children but the school will not take financial responsibility for such services.

There is a variety of mental health services provided by

school systems to students whose emotional difficulties are interfering with learning. These include the following:

Classes or Programs for Youngsters with Emotional or Behavioral Difficulities

These classes are taught by teachers who have received special training and certification to work with troubled children. Some of these classes are designed to serve a limited number of students (approximately four to eight students per teacher). In these self-contained classrooms the teacher provides most or all of the youngsters' academic curriculum. In another kind of class, sometimes called "a resource room," youngsters come and go for periods of time, usually to work on specific subjects. A child who loses his temper and strikes out whenever frustrated might go to a resource room for his two poorest subjects—reading and math, for instance. He would attend regular classes for the rest of the day.

Individual or Group Counseling

School systems generally employ a number of different professionals to provide counseling to students. These include, guidance counselors, school social workers, and school psychologists. Depending on the school, any one of these professionals might provide individual or group counseling to a youngster in need of help.

Mental Health Services Not Provided by Local School Systems

There are many kinds of mental health services which are not provided by local school systems. For example, long-term therapy is typically not provided at schools. When a youngster's emotional problems seem to be deep seated or when it appears that it will take a long time before they can be remedied, youngsters are usually referred to private therapists or to mental health clinics.

At times a youngster's behavior is so disruptive or atypical that he or she cannot be helped, even with the special attention provided in a resource room or a self-contained classroom. In such instances it may be recommended that the child be considered for inpatient or residential treatment. A discussion of these kinds of treatment, and a description of the kinds of facilties which provide them, will be the topic of the next chapter.

Chapter 14

OBTAINING HELP IN AN INPATIENT OR RESIDENTIAL SETTING

I hope that you will never face the prospect of needing to send your child away from home for psychiatric evaluation or treatment. Residential treatment or psychiatric hospitalization cannot help but be an upsetting experience for youngsters, their parents, and other family members. On the other hand, in some instances such a placement is the best course of action available to parents and professionals in their efforts to help troubled children.

The purpose of this chapter is to provide you with information about the variety of inpatient and residential treatments. I'll address such questions as how to decide if such help is necessary and what to expect if your youngster is placed in this kind of setting.

DISTINCTIONS BETWEEN INPATIENT AND RESIDENTIAL TREATMENT

There are a number of terms which are generally used to describe psychiatric care which is provided to youngsters while they live away from home.

Two of these terms, "inpatient treatment" and "psychiatric hospitalization," are generally used interchangeably. Both refer to an entire range of services which are provided to a child or adolescent while he stays in a hospital. Both of these terms are distinguished from the term "residential treatment," which refers to therapeutic help which is provided in what are called "residential treatment centers" or "residential schools for disturbed children."

Although it is possible to draw many distinctions between "inpatient" and "residential" treatment, it is important to keep in mind that these kinds of help are similar in certain basic ways. The basic similarity lies in the fact that both inpatient help and residential help are designed for youngsters who are experiencing significant difficulty in coping with their environment and who need a safe, secure, and protective setting in which to get help.

Inpatient Treatment

There are a number of different kinds of settings in which children and adolescents can be placed for inpatient help. These include:

1) A psychiatric hospital
2) A pediatric unit of a general hospital
3) A psychiatric unit of a general hospital

A further distinction can be made between psychiatric hospital settings which are designed especially to house youngsters and those which provide care primarily for adults, but which admit children and adolescents when no other more appropriate setting is available.

Although you will naturally be interested in finding out about the type of unit in which your child might be placed, you should also remember that in many parts of the country there are so few inpatient psychiatric facilities that you will have little or no choice of hospital setting. Indeed, in some instances, though hospitalization may be indicated, parents refuse this help because they feel that no adequate facility is available.

In general, hospital settings attempt to provide a secure

and protective environment for youngsters who are evidencing some serious emotional distress. Some of these facilities, typically those on pediatric or psychiatric units of a general hospital, furnish various kinds of relatively short-term help, generally lasting for a period of time ranging from a few days to a number of weeks. Other inpatient settings, typically those at psychiatric hospitals, generally expect their patients to stay for a minimum of six to eight weeks so that a thorough psychiatric evaluation can be performed.

One important function of inpatient settings is to provide *diagnostic and evaluation services* for troubled children. A hospital is usually the only single place where a wide variety of professionals (including psychiatrists, psychologists, psychiatric social workers, psychiatric nurses, pediatricians, neurologists, and occupational, recreational, and speech therapists) can collaborate on an evaluation of a youngster in a relatively short period of time. The observations and impressions of these specialists can then be brought together so as to provide a clear picture of the child's problems and some reasonable recommendations about what kind of treatment will be most helpful.

The other major function of inpatient settings is to provide *treatment* for troubled children. Hospital treatment is so expensive that only the wealthiest of parents, or those with the most extensive of insurance coverage, can afford such help in private hospitals. Publicly financed hospitals, on the other hand, do provide long-term treatment for some children in need of this kind of help.

Residential Treatment Centers

Unlike hospitals, residential treatment centers typically do not provide extensive diagnostic services. Rather, they are intended to provide psychological treatment and educational programs.

The length of time that a youngster will stay in a residential treatment center (or RTC) will depend on the nature of his problems. In general, however, youngsters stay for at least the equivalent of one school year (nine to eleven months). This is considered the minimum amount of time necessary for a child to become acclimated to a new environment, learn new ways of dealing with the stresses and conflicts in his life, and be prepared to return home.

RTC's are designed to provide for all of a youngster's needs, including living accommodations, educational services, recreational activities, and therapeutic help. Some centers physically resemble boarding schools or summer camps, with children housed in cabins or cottages.

In many instances it is preferable, when possible, to provide longer-term treatment in residential settings rather than in hospital facilities. This is not only because residential treatment is much less expensive, but also because it can be provided in a relatively more homelike environment.

On the other hand, since most residential facilities cannot provide the kind of round-the-clock medical and nursing supervision available at hospitals, youngsters who need such constant monitoring or close medical attention may need to be placed in the more protective hospital environment.

Summary

In summary, inpatient facilities can be used to provide diagnostic services, short-term help, or long-term help. Because hospitals are expensive and physically restrictive, long-term treatment is generally recommended only when a youngster needs a very protective environment, or constant medical attention, or when residential treatment facilities are not available.

Residential treatment centers generally provide longer-term treatment services. The advantages of these facilities are that they are less expensive than hospitals and can provide therapeutic care in somewhat more of a homelike atmosphere.

UNDER WHAT CIRCUMSTANCES IS INPATIENT OR RESIDENTIAL TREATMENT RECOMMENDED?

Psychiatric hospitalization or residential treatment is generally not something which parents seek out on their own. In most cases such care has been recommended to them by a therapist or physician from whom they've sought help. The concerns that generally would lead one of these professionals to recommend impatient or residential care fall into the following categories:

Concerns About the Welfare of the Child

Some children are referred to hospitals or RTC's because there is concern that without special observation, treatment, or protection, they could be of danger to themselves. Included in this category are:

SUICIDAL YOUNGSTERS

Suicidal behavior and ideation was discussed in Chapter Two. As was discussed in that section, it is sometimes very difficult for a professional, much less a parent, to determine if a child who is expressing suicidal thoughts is truly a danger to himself. If there is any chance that a youngster might harm himself, placement in a more protective setting is often recommended. A case example:

> Frankie, aged twelve, was an angry youngster who had been repeatedly suspended from school for fight-

ing. In addition, he was part of a group of youngsters who had been involved in petty vandalism and stealing. His mother and father had tried talking to him on many occasions but these conversations usually ended in angry arguments. One night after a heated discussion of his poor report card, Frankie was sent to his room for the night.

Angry at his parents for what he saw as their constant picking on him, Frankie decided to get back at them, by hurting himself. Then, without much further thought, he jumped out of his second-story bedroom window.

Although he appeared unhurt from the fall, Frankie's parents were rightfully quite concerned and called their pediatrician. Their physician advised them to take Frankie to the emergency room of the local hospital, not only to check on his physical condition, but also to evaluate his mental state. The psychiatrist-on-call at the emergency room recommended that Frankie be admitted to the pediatric unit of the hospital for a period of observation and evaluation. Over the course of ten days Frankie and his parents met with the staff of the hospital to discuss various problems. Frankie agreed not to try to hurt himself again and it was decided that it would be safe for him to return home with the understanding that his parents would arrange for outpatient therapeutic help for him and themselves.

YOUNGSTERS WITH SERIOUSLY IMPAIRED JUDGMENT

Youngsters whose behavior is so unpredictable that they might be unable to protect themselves from external dangers sometimes need the security of an inpatient or residential setting. A case example:

Julie, aged eight, was a quiet girl who throughout her school years preferred to draw or daydream rather than play with friends. In the third grade she began to talk increasingly about cartoon characters that she watched on TV and she began to wander off into some woods near her school during recess. Her parents noticed that her talk was increasingly peculiar and after a discussion with the school guidance counselor decided to get professional help.

The psychologist who evaluated Julie found her to be so out of touch with reality that he recommended that she be taken to a psychiatric hospital for a more thorough evaluation. The recommendation from the hospital staff was that Julie remain in an inpatient setting until she was well enough to return home for outpatient therapy.

SERIOUSLY ABUSED OR NEGLECTED CHILDREN

Hospitalization is sometimes necessary for youngsters who are in serious danger of being psychologically or physically harmed if left in their home. A hospital may then be used as a temporary refuge until a suitable alternate living arrangement can be found. Since hospitals are so expensive and bed space is in such demand, this use of a hospital setting should be considered only when no other alternative exists.

Concerns About the Welfare of Others

Hospitalization is sometimes necessary for the protection of others in the child's environment. Youngsters who may arouse such concerns are:

VIOLENT OR DANGEROUS YOUTHS

Children and adolescents can be capable of doing serious physical harm to others. (See Chapter Two for a discussion of violence and aggression in children and adolescents.) Youngsters who behave violently or who appear likely to behave violently, in some cases need to be placed in a protective environment while the severity of their problems is evaluated. A case example:

> James, aged fifteen, had been in trouble with the police since he was eleven. His mother and father had separated when he was four and his mother, who had had to work ever since, had recently grown quite concerned about her inability to control her son's actions. She had, on a number of occasions, taken James to their local community mental health center, but he had always denied having any problems and the attempts to help him had proven unsuccessful.
>
> One day James was arrested with two other boys for assaulting and robbing an elderly woman. James's probation officer referred him back to the mental health center for a complete evaluation. The recommendation of the evaluator was that James be placed in a residential treatment center for long-term therapy.

YOUNGSTERS WHOSE PRESENCE AT HOME IS INTOLERABLE

In some families one youngster is experienced as such a threat to a family harmony that he or she needs to be placed out of the home. As is the case with abused or neglected youngsters, hospitalization may be the only temporary refuge for these children.

Necessity for Diagnostic or Therapeutic Intervention in a Hospital Setting

In certain situations diagnostic or treatment services cannot be properly provided in any but a hospital setting. This can be the case for:

YOUNGSTERS WHOSE EMOTIONAL AND MEDI-

CAL PROBLEMS REQUIRE MEDICAL AS WELL AS PSYCHIATRIC ATTENTION

A case example:

Tommy aged thirteen, had a long history of functioning poorly in school. He had an especially difficult time sitting still or paying attention to his teachers. As his grades steadily fell, he began to develop the conviction that his teachers not only were picking on him but were out to hurt him.

Tommy also began to resist taking the medication he had been on since age seven to control his epileptic seizures.

Because his problems at school were growing progressively worse and because he hadn't had a complete neurological examination since he was seven, his family decided to obtain a complete psychiatric and neurological evaluation for Tommy at a psychiatric hospital. The result of the evaluation was that Tommy's medication was readjusted and he was referred for outpatient therapy.

YOUNGSTERS WHO ARE PLACED ON THERAPEUTIC PROGRAMS WHICH MUST BE CAREFULLY MONITORED

A case example:

Andrea, aged eight, was described by her parents as always having been somewhat peculiar. Unlike her brothers and sisters she didn't participate in many social activities. Although she was usually well behaved, when frustrated she could throw severe temper tantrums.

A few weeks after her eighth birthday she began to pull out her hair whenever she was frustrated. Despite attempts by her parents and family physician to control this behavior, it worsened. Finally her physician recommended that she be hospitalized for a complete psychiatric evaluation. It was felt that this could be done most easily on the pediatric unit of the local hospital. In this setting a therapeutic program was instituted to help Julie stop pulling out her hair. After two weeks the program was successful enough to allow her to return home for further outpatient treatment.

The preceding are two of the most common reasons for youngsters to be recommended for inpatient help. Of course, all such recommendations are made on an individual basis. You will need to discuss carefully the reasons for *your* child's hospitalization or residential treatment with the person who has made this suggestion.

WHAT TO DO WHEN A PROFESSIONAL RECOMMENDS INPATIENT TREATMENT

You are most likely to be told that your child needs inpatient or residential care by your physician or by a psychiatrist or psychologist who knows your youngster. Ideally the recommendation will be made before things have reached crisis proportions, so that you will have time to ask questions and to consider the advantages and disadvantages of such a placement. It is usually a good idea to visit the facility that is being suggested, before placing your child there.

What to Ask the Recommmending Professional

Upon hearing the recommendation that your child receive treatment out of the home you may find it helpful to ask some or all of the following questions:

1) Exactly why are you recommending that my child go to a hospital or residential treatment center?

2) Is there something else that can be done to help without having to take her out of our house?

3) Does this mean that my child is crazy?

4) What do you think will happen if I don't accept this recommendation?*

5) Can't the hospitalization do more harm than good?

Parents are often rightfully concerned that a hospital or RTC might have more negative than positive consequences. You should feel free to ask about any negative consequences that you fear will result from such a placement.

6) Can we get another opinion about the need for inpatient or residential help?

This need not even be a question: You have every right to seek another professional opinion whenever you have any question about a professional's recommendation.

What to Ask at Preadmission Visits

I advise that, if at all possible, you visit the recommended hospital or residential treatment center before deciding to

* It is possible, but not at all likely, that a therapist will feel so strongly that a child needs the protection of a hospital or RTC that he or she will be prepared to try to arrange this even against a parent's wishes. This becomes a legal matter and laws regarding this vary from state to state.

In general, except for emergency cases (in which youngsters can be hospitalized for anywhere from twenty-four hours to three days), hospitalization against your wishes is only possible after a formal court hearing, in which you should have legal counsel.

There is a separate and growing legal question about *children's rights to legal representation* in the matter of their hospitalization. The major issue revolves around children's rights to challenge hospitalization when their parents have requested this kind of assistance.

place your youngster there. These facilities welcome and encourage such visits. At this time you can ask some other questions, as follows:

1) What will her day be like at the hospital or RTC?
2) Who will be supervising her? What is their training and experience?
3) When will we be allowed to visit?
4) What arrangements will be made for her schooling?
5) Will she be put on medications while in the hospital?

Medications are not a necessary part of every hospitalization. Decisions about medication are totally separate from decisions about whether or not to hospitalize a child. On the other hand, if medications are necessary, a hospital setting is a good place to begin them, as your child's reaction to them can be carefully monitored and changes in dosages or in the type of medication can be quickly arranged.

6) How long will she need to be here, if we do agree to such a placement?
7) Will we be asked to meet with someone while our youngster is here? If so, how often?
8) How much does this cost? Will our insurance cover the cost? What if we can't afford to pay for this care?
9) What will happen after the hospitalization or residential treatment?
10) Finally (if you have decided to agree to inpatient or residential treatment), What should I tell my youngster?

Parents reasonably want some advice about what to tell their child about why such a placement is necessary. Often they worry that their child will never love or trust them again if they send her to a hospital or RTC. Indeed, some children voice these sentiments directly. They may protest, "You wouldn't do this to me, if you really loved me!" or "You're just trying to get rid of me because you hate me!" You should realize that after voicing some initial feelings along these lines, many children come to accept that you have made your decision with their best interests at heart.

What to Tell Your Youngster

The most important thing is to tell your child the truth.

> Your mother and I and Dr. Roberts have all talked at length and believe that you can't solve your problems without some more special help. So we've decided that you will need to go to Children's Hospital. We're not exactly sure how long you'll stay. We do know that your mother and I will be meeting after two months with your doctors and other hospital people to see if you could come home then. Of course, we'll visit you as often as possible and talk to you by phone a lot.

Of course, exactly what you'll say will depend on your child's age, the nature of her problems, and other factors that will be important to you. In many instances you will also want to accompany your child on a preadmission visit arranged for her benefit. Finally, you should be sure to let your child ask as many questions as she needs to.

In some cases parents will prefer to tell their child about the hospitalization with the youngster's therapist present. This is often an excellent idea.

Some parents try to spare their youngster's feelings by not telling her about the hospitalization until the last minute, or by telling her that they are going to the hospital for a checkup. If you can imagine how betrayed and abandoned a youngster will feel when the truth is revealed, you will see why such deceptions are not a good idea.

WHAT HAPPENS DURING A HOSPITALIZATION

What will happen during a hospitalization will vary depending on whether your youngster was placed there for a temporary stay, which can be relatively short, or for a comprehensive evaluation, which will be more lengthy.

A *complete psychiatric evaluation* in a hospital will average between six and eight weeks, although the evaluation will sometimes be extended in cases where special tests are necessary. A complete evaluation should include all of the following:

1) A thorough pediatric evaluation, the purpose of which is to establish that a youngster's health is good and that no medical problem is contributing to his emotional difficulties. When indicated, this will include a neurological evaluation.

2) A complete psychological test battery, especially including personality tests. For a description of these tests, see Chapter Eight.

3) An educational evaluation, including all relevant information from school.

4) Interviews with the youngster conducted by a staff psychiatrist, psychologist, or social worker.

5) Interviews with parents to obtain information about the youngster's developmental history and functioning at home.

6) Continual observation. The staff of the hospital will observe a child to see how he relates to peers and adults in a living situation. Some children go on their best behavior immediately after hospitalization in order to convince staff that they no longer need to be there. After a while, when this technique does not succeed in getting them discharged, they will begin to act more naturally.

7) A large conference between parents and professional staff, in which all assessments, tests, and observations are reviewed and discussed.

If your youngster is hospitalized for a shorter stay, some of the above procedures will not be conducted. In general, *shorter-term evaluations* include: 1) any necessary medical examinations; 2) interviews with the child; 3) interviews with parents; 4) continual observation of the youngster; and 5) a conference to discuss recommendations for the child's care.

Many parents feel intimidated by large meetings at which a number of professionals discuss their child. If you are likely to feel this way, one thing you can do is to bring along a friend or relative to give you moral support and to help you ask any questions that may be on your mind. There are parents who feel embarrassed to have someone attend a meeting with them. However, if they are able to get over this embarrassment, they usually find a friend's presence to be surprisingly helpful.

The primary purpose of these large conferences—which conclude both long-term and short-term hospital evaluations—is to determine what kind of treatment will be most helpful for a youngster and in what setting that treatment should be provided. Typical places that may be selected for further treatment are as follows:

1) A hospital setting
2) A residential treatment center
3) A partial hospitalization program
4) A halfway house
5) Any of a variety of outpatient facilities.
6) If a youngster has had a brief evaluation in a general hospital, it may be recommended that he be placed in a psychiatric hospital for a more complete evaluation.

WHAT HAPPENS DURING RESIDENTIAL TREATMENT

Although procedures at different residential treatment centers vary tremendously, there are some general things which you can prepare yourself for.

The early weeks of a youngster's stay at an RTC are generally devoted to helping him adjust to a radically different living situation. It is often believed that the best way to do this is to put severe limits on a youngster's contact with his parents, siblings, or friends. During the first two to six weeks, for example, a youngster may be allowed absolutely no visitors and only one phone call a week from his parents. Contact via letters is usually not restricted, however.

There are many reasons for such a policy. First, it is felt that a youngster, in order to adjust more quickly to a new living situation, should devote his total attention to interacting with the staff and residents at the center. Visits by parents, it is believed, will tend to channel a youngster's attention back to his home situation and thus make it more difficult for him to adjust to the new environment. Second, since the first weeks of residential treatment can be difficult for a youngster, it is feared that visits by parents will only increase a youngster's resentment about having had to leave home—as well as make the parents feel even more guilty.

After this initial period is over, visits and calls are allowed according to the age and the nature of the problems of the youngster. Eventually other privileges, such as visits home, are granted. As time goes on, these visits can be extended in length, as one way of preparing the child for his eventual return home.

One of the most difficult things for parents to cope with is that some youngsters, throughout their stay at an RTC, protest that they hate the center and want to return home.

Most parents, however, can reassure themselves with the knowledge that these protestations generally become less intense as time passes.

In general, you should expect a residential treatment center to provide the following services for your youngster:

1) Adequate living accommodations
2) Opportunities for recreational activities
3) A complete educational program
4) Therapeutic help: At an RTC, therapeutic help often takes the form of what is called "milieu therapy." Typically this means that all of a youngster's behaviors in the course of his day are subject to observation and discussion by the professional staff, as well as by other residents. On some regular basis the staff and residents meet to discuss the problems and improvements of each youngster. Individual therapy is not necessarily part of the treatment program at an RTC, though this may also be available, if it is indicated.
5) Regular contact with parents: You should have the opportunity to meet with the staff at a center to discuss your youngster's progress and to inform the staff about how he is behaving during visits home. Family meetings are sometimes held to help work out any problems that are experienced during these visits.
6) Contact with other professionals: Near the end of a youngster's stay at least one meeting should be held with appropriate school personnel or mental health professionals to discuss how best to reintegrate a youngster into his home environment.

HOW YOU MAY REACT TO THE IDEA OF YOUR CHILD'S HOSPITALIZATION OR RESIDENTIAL PLACEMENT

So far this chapter has focused on a variety of details about hospitalization and residential treatment. As I mentioned at the start, however, such out-of-home placements are often disruptive and upsetting for children, parents, and other family members.

Different parents experience different reactions when they are told that their child will need to be treated outside of their home. Usually, after a period of shock, they feel either strong resistance to this idea, or some relief that someone will finally help their youngster get back in control.

Relief Reaction

Parents who have felt totally unable to control, much less help, their youngster, often feel a measure of relief that their child will be placed in a safe and secure environment.

Resistance Reactions

Many parents understandably resist the idea of having their youngster removed from their home. Some of their reasons for this opposition can be characterized as follows:

1) *"It's impossible":* Parents often have numerous prac-

tical reasons why a hospitalization or residential placement would be impossible, as illustrated by the following comments: "He'd never agree to go. As defiant and rebellious as he is, he's very dependent on me. He's never been away from home at night, except to stay with his grandparents." Or, "I don't know if such a placement is a good idea or not, but I know it would kill her grandparents to find out that she had to be put there. They'd never speak to me again if I agreed to this." Or, "It will interrupt his schoolwork [or sports activities or friendships.] It'll do more harm than good to do that to him."

2) *"It's not that serious":* Some parents, in the face of hospitalization or residential treatment, begin to deny or minimize the seriousness of the child's problems with arguments like these: "All kids cause parents to worry." Or, "All kids get depressed. He talks of hurting himself, but you yourself said that he probably wouldn't do anything." Or, "I know plenty of kids that are far worse off than my daughter. They don't even see a psychologist, much less go into a hospital."

Guilt Reaction

Parents often feel guilty about whatever they might have done to their child to make her have such serious problems. "Put me in the hospital, not her. It's probably all my fault that she got so messed up in the first place."

Blame Reaction

It's also fairly common for parents to try to find someone to blame for their youngster's difficulties. Sometimes they blame themselves, as in the guilt reaction. Sometimes they blame others, often their spouse. "If she hadn't babied him so much, he'd be able to solve his problems on his own, he wouldn't have to go to the hospital."

Some parents blame the therapist who is making the recommendation: "He was much better before he started to see you. Ever since his visits to you, things have been going downhill. This would probably blow over, if he just stopped talking to you."

Whether you have these reactions or others, please feel free to discuss your feelings and concerns openly with your child's therapist or pediatrician, or with whoever recommends residential or hospital treatment, and be sure to get all your questions answered before making your decision.

HOW YOUR CHILD MAY REACT TO THE IDEA OF HOSPITAL OR RESIDENTIAL PLACEMENT

Youngsters' initial reactions to a recommendation of *hospitalization* are widely varied. Some react very negatively, crying bitterly or threatening that they'll try to run away. They may protest that they're OK now, or that their therapist is making a mountain out of a molehill. They may accuse you of not loving them or of wanting to get rid of them.

These strong negative reactions are completely natural. It's scary for anyone, especially a child, to face the unknown of a hospital stay. The prospect of a psychiatric hospitalization is even more frightening, with its implication that the youngster is either crazy or about to go crazy. And many youngsters can't help fearing that by placing them in a hospital you are indicating that you no longer love them and are rejecting or abandoning them.

These feelings and fears will often last through the first few days or even weeks of a hospitalization. However, for many youngsters these reactions begin to diminish as they realize, through your calls and visits, that you are not abandoning them; and, through the care and concern of the hospital staff, that you have placed them in the hands of people who are trying to help.

In some instances, though, youngsters continue to feel negatively throughout their hospital stay. This places a great strain on parents. They will want and need to stay in close touch with the hospital staff to assess whether continued hospitalization is still indicated.

On the other hand, many youngsters react positively, even with relief, to a proposed hospitalization, especially if it's designed to be for a relatively brief period of time. These children look forward to a respite from the pressures in their everyday life. They welcome the prospect of being in a safe environment with many people available round the clock to take care of them.

Youngsters' reactions to *residential treatment,* however, generally tend to be negative. The long period of time away from home that such a placement entails, often leaves them feeling that their parents are trying to get rid of them. In addition, youngsters typically have a host of worries about adjusting to a new living situation, perhaps in a different city or even a different state; to new friends; to a new school; and so on. Since most residential placements entail strict rules, many youngsters, especially adolescents, feel that they are being punished and protest that they are being placed in a prisonlike atmosphere.

As was mentioned before, these negative feelings can persist through much or all of a youngster's stay, and this imposes quite a strain on parents—who often are already feeling some guilt about their child's predicament.

It may help you to know that your youngster's protests are apt to be more vehement when you are present than at other times. In addition, if your youngster's behavior does improve over time, you can reassure yourself that, despite his protestations, the center is providing much-needed help.

OTHER KINDS OF OUT-OF-HOME PLACEMENTS

In addition to hospitals and residential treatment centers, there are a number of other kinds of settings which provide help for youngsters who need to live away from home. Two of these are halfway houses and foster homes.

Halfway Houses

"Halfway houses" are residential facilities in operation seven days a week, with around-the-clock supervision. "They are differentiated from other mental health facilities in that their primary focus is on the provision of room and board, and assistance in the activities of daily living rather than on the provision of a planned treatment program."[1] Residents who are in need of individual or group therapy are expected to receive such assistance at other facilities. Residents live as though they were in their own homes, working or otherwise occupying themselves during the day. This being the case, halfway houses are not designed for children or younger adolescents. Indeed, most halfway houses will not accept adolescents younger than seventeen or eighteen.

Such facilities can, however, be the perfect place for adolescents who need some support in order to function in the community, but who do not need inpatient treatment and who do not wish to return to their parents' home.

Foster Homes

There are cases where parents find that their youngster, although not seriously enough troubled to warrant inpatient or residential treatment, is continually disrupting family life over a long period of time. (To be fair to the youngster, he usually feels that it is the parents who are causing the disruption in the family.) In such cases the youngster often seems to need another family situation in which to live, and foster care may be recommended.*

One purpose of foster care is to help a youngster, in the context of another family-living situation, learn enough about himself and his family to be able to return home with more ability to cope with everyday stresses and conflicts. During this same period of time, parents, too, can try to understand the difficulties in the family, and make changes which will help make it easier for their youngster to return.

Counseling in Foster Care

Obviously, for such foster care to be fully effective, the youngster, his foster parents, and the natural parents must all be willing to accept counseling services; and such counseling help must be made available to them.

In point of fact, counseling for all concerned in a foster-care situation is not always available—or if available is not always utilized. Without such help foster care is often unsuccessful. In foster-care circumstances the youngster typically experiences a four- to six-week period of tranquility and happiness. During this "honeymoon period" a youngster may say that his foster parents are just marvelous and that all his problems are now solved. Often, however, a youngster's old patterns of behavior will resurface during the next month or two, creating tensions in the foster home. Without some professional support this all too often leads the foster parents to ask that the youngster be removed from their home.

A different difficulty can arise if the foster placement

* I do not address, in this section, foster care which is provided in cases where children are removed from their homes because of neglect or abuse, or in cases of parental death or desertion.

proves successful. In such instances the natural parents often feel inadequate compared to the foster parents; and some are prone to deal with this feeling by demanding that their youngster return home.

How to Find Out About Foster Care

The easiest way to find out about agencies in your area that provide foster-care services is to call your local Mental Health Association or your local United Way or Community Chest. They will be able to put you in touch with either a child-welfare or family-service agency which can help you locate such assistance.

Chapter 15

PSYCHIATRIC EMERGENCIES

Throughout this book I have encouraged parents to be careful and thoughtful when selecting mental health services for their children or families. In times of psychiatric emergency, however, parents will have to act quickly.

A psychiatric emergency can be defined as any situation which requires immediate therapeutic intervention to protect the safety or psychological equilibrium of a youngster, his family, or someone else.

GENERAL CONSIDERATIONS

Parents are not always sure whether their child's or adolescent's behavior is serious enough to be considered an "emergency." They may hesitate to call (and "bother") a physician or mental health professional unless there is a "real crisis."

My advice to such parents is that, in general, if you have any question about whether or not your youngster may need immediate help, you should call someone (that is to say, a physician or a therapist) or some place (such as the emergency room of a nearby hospital or the local police) so that they can help you assess the seriousness of the situation. In times of stress it is often difficult for parents to determine, on their own, whether or not their youngster is in need of immediate help, and a call to an appropriate professional is the most reasonable first step to take in such circumstances.

Physicians, mental health professionals, clinics, and hospitals all make provisions for handling potential and actual crises and you need to realize that you are not "bothering" anyone when you make use of these emergency services.

In the actions below I'll outline the major kinds of psychiatric emergencies and detail what parents should do in each of these circumstances.

SUICIDE

Suicide Attempts

If your youngster has done something to hurt himself such as cutting himself with a sharp instrument or ingesting some dangerous substance, there are a few logical things to do.

First, follow your common sense in providing any first aid that may be necessary; for example, stopping bleeding. Then call your physician or the emergency room of the nearest hospital. If neither of these is available, call your local police. Tell whomever you speak to, as concretely as possible, what has happened. They will advise you about what to do next. Then stay with your youngster and try to calm him as much as possible. This is not the time to try to find out why your child did what he did. There will be time and opportunity for that kind of discussion after the crisis has passed.

Suicide Gestures

Obviously all suicide attempts are not equally life-endangering. A ten-year-old boy who nicks his hand with his penknife and then shows the cut to his mother is far different from a teenager who slits her wrists and goes into her room quietly to die. The teenager is obviously in danger and needs immediate medical, and subsequently psychiatric help. "But what about the boy" you might ask. "Wouldn't it be better to ignore his behavior, since he might just be trying to get attention?" My answer is no, you should not ignore suicidal behavior, even when convinced that your youngster had no "real intention" of hurting himself. An immediate call to a professional, in such instances, serves a number of purposes. First, it provides you with another opinion about how to handle the situation. After all, you might be told that your youngster's behavior is more serious than you thought. Second, it lets your youngster know that you have taken his behavior seriously; that you understand that he must be very unhappy or very angry or very disappointed in order to have made even an apparently harmless suicide gesture. On the other hand, ignoring such behavior so as not to "give in" to a youngster's "manipulations" may be a serious mistake. For it is possible that if you respond with apparent indifference to such behavior, your youngster may feel the need to engage in more life-threatening behavior in order to get you to notice that something is seriously wrong. Punishment in such circumstances usually is equally unhelpful, and may also lead to more dangerous suicidal behavior.

Suicide Threats

As in the case with suicide attempts, parents may sometimes wonder whether their youngster is really serious about a suicide threat. Again my advice is that a parent should not take sole responsibility for trying to decide whether or not such a threat is likely to lead to immediate action. This determination should be made after seeking a professional opinion.

If your youngster makes a suicide threat, I advise you to do the following:

1) Let her know that you are taking the threat seriously. (*Never* challenge a youngster to "prove" that she is serious, because this may back her into a corner, leaving her feeling that she must do something in order to save face.)

2) Make sure that someone stays with the youngster until professional help is obtained.

3) Call the family doctor; your youngster's or family's therapist, if there is one; or the emergency room of the nearest hospital. They will advise you what to do next.

Of course, all suicide threats are not equally ominous. One can, for instance, distinguish between "threatening to commit suicide" (for example, "I've got a gun in my room—I've been so depressed for so long that I just can't take it anymore") and "threatening parents with suicide" (for example, "If you don't let me see Johnny again, I swear I'll kill myself").

When a youngster threatens to commit suicide, as in the example above, parents are obviously facing a very serious and life-threatening situation, and should follow the steps already outlined. However, a youngster's angry threat to commit suicide if he or she is not allowed to do something, is a somewhat different matter. In such a circumstance I recommend the following course of action:

1) Tell your youngster that you're concerned about her making such a drastic statement.

2) Ask her if she's serious about what she said.

3) If she says she is, or if you suspect she is, treat the situation as a potential crisis and call someone for some immediate advice. (Most likely this will lead to an appointment with a mental health professional so that your conflict with your daughter can begin to be resolved.)

Suicidal Thoughts

Suicidal thoughts or ideas are *not* psychiatric emergencies, when the child is expressing general unhappiness and distress, as opposed to an intention to seriously harm herself. When your child fails an important test or doesn't get asked to the prom or doesn't make the high school team, it is natural for her to feel depressed. "Oh, I wish I were dead" is not normally a statement of intention to harm oneself.

However, if your youngster is continuously depressed *and* begins to talk of suicide, you should take this as an indication of significant distress. You should arrange for psychiatric evaluation to assess her overall emotional state (as well as the likelihood of her being in real danger to herself). If you have *any* doubts about whether or not she is about to try to harm herself, the situation should be treated as an emergency, as described above.

Myths about Suicide

All too many people still believe in some myths about suicide: ideas which experts in the field have long since proved false.

The most dangerous myth is that people who talk about suicide don't commit it. The fact is that of any ten adults who kill themselves, eight have given some definite warnings of their suicidal intentions.[1] In one study of children who killed themselves, at least one half of them had previously discussed, threatened, or attempted suicide.[2]

Another dangerous and erroneous myth is that children are incapable of killing themselves. Although it is true that childhood suicide is fairly rare,[3] the fact is that youngsters *are* capable of killing themselves and sometimes do. Adolescent suicide is not rare; adolescents can and do kill themselves.

PHYSICAL VIOLENCE

Actual Physical Violence

Violent outbursts, especially when they involve adolescents, present parents with a need to seek immediate help. Such outbursts may be directed at property for example when a teenager starts to destroy things in his house, or it may involve another person as when a teenage boy and his father come to blows.

Whatever the exact circumstances, a parent's behavior needs to be directed toward helping the young person get back into control. This obviously needs to be done in such a fashion that the teenager is not provoked into further violence. After the youngster is calmed, a parent should call the emergency room of a hospital or the emergency service of a local mental health clinic, in order to get professional advice about what to do next.

Threats of Physical Violence

Threats of physical violence should be treated with the same amount of concern and reasoned action as threats of suicide.

If you have any reason to believe or suspect that your youngster is planning to try to hurt someone, you should take the following action:

1) Stay with your youngster.
2) Call your physician; your youngster's therapist,

if there is one; the emergency room of the nearest hospital; or the police.

It is important for you to let your youngster know that you are taking his threats seriously, and that for his own protection, as well as his intended victim's, you are arranging for some help. It is important not to challenge or threaten your youngster at such times, for fear that he may feel it necessary to prove that he's capable of doing what he's threatening.

As is the case with suicide threats, threats of physical violence usually reflect ambivalent urges in a youngster. At one and the same time he wants to do something, and wants someone to stop him from doing something. If attempts are not made to intervene, he may go ahead and hurt someone else.

VICTIMS OF PHYSICAL OR SEXUAL VIOLENCE

If your child is a victim of physical or sexual assault, your first responsibility is to get her medical assistance as quickly as possible. In addition, victims of assaults, especially victims of rape, are in need of *immediate* counseling and support to minimize the traumatic effects of what has happened to them. Some communities have twenty-four-hour crisis "hot lines" or rape "hot lines" where you can get information or assistance of this kind. If no such services exist in your area, your physician, your hospital staff, or the local police ought to know how and where to obtain help.

ACUTE PANIC OR ANXIETY ATTACKS

Anxiety attacks are characterized by the following: There is shallow breathing, rapid heartbeat, and trembling, and the child acts panic stricken. Often the child becomes fearful that she is about to die, or that someone close to the child is going to die. She may have visual distortions or feelings that everything is unreal or strange. The attack may be accompanied by physical sensations of dizziness or light-headedness; sweating; and stomach distress, including vomiting. An anxiety attack may last only a few minutes or go on as long as an hour, and attacks may occur repeatedly over the course of a day.

When an attack is occurring, stay with your child. Try to reassure her that you will stay with her, and that she will soon be feeling better. If you feel that you cannot calm your child yourself, you should call your family physician or the hospital emergency room for advice about what to do.

During an anxiety attack it may be necessary to restrain a child physically to keep her from harming herself or someone else. Use as little restraint as is possible, and do so in a calm, matter-of-fact manner to show that you are trying to protect and not harm her. Such restraint should be stopped as soon as she is back in control.

ACUTE DISORGANIZED BEHAVIOR

At times youngsters begin to act in a bizarre, incoherent, or disorganized manner. Especially with adolescents, it is often difficult to know whether such behavior is caused by the ingestion of a drug, by some medical problem, or by emotional difficulties. Therefore you should call your physician or the emergency room of the nearest hospital for advice about what to do. As is the case with all other emergencies, someone should stay with your child so as to calm her and to protect against harm to herself or to someone else.

AFTER THE CRISIS HAS PASSED

Often, after your child has calmed down, she will seem particularly tranquil and contented, say that everything is fine, and refuse any offers of further help. You should be aware that it is almost never the case that the problems which led to the emergency have disappeared. Indeed, psychiatric crises are almost always the culmination of a long period of mounting emotional distress. During the acute phases of the emergency, a youngster discharges a great deal of tension, which explains why she feels so calm immediately after the crisis. If the child's underlying problems are not resolved, however, the tension will eventually begin to build again. Therefore the most reasonable thing for you to do, as soon as it is convenient, is to obtain an evaluation of your child's emotional functioning. Earlier chapters of this book can provide you with information about how to obtain such help.

Appendix A

NATIONAL ORGANIZATIONS

I. GENERAL INFORMATION

Closer Look Information Center, Box 1492, Washington, D.C. 20012. Telephone (202) 833-4160. Closer Look is a service set up to help parents of children with emotional, physical, and mental handicaps find educational and related services. Closer Look is *not* a referral and placement service, but they will be happy to provide parents with names of local organizations, agencies, schools, and individuals who may be able to assist with the many problems which confront the parents of a child with special needs.

Council for Exceptional Children, 1920 Association Drive, Reston, Virginia 22091. Telephone toll free (800) 336-3728. The Council for Exceptional Children, among its other functions, serves as a clearinghouse of information on the education of handicapped and gifted children.

Mental Health Association, 1800 North Kent Street, Arlington, Virginia 22209. They can provide you with information about how to contact your local Mental Health Association.

II. INFORMATION PERTAINING TO SPECIFIC DISABILITIES

Autism

National Society for Autistic Children, 1234 Massachusetts Avenue N.W., Suite 1017, Washington, D.C. 20005. Telephone (202) 783-0125. Among its many functions the NSAC maintains an information and referral service. Interested parents can write or call NSAC for information about 1) private and public schools which accept mentally ill children; 2) public mental hospitals with children's units; 3) other parents in the same area with similar problems; 4) diagnostic and evaluation centers; and 5) a variety of other information.

Child Abuse or Neglect

Parents Anonymous, 22330 Hawthorne Boulevard, Suite 208, Torrance, California 90505. Telephone toll free (outside California) 800-421-0353, (in California) 800-352-0386. For information or help, if you are abusing (or afraid you may begin to abuse) your child. All calls to Parents Anonymous are confidential and callers are not asked to identify themselves.

Epilepsy

Epilepsy Foundation of America, 1828 L Street N.W., Suite 406, Washington, D.C. 20036. Telephone (202) 293-2930.

Hearing Impairments

The International Association of Parents of the Deaf, 814 Thayer Avenue, Silver Spring, Maryland 20910. Telephone (301) 585-5400.

The International Parents' Organization, Alexander Graham Bell Association for the Deaf, 3417 Volta Place N.W., Washington, D.C. 20007. Telephone (202) 337-5220.

Learning Disabilities

Association for Children with Learning Disabilities, 4156 Library Road, Pittsburgh, Pennsylvania 15234. Telephone (412) 341-1515. The purpose of ACLD is to advance the education and general well-being of children with learning disabilities. Through its local chapters ACLD provides parents with information about educational, psychological, and medical services.

Physical Handicaps

The National Easter Seal Society, 2023 West Ogden Avenue, Chicago, Illinois 60612. Telephone (312) 243-8400. Their local offices will provide parents with information on services and programs for children with a variety of handicaps. They will also offer guidance and assistance in selecting and using the most appropriate resource.

Retardation

The National Association for Retarded Children, 2709 Avenue E, East Arlington, Texas 76011. Telephone (817) 261-4961. Their local offices will provide parents with information on services and programs for mentally retarded youngsters.

Visual Impairments

American Foundation for the Blind, Incorporated, 15 West Sixteenth Street, New York, New York 10011. Telephone (212) 620-2000. The AFB serves as a national clearinghouse of information for the blind.

National Federation of the Blind, 1800 Johnson Street, Baltimore, Maryland 21230. Telephone (301) 659-9314. The NFB is an organization of blind persons, one of whose purposes is to serve as a consumer advocate for blind youngsters and adults.

Appendix B

NATIONAL DIRECTORIES*

I. ASSORTED DISABILITIES

Directory for Special Children. 1975. American Association of Special Educators, Box 168, Fryeburg, Maine 04037. A national geographic listing of facilities and services for the handicapped.

The Easter Seal Directory of Resident Camps for Persons with Special Health Needs (tenth edition). 1977. National Easter Seal Society, 2023 West Ogden Avenue, Chicago, Illinois 60612. A list of resident camps for persons with physical or emotional disabilities.

Directory for Exceptional Children (eighth edition). 1978. Porter Sargent Publisher, Incorporated, 11 Beacon Street, Boston, Massachusetts 02108. Concise descriptions of approximately three thousand schools, hospitals, clinics, and other treatment centers for emotionally disturbed, learning-disabled, or physically handicapped youngsters.

* For a complete and more up-to-date list of national directories, write to the National Easter Seal Society, 2023 West Ogden Avenue, Chicago, Illinois 60612. The information provided in this appendix is excerpted from information provided by the National Easter Seal Society.

II. EMOTIONAL DISORDERS

Mental Health Programs for Preschool Children. 1974. Mental Health Association, 1800 North Kent Street, Arlington, Virginia 22209.

U.S. Facilities and Programs for Children with Severe Mental Illnesses—A Rirectory. 1974. Single copy is free. National Institute for Mental Health, 5600 Fishers Lane, Rockville, Maryland 20857.

Mental Health Services: Information and Referral Directory. (Four regional editions—Eastern, Southern, Central, and Western.) 1978. Ready Reference Press, 100 East Thousand Oaks Boulevard, Suite 224, Thousand Oaks, California 91360.

III. LEARNING DISABILITIES

Directory of Educational Facilities for the Learning Disabled (seventh edition). 1978–9. Issued biennially. Academy Therapy Publications, P.O. Box 99, San Rafael, California 94901.

A National Directory of Four-Year Colleges, Two-Year Colleges, and Post-High School Training Programs for Young People with Learning Disabilities (third edition). 1977. Partners in Publishing, P.O. Box 50347, Tulsa, Oklahoma 74150.

The Association for Children with Learning Disabilities, 4156 Library Road, Pittsburgh, Pennsylvania 15234, publishes directories of private schools, summer camps, and colleges.

Appendix C

SOME HELPFUL READINGS

The following are some books which may be of general interest. Writings pertaining to more specific topics are discussed throughout this book and are referenced in the "Notes" section.

I. BOOKS ABOUT EARLY CHILDHOOD DEVELOPMENT

BRAZLETON, T. BERRY, *Infants and Mothers,* published in paperback by Delta Books, 1969.

BRAZLETON, T. BERRY, *Toddlers and Mothers,* published in paperback by Delta Books, 1974.

CHESS, STELLA, THOMAS, ALEXANDER, AND BIRCH, HERBERT, *Your Child Is a Person,* published in paperback by Penguin Books, 1977.

SPOCK, BENJAMIN, *Baby and Child Care,* published in paperback by Pocket Books, 1976.

WHITE, BURTON, *The First Three Years of Life,* published in paperback by Avon Books, 1975.

II. BOOKS ABOUT COMMON CHILDHOOD PROBLEMS

FRAIBERG, SELMA, *The Magic Years,* published in paperback by Charles Scribner's Sons, 1968.

ILG, FRANCES, AND AMES, LOUISE BATES, *Child Behavior,* published in paperback by Harper and Row, 1966.

III. BOOKS ABOUT PSYCHOTHERAPY

Portrayal of Child Psychotherapy

AXLINE, VIRGINIA, *Dibs: In Search of Self,* published in paperback by Ballantine Books, 1976.

BARUCH, DOROTHY, *One Little Boy,* published in paperback by Dell Publishing Company, 1964.

Portrayal of Family Therapy

NAPIER, AUGUSTUS, AND WHITAKER, CARL, *The Family Crucible,* published in hardcover by Harper and Row, 1978.

Portrayal of the Treatment of a Seriously Disturbed Adolescent

GREEN, HANNAH, *I Never Promised You a Rose Garden,* published in paperback by the New American Library, 1964.

IV. BOOKS BY PARENTS ABOUT THEIR ATTEMPTS TO HELP THEIR SERIOUSLY DISTURBED CHILD

GREENFIELD, JOSH, *A Child Called Noah,* published in paperback by Pocket Books, 1979.

KAUFMAN, BARRY, *Son-Rise,* published in paperback by Warner Books, 1977.

PARK, CLARA, *The Siege: The First Eight Years of an Autistic Child,* published in paperback by Atlantic-Little, Brown, 1972.

V. BOOKS FOR PARENTS ABOUT LEARNING DISABILITIES AND HYPERACTIVITY

Learning Disabilities

BRUTTEN, MILTON, RICHARDSON, SYLVIA, AND MANGEL, CHARLES, *Something's Wrong with My Child,* published in hardcover by Harcourt Brace Jovanovich, 1973.

OSMAN, BETTY, *Learning Disabilities: A Family Affair,* published in hardcover by Random House, 1979.

ROSS, ALAN, *Learning Disability: The Unrealized Potential,* published in hardcover by McGraw Hill, 1977.

Hyperactivity

STEWART, MARK, AND OLDS, SALLY, *Raising a Hyperactive Child,* published in hardcover by Harper and Row, 1973.

WENDER, PAULA, AND WENDER, ESTHER, *The Hyperactive and the Learning Disabled Child,* published in hardcover by Crown, 1978.

VI. ASSORTED CONSUMER GUIDES

Mental Health Services for Adults

ADAMS, SALLIE, AND ORGEL, MICHAEL, *Through the Mental Health Maze,* available from The Health Research Group, 2000 P Street N.W., Washington, D.C., 20036.

EHRENBERG, OTTO, AND EHRENBERG, MIRIAM, *The Psychotherapy Maze,* published in hardcover by Holt, Rinehart and Winston, 1977.

KOVEL, JOEL, *A Complete Guide to Therapy,* published in paperback by Pantheon Books, 1977.

PARK, CLARA, AND SHAPIRO, LEON, *You Are Not Alone,* published in paperback by Atlantic-Little, Brown, 1976.

Mental Health Services for Children

BREHM, SHARON, *Help for Your Child,* published in paperback by Prentice-Hall, Inc., 1978.

Psychological Testing of Children

KLEIN, STANLEY, *Psychological Testing of Children: A Consumer's Guide,* published in paperback by the Exceptional Parent Press, 1977.

Notes

CHAPTER TWO

[1] This classification system is an amalgram derived from many different sources. Two of these sources are Chess, S., and Hassibi, M., *Principles and Practice of Child Psychiatry* (New York: Plenum Press, 1978), and Josephson, M., and Porter, R. (eds.) *Clinician's Handbook of Childhood Psychopathology* (New York: Pocket Books, 1976). Both of these books are referred to throught this chapter.
[2] Spock, Benjamin, *Baby and Child Care,* published in paperback by Pocket Books, 1976, p. 480.
[3] Bruch, H., *The Golden Cage: The Enigma of Anorexia Nervosa,* published in paperback by Vintage Books, 1979, p. ix. This book is designed to be read by parents as well as professionals.
[4] *Ibid.,* pp. 8–9.
[5] *Ibid.,* p. 6.
[6] Bruch, H., *Eating Disorders: Obesity, Anorexia Nervosa, and the Person Within,* published in paperback by Basic Books, Inc., 1973, p. 253.
[7] Stunkard, Albert, "Obesity," in Freedman, A. M., Kaplan, H. I., and Sadock, B. J., *Comprehensive Textbook of Psychiatry,* volume II, second edition (Baltimore: Williams and Wilkins Company, 1975), p. 1649.
[8] *Ibid.,* p. 1648.
[9] Bruch, H., *Eating Disorders, op. cit.,* p. 134.
[10] Stunkard, A., *op. cit.,* p. 1649.
[11] Spock, B., *op. cit.,* p. 489.
[12] *Ibid.,* p. 491.

[13] Bruch, H., *op. cit.*, p. 309.
[14] *Ibid.*, p. 336.
[15] In their book *Child Behavior*, published in paperback by Harper and Row, Dr. Frances Ilg and Dr. Louise Ames of the Gesell Institute discuss common childhood problems. Interested readers may wish to refer to this book or to the sections on sleep problems in Spock's *Baby and Child Care*.
[16] Ilg, F., and Ames, L., *op cit.*, pp. 95–7.
[17] Cohen, A., "Enuresis," in Josephson, M., and Porter, R., *op. cit.*, p. 169.
[18] Chess, S., and Hassibi, M., *op. cit,*, p. 224.
[19] Ilg, F., and Ames, L., *op. cit.*, p. 114.
[20] Chess, S., and Hassibi, M., *op. cit.*, p. 225.
[21] *Ibid.*, p. 224.
[22] Levine, M. D., "Children with Encopresis: A Descriptive Analysis," *Pediatrics*, vol. 56, no. 3, Sept. 1975, p. 412.
[23] Halpern, W. I., "The Treatment of Encopretic Children," *Journal of the American Academy of Child Psychiatry*, vol. 16, 1977, p. 480.
[24] Levine, M. D., and Bakow, H., "Children with Encopresis: A Study of Treatment Outcome," *Pediatrics*, vol. 58, no. 6, Dec. 1976, pp. 845–52.
[25] Chess, S., and Hassibi, M., *op. cit.*, pp. 231–2.
[26] Newman, L. E., "Treatment for the Parents of Feminine Boys," *American Journal of Psychiatry*, vol. 133, no. 6, June 1976, p. 685.
[27] Chess, S., and Hassibi, M., *op. cit.*, p. 233.
[28] Porter, R. T., "Gender Disturbances," in Josephson, M., and Porter, R., *op. cit.*, p. 211.
[29] Fairchild, B., and Hayward, N., *Now That You Know: What Every Parent Should Know About Homosexuality* (New York: Harcourt, Brace and Jovanovich, 1979), p. 72.
[30] Straker, N., "Bronchial Asthma: An Example of Psychosomatic Disorder," in Josephson, M., and Porter, R., *op. cit.*, p. 195.
[31] Minuchin, S., et al., "A Conceptual Model of Psychosomatic Illness in Children," *Archives of General Psychiatry*, vol. 32, no. 8, August 1975, pp. 1031–38; and Minuchin,

S., et al., *Psychosomatic Families: Anorexia Nervosa in Context* (Cambridge, Massachusetts; Harvard University Press, 1978).
[32] Kanner, L., *Child Psychiatry,* fourth edition (Springfield, Illinois: Charles Thomas, 1972), p. 518.
[33] Spock, B., *op. cit.,* p. 256.
[34] Ilg, F., and Ames, L., *op. cit.,* p. 139.
[35] Ilg, F., and Ames, L., *op. cit.,* pp. 142–3.
[36] de Lissovoy, V., "Headbanging in Early Childhood," *Journal of Pediatrics,* vol. 58, no. 6, June 1961, p. 805.
[37] Spock, B., *op. cit.,* p. 262.
[38] Mannino, F. V., and Delgado, R. A., "Trichotillomania in Children: A Review," *American Journal of Psychiatry,* vol. 126, no. 4, Oct. 1969, p. 505.
[39] Ilg, F., and Ames, L., *op. cit.,* p. 146.
[40] Shapiro, E. S., and Shapiro, A. K., "Tic Disorders," in Josephson, M., and Porter, R., *op. cit.,* p. 326.
[41] *Ibid,,* pp. 327–9
[42] *Ibid.,* p. 245.
[43] *Ibid.,* p. 247.
[44] *Ibid.,* p. 247.
[45] *Ibid.,* p. 248.
[46] *Ibid.,* pp. 241–2.
[47] *Ibid.,* p. 243.
[48] *Ibid.,* p. 242.
[49] Karush, R. K., "Obsessive-Compulsive Syndromes," in Josephson, M., and Porter, R., *op. cit.,* p. 87.
[50] Chess, S., and Hassibi, M., *op. cit.,* p. 250.
[51] Shaffer, D., "Suicide in Childhood and Early Adolescence," *Journal of Child Psychology and Psychiatry,* vol. 15, 1974, p. 275.
[52] Shneidman, E. S., "Suicide," in Freedman, A. M., Kaplan, H. I., and Sadock, B. J., *op. cit.,* p. 1780.
[53] Shaffer, D., *op. cit.,* p. 280.
[54] *Ibid.,* p. 275.
[55] Hoffman, L., "Speech Disorders: Stuttering and Elective Mutism," in Josephson, M., and Porter, R., *op. cit.,* p. 139.
[56] Spock, B., *op. cit.,* p. 276.
[57] *Ibid.,* p. 276.

[58] Chess, S., and Hassibi, M., *op. cit.*, p. 314.
[59] de Hirsch, K., "Language Disturbances," in Freedman, A. M., Kaplan, H. I., and Sadock, B. J., *op. cit.*, p. 2111.
[60] *Ibid.*, p. 2111.
[61] Chess, S., and Hassibi, M., *op. cit.*, p. 257.
[62] Straker, N., "Impulse and Conduct Disorders," in Josephson, M., and Porter, R., *op. cit.*, p. 351.
[63] Wolff, P., "The Natural History of Crying and Other Vocalizations in Early Infancy," in Foss, B. M. (ed.) *Tavistock Study Group on Mother-Infant Interaction, London, 1959–63. Determinants of Infant Behavior,* vol. IV, 1969, p. 841.
[64] Spock, B., *op. cit.*, pp. 349–50.
[65] *Ibid.*, pp. 293–4.
[66] Vandersall, T., and Wiener, J., "Children Who Set Fires," *Archives of General Psychiatry,* vol. 22, Jan. 1970, pp. 63–71.
[67] Krakauer, W., "Delinquency," in Josephson, M., and Porter, R., *op. cit.*, p. 366.
[68] Chess, S., and Hassibi, M., *op. cit.*, p. 449.
[69] *Ibid.*, p. 449.
[70] *Ibid.*, p. 263.
[71] Kanner, L., "Early Infantile Autism," *Journal of Pediatrics,* vol. 25, 1944, p. 211.
[72] Ainsworth, M. D., "The Development of Mother-Infant Interaction Among the Ganda," in Foss, B. M., *Determinants of Infant Behavior,* vol. II (New York: John Wiley and Sons, 1967), pp. 76–80.
[73] Kanner, L., "Early Infantile Autism," *op. cit.*, p. 211.
[74] Reich, R., "Early Onset Psychosis—Autistic," in Josephson, M., and Porter, R., *op. cit.*, p. 39.
[75] *Diagnostic and Statistical Manual of Mental Disorders, Third Edition, Draft,* prepared by the American Psychiatric Association, 1978, p. M:12.
[76] *Ibid.*, p. M:13.
[77] Reich, R., "Early Onset Psychosis—Symbiotic," in Josephson, M., and Porter, R., *op. cit.*, p. 45.
[78] Chess, S., and Hassibi, M., *op. cit.*, pp. 385–6.
[79] APA Manual, *op. cit.*, pp. C:2–3.
[80] Chess, S., and Hassibi, M., *op. cit.*, p. 278.

[81] *Ibid.*, pp. 345–6.
[82] *Ibid.*, pp. 331–2.
[83] *Ibid.*, p. 321.
[84] *Ibid.*, p. 322.
[85] Spock, B., *op. cit.*, p. 576.
[86] Chess, S., and Hassibi, M., *op. cit.*, pp. 325–6.
[87] *Ibid.*, p. 326.
[88] Turecki, S., "Mental Retardation," in Josephson, M., and Porter, R., *op. cit.*, p. 337.
[89] *Ibid.*, p. 341.
[90] Chess, S., and Hassibi, M., *op. cit.*, p. 375.
[91] Golombeck, H., et al., "The Developmental Challenges of Adolescence," in Steinhauer, P., and Rae-Grant, Q., *Psychological Problems of the Child and His Family* (Toronto: Macmillan of Canada, 1977), p. 30.
[92] *Ibid.*, p. 30.
[93] *Ibid.*, p. 30.
[94] *Ibid.*, pp. 30–1.
[95] Chess, S., and Hassibi, M., *op. cit.*, p. 384.
[96] Golombeck, H., et al., *op. cit.*, pp. 31–2.
[97] *Ibid.*, p. 35.
[98] Chess, S., and Hassibi, M., *op. cit.*, p. 385.

CHAPTER THREE

[1] Cruikshank, W. M., *The Brain-Injured Child in Home, School, and Community* (Syracuse: Syracuse University Press, 1967), p. 2.
[2] Farnham-Diggory, S., *Learning Disabilities: A Psychological Perspective,* published in paperback by Harvard University Press, Cambridge, Mass., 1978, pp. 9–11.
[3] Ross, A. O., *Learning Disability: The Unrealized Potential* (New York: McGraw Hill, 1977), pp. 44–60.
[4] Wender, P., *Minimal Brain Dysfunction in Children* (New York: John Wiley and Sons, 1971).
[5] *Diagnostic and Statistical Manual of Mental Disorders, Third Edition, Draft,* prepared by the American Psychiatric Association, 1978, pp. M:26–33.

[6] Farnham-Diggory, S., *op. cit.*, p. 5.
[7] Kinsbourne, M., "Hyperactivity: Diagnosis," *The Exceptional Parent Magazine,* August 1978, p. 9.
[8] Millichap, J. G., *The Hyperactive Child with Minimal Brain Dysfunction* (Chicago: Year Book Medical Publishers, Inc., 1975), p. 1.
[9] Kinsbourne, M., *op. cit.*, p. 11.
[10] Kinsbourne, M., "Hyperactivity: Treatment," *The Exceptional Parent Magazine,* October 1978, p. 7.
[11] Feingold, B., *Why Your Child is Hyperactive* (New York: Random House, 1974).
[12] Ross, A. O., *op. cit.*, p. 4.

CHAPTER FIVE

[1] A section similar to this appears in Ehrenberg, O., and Ehrenberg, M., *The Psychotherapy Maze* (New York: Holt, Rinehart and Winston, 1977), pp. 59–61. Their writing was helpful to me in the presentation of my own thoughts in this area.
[2] Paraphrased from Friedman, M., *Capitalism and Freedom* (Chicago: University of Chicago Press, 1962), pp. 144–5, as quoted in Gross, Stanley, J., "The Myth of Professional Licensing," in the *American Psychologist,* vol. 33, no. 11, November 1978, p. 1009.
[3] Interested readers are referred to Gross's article, cited above.

CHAPTER SIX

[1] Kovel, Joel, *A Complete Guide to Therapy,* published in paperback by Pantheon Books, 1977, p. 43.
[2] *Ibid.*, p. 226.
[3] *Ibid.*, p. 223.
[4] Anna Freud is a prolific writer (International Universities Press has published a seven-volume series of her

writings). If you are interested in a general introduction to child psychoanalysis I recommend her book entitled *The Psychoanalytic Treatment of Children,* published in paperback by Schocken Books, New York, 1964.

[5] Dorothy Baruch presents a vivid account of the psychoanalytically oriented psychotherapy of an asthmatic boy in a book entitled *One Little Boy,* published in paperback by the Dell Publishing Company, 1964.

[6] Dr. Bruno Bettelheim has written extensively about the application of psychoanalytic treatment techniques in working with severely disturbed youngsters. Bettelheim founded a residential school in Chicago, called the Sonia Shankman Orthogenic School, to treat such children. Interested parents may want to read his book *Love is Not Enough,* published in paperback by Avon Books, 1971, which describes the work of this school.

[7] Interested parents may wish to read Rogers's book entitled *Client-Centered Therapy,* published in paperback by the Houghton Mifflin Company, 1965, for a description of his theory and techniques.

[8] Axline has written two books which may be of interest to parents: *Play Therapy,* published in paperback by Ballantine Books, 1974, which describes the theory and technique of client-centered play-therapy, and *Dibs: In Search of Self,* also published in paperback by Ballantine Books, 1976, which details Axline's treatment of a troubled boy.

[9] Kovel, *op. cit.,* p. 112, quoting Carl Rogers, *On Becoming a Person,* pp. 90–91.

[10] Axline, V., *Dibs: In Search of Self,* p. 49.

[11] Gordon, Thomas, *Parent Effectiveness Training,* published in paperback by the New American Library, 1975.

[12] Parents may wish to read *Parents are Teachers* by Wesley Becker, published in paperback by the Research Press, 1971, or *Families* (revised edition), by Gerald Patterson, also published in paperback by the Research Press, 1975, for a description of behaviorally oriented treatment of children and families.

[13] A pioneer in the behavioral analysis and treatment of stuttering behavior is Dr. Ronald Webster. For informa-

tion about his treatment approaches and locations of programs which utilize his methods you can write to: Dr. Ronald Webster, Hollins Communications Research Institute, P. O. Box 9684, Roanoke, Virginia 24020.

[14] Two books, written for therapists, but perhaps of interest to parents, about structural family therapy are Minuchin, S., *Families and Family Therapy,* available in hardcover only from Harvard University Press, 1974, and Haley, J., *Problem-Solving Therapy,* published in paperback by Harper and Row, 1978. A reporter's account of one family's experience with structural family therapy appears in the magazine *The New Yorker,* in its May 15, 1978, edition beginning on page 39.

[15] Berne, Eric, *Games People Play,* published in paperback by Ballantine Books, 1978.

[16] Harris, Thomas, *I'm OK, You're OK,* published in paperback by Avon Books, 1973.

CHAPTER SEVEN

---

[1] Wiener, J. M., *Psychopharmacology in Childhood and Adolescence* (New York: Basic Books, Inc., 1977).

[2] Kinsbourne, M., "Hyperactivity: Treatment," *The Exceptional Parent Magazine,* October 1978, p. 8.

CHAPTER EIGHT

---

[1] Klein, S., *Psychological Testing of Children: A Consumer's Guide* (Boston: The Exceptional Parent Press, 1977), p. 6.

[2] *Ibid.,* p. 20.

[3] Ross, Alan O., *Learning Disability: The Unrealized Potential* (New York: McGraw Hill, 1977), p. 4.

CHAPTER ELEVEN

[1] A chapter similar to this appears in Ehrenberg and Ehrenberg, *op. cit.*, pp. 86–98. Although their book focuses exclusively on psychotherapy for adults, their ideas were helpful to me in the organization of my own thoughts.

[2] I would like to thank the Health Research Group for permission to paraphrase from *Through the Mental Health Maze.*

CHAPTER TWELVE

[1] Ehrenberg, O., and Ehrenberg, M., *op. cit.*, have an excellent chapter in their book on how adult clients can distinguish between signs of resistance and signs of incompatibility in their own therapy. The Ehrenbergs' writing was helpful to me in my presentation of this issue with regard to child and family therapy.

CHAPTER FOURTEEN

[1] Quoted from National Institute of Mental Health, *Halfway Houses Serving the Mentally Ill and Alcoholics, United States,* 1973 DHEW Publication No. (ADM) 76-264, Superintendent of Documents, U.S. Government Printing Office, page 1.

CHAPTER FIFTEEN

[1] Shneidman, Edwin S., "Suicide," in Freedman, A. M., Kaplan, H. I., and Sadock, B. J., *Comprehensive Textbook*

of Psychiatry, vol. II, second edition (Baltimore: William and Wilkins Company, 1975), p. 1780.

[2] Shaffer, David, "Suicide in Childhood and Early Adolescence," *Journal of Child Psychology and Psychiatry*, vol. 15, 1974, p. 280.

[3] *Ibid.*, p. 275.

INDEX

abused children, 59–60, 285
academic: problems, 17, 46; skills, 193–95
Academy of Certified Social Workers (ACSW), 129, 130, 131
achievement tests, 193–95
acute disorganized behavior, 310–11
acute panic. *See* anxiety attacks
acute transient tic disorder of childhood, 41–42
adolescence: biological and physical maturation in, 73–74; drug or alcohol abuse in, 149; emotional problems of, 21–76; sexual preferences in, 35; subperiods of, 72–73; tasks of, 73–76; and therapy, 212–13, 217–19
adolescent onset psychosis, 62, 65–66
"adult," in Transactional Analysis, 168
aggressive behavior, 55–56
American Board of Psychiatry and Neurology, 125
American Nurses Association, 131
American Psychological and Psychiatric Associations, 35
amitriptyline (Elavil), 177
analyst, definition of term, 120, 121–122. *See also* therapist
anemia, 26
anger, 55
anorexia nervosa (self-starvation), 23, 25–26, 166; medications for, 180
antidepressants, 175, 179, 180; tricyclic, 177
antipsychotic medications, 175, 176, 179
antisocial behaviors or conduct disorders, 54–59
anxiety and anxiety attacks, 37, 41, 43*n*., 44, 45–47, 310; medications for, 178
arithmetic, 83, 93; tests on, 193
arson, 54, 56, 57–58
articulation or pronunciation problems, 51, 52
artificial food flavorings and colorings, 88, 175
assault (physical harm), 54, 56, 59–60, 309
asthma, bronchial, 37
attention deficit disorder, 78, 82
attorney, 119
atypical childhood psychosis. *See* developmental child psychosis
audiologist, role in formal examination, 271
auditory memory deficit, 91
auditory-perception tests, 191
aural information, 90, 91–92
autism, early infantile, 62–64
Axelrod, Joan, 79*n*.
Axline, Virginia, 150, 152–53

baby talk. *See* articulation or pronunciation problems

Bayley Scale of Infant Development, 184
bedwetting, 30–31, 160. *See also* enuresis
behavioral therapy, 137, 155–61, 164–65
behavior problems, 79; and learning difficulties, 96; in school, 54
Bender Visual-Motor Gestalt Test, 191
Berne, Eric, *Games People Play,* 167
biological and physical maturation in adolescence, 73–74
biological function, disorders of, 21, 22–32
biting, 55
Blacky pictures, 188
bowel syndrome, irritable, 37
Bowen, Murray, 161, 165
Bowenian therapy. *See* Family Systems Therapy
brain, assessment of functioning, 272; effects of injuries, 80–81
brain damaged, 149
brain dysfunction, 79, 81, 82, 271
brain injured, 79, 80; and behavioral therapy, 160
Brokowski, Helen, 137*n.*
Bruch, Dr. Hilde, 25–28
Bucks County, Penn., 80
bullying, 54

California, 80
California Achievement Tests, 193
Catell Infant Intelligence Scale, 184
cerebral palsy, 270
certification of mental health professionals, definition of, 122–23
Chess, S., and M. Hassibi, *Principles and Practices of Child Psychiatry,* 44, 52
chest, heaviness in, 45
child, role in Individualized Education Plan, 273–75
"child," in Transactional Analysis, 167–68
child abuse. *See* abused children
child-guidance clinics, 100–101; referrals from, 206–207
child-guidance model, 145
childhood, emotional problems of, 21, 32–59, 61–72, 307–308; normal problems of, 15
child neglect. *See* neglected children
child psychiatrist, 125–26
child psychiatry department of a teaching hospital, 207
child psychoanalysis. *See* psychoanalytic approaches
children: and attitudes about medication, 172; and complaints about therapy, 258–61; and residential treatment, 283–86, 291–92, 298–99
Children's Apperception Test (CAT), 188
child therapist, 56–57. *See also* child psychiatrist
chloral hydrate, 179
chlordiazepoxide (Librium), 178
chlorpromazine (Thorazine), 178
chronic multiple tic. *See* Gilles de la Tourette's syndrome
chronic overeating. *See* obesity
clergyman, 19, 104, 119
client-centered therapy, 150
clinical child psychologist, 128
clinical psychology, 126
clinician, definition of term, 120, 121
clinics: fees and insurance, 134; in psychiatric emergencies, 305, 308, 309. *See also* community sponsored clinics
Closer Look Information, 274*n.*
colitis, ulcerative, 37
Columbia Maturity Scale, 185
Community Chest, 104; referrals through, 223

community mental health centers, 100–101, 103
community-sponsored clinics, 100–101, 109, 110, 111–15
Complete Guide to Therapy, Dr. Joel Kovel, 138, 140
compulsive behavior. *See* obsessive-compulsive syndrome
Computerized Axial Tomography (CAT) scan, 271*n.*
conditioned stimulus, 155
conduct disorders. *See* antisocial behaviors or conduct disorders
conflict theory of personality development, 143–44
contract, therapy and a written, 243–45
coordination, poor, 79
counseling psychologists, 126–27
counselor, definition of, 120, 121

defiance, 54
delinquency, juvenile, 58–59, 149
delinquent youth, 149
dentist, 100
depression: in adolescence, 48–49; and behavioral therapy, 160; medication for, 177
depressive reactions, 48
desensitization techniques, 159–60
Detroit Test of Learning Aptitude, 191
developmental child psychosis, 62, 64–65
developmental dyslexia, 80, 82–83, 95
developmental history, in formal evaluation, 269
developmental optometrists, 272*n.*
Developmental Test of Visual Motor Integration, 191
dextroamphetamine (Dexedrine), 174
diagnostic and counseling services, in hospitals, 286–87; in schools, 101
diazepam (Valium), 178
diet, additive free, 88, 175
difficulties (academic, behavioral, emotional), nature, causes, and treatment of, 83, 84, 87; symptoms of, 79, 80
diphenhydramine (Benadryl), 179
Diploma of the American Board of Professional Psychology, 127–28
Directory for Exceptional Children, Porter Sargent, 102*n.*
disorders of biological function, 21, 22–35
distractibility, 79, 80, 82, 88
dizziness, 46
Draw-a-Person Test, 188
drugs, 310
drug treatment in therapy, 154, 171–80
duodenum, 37
dyslexia, 80, 82–83, 95–96

eating; difficulties associated with, 8, 22–28; disturbances and causes, 23–24
echolalia, 63, 65
educational and vocational choices in adolescence, 75–76
educational evaluation, 269–70, 292
educationally handicapped, 79
educational programs in residential treatment centers, 281, 282
Education for All Handicapped Children Act (Public Law 94–142), 101, 263–64, 265, 269
educators, children's difficulties and, 79. *See also* guidance counselor; principal; school personnel; teacher
effeminate behaviors, 32, 33–34
elective mutism, 54

electroencephalogram (EEG), 271*n.*
elimination, 23, 30–32
emergencies, psychiatric, 303–11
emotional difficulties, 311; and school's role, 276. *See also* adolescence, emotional difficulties in; childhood, emotional difficulties in
encopresis, 31–32
enteritis, regional, 37
enuresis, 30–31, 39; medication for, 179; *See also* bedwetting
epilepsy, 69–70, 271*n.*
Experimental Test of Comprehension and Linguistic Structure, 191
experimental psychologists, 126
evaluation: educational, by school, 269–70; 292; in inpatient hospitalization, 292–93

family, reaction to problems by, 19. *See also* parents
family doctor, 104, 105, 119, 205–206; advice of, 19, 23, 47, 69, 78; and information, 242; and inpatient treatment, 288. *See also* physician
family history, in formal evaluation, 269
family-service agencies, 100
Family Systems Therapy, 109, 137, 161–67
family therapy, 146, 148, 170
fatigue, 36, 45
fears, 15, 42–43
fees, 100–101, 105–108, 111–12, 134, 199, 209, 210, 221, 224, 225, 226, 238–39
Feingold, Dr. Ben, *Why Your Child Is Hyperactive,* 88, 175
fighting, 17, 55. *See also* physical violence
financial considerations, 105–108, 111–12, 134–35, 199, 281; cost of therapy, 238–39; in residential treatment, 282
fire setting. *See* arson
formal evaluation of child by school, 269–70
foster care, 301–302
foster homes, 300–301
Freud, Anna, 143
Freud, Dr. Sigmund, 142–43
Freudian theory, 121
frustration, 55, 56; headbanging as indication of, 40; in hyperactivity, 87

Games People Play, Eric Berne, 167
general systems theory, 161–62
genitals, 32, 33
Gestalt therapy, 137, 167, 168–69
Gilles de la Tourette's syndrome, 41–42; medication for, 180
glandular disorder, 27
Goodman-Fristoe-Woodcock Auditory Skills Test Battery, 191
Gordon, Thomas, 153
grand mal. *See* epilepsy
Griffiths Mental Development Scale, 184
group counseling in school systems, 276
group homes, residences, and shelters, 103
group psychiatric practices, 100
group therapy, 110, 130, 146, 148, 151, 170
guidance counselor, 19, 104, 121, 276; referrals from, 206; role in help of child, 268. *See also* school personnel
guidelines determining need for help, 16–19

habit: disorders of, 37–42; disturbances, 45
hair pulling, 38, 40
Haldol. *See* haloperidol

halfway houses. *See* therapeutic communities
haloperidol (Haldol), 42, 176, 180
handicapped children, definition of, 263*n.*
handwriting, 83
Harris, Thomas A., *I'm O.K.—You're O.K.*, 167
headache, 36, 44, 45, 48
head banging, 39–40
Health Research Group, *Through the Mental Health Maze: A Consumer's Guide to Finding a Psychotherapist*, 243
health insurance. *See* medical health insurance
hearing: assessment of, 271; impairments, 67
help, places to go for, 99–108
heterosexuals, 35
hitting, 55. *See also* physical violence
homosexuality (gay orientation), 33, 34–35
hospital, 102, 293; hospitalization in, 135; in psychiatric emergencies, 304–305, 309, 310, 311
"hot line" for crisis or rape, 309
humanistic therapy, 137, 150–54
hyperactivity, 26, 70, 79, 80, 81–82, 84–90; activity level of, 84–86; and difficulties in attending, 86; and medication, 172–76; and social difficulties, 87; treatment of, 87–89
hyperactivity syndrome, 79, 82, 84–90
hyperkinetic syndrome, 79, 81, 84. *See also* hyperactivity syndrome
hypersomnia (excessive sleep), 29–30

identity: adolescent formation of, 76; and behavioral therapy, 160; in humanistic therapy, 153–54
Ilg, Dr. Frances, and Dr. Louise Ames, *Child Behavior*, 30, 38–39, 40
Illinois Test of Psycholinguistic Abilities (ITPA), 190–91
imipramine (Tofranil), 177, 179
immaturity, 39; in retarded youngsters, 71; in school phobia, 44
impulsivity, 79, 82, 83, 87
independence in adolescence, 74–75
individual counseling in school systems, 276
Individualized Educational Plan (IEP), 273–75
individual therapy, 110, 145, 148, 151, 170
information processing in learning disabilities, 90–91, 96, 98
ingestion of dangerous or poisonous materials. *See* pica
inpatient services. *See* residential treatment centers
inpatient treatment, 280–81
insurance coverage, 106*n.*, 106–108, 134, 215, 238, 281
intake worker, 224–25
intelligence, 79
Intelligence Tests (IQ tests), 183–87
Interim Hayes-Binet Intelligence Test, 184
Internal Revenue Service, 134–35
internship, 124
Iowa Tests of Basic Skills, 193, 194
irrational fears, 15
insomnia or sleep disturbances, 28–30

Jacksonian seizures. *See* epilepsy
Jungian theory, 121
juvenile delinquent or offender. *See* delinquency, juvenile

Kanner, Dr. Leo, 38, 62
Kinsbourne, Dr. Marcel, 87–88, 173*n.*
Klein, Stanley D., *Psychological Testing for Children*, 181*n.*
Kovel, Dr. Joel, *A Complete Guide to Therapy*, 138–39, 140

language arts (spelling, punctuation, and sentence structure), 193
language disorders, 80
language function testing, 191
language (auditory) processing disorders, 91–92, 94
law of conditioned reflexes, 155
law of effect, 155–56
laxatives or diuretics, excessive use of, 25
learning difficulties, 17, 80, 82–84, 86, 87, 90–91
learning disabled children. *See* Learning Disabilities
Learning Disabilities (LD), 79, 80, 82–98; definition of, 191; tests for, 189–93
learning disabilities specialists, 191
Leiter International Performance Scale, 184–85
licensing mental health professionals, definition of, 122
lightheadedness, 46
Lithium salts, 177
lying, 54, 56–57

malnutrition, 25
maltreated child. *See* neglected children
Marianne Frostig Developmental Test of Visual Perception, 191
marital therapy, 170
masturbatory behavior, 32–33, 34*n.*
math, 83, 93; tests on, 193
mathematical psychologists, 126
medical examination in formal evaluation, 269
medical health insurance, 106*n.*, 106–108, 134, 215, 238, 281
Medicaid, 221
Medicare, 221
medication, 69, 87–88; and childhood psychosis, 67; psychiatrists and, 135; in psychotherapeutic treatment, 171–80
menstruation, 26
Mental Health Association (MHA), 103–104, 105–106; referrals from, 206–207, 223
mental health clinic, 277; obtaining help in a, 221–33
mental health insurance coverage, 106*n.*, 106–108
mental health professional, 100, 104; advice of, 19–20, 31, 33, 34, 35, 39, 40, 43, 46, 48, 49, 50, 52, 55, 60, 71, 78; definition of, 119, 120–122; children's difficulties and, 79; licensing and certification for, 122–33; in psychiatric emergencies, 303–304, 308; referrals to, 49
mental health professions and services, 103–105; location of, 99–135; and schools, 275–76
mental hospitals, 103
mental retardation, 70–72, 149, 160
methylphenidate (Ritalin), 174
Metropolitan Achievement Tests, 193
Michigan, 80
minimal brain damage, 79, 80–81
minimal brain dysfunction (MBD), 79, 81
minimal cerebral dysfunction, 79, 81
minister. *See* clergyman
Minuchin, Dr. Salvador, 37
monoamine oxidase inhibitors, (MAO inhibitors), 177

Montgomery County, Maryland, 80
moral values in adolescence, 75
motor coordination deficiencies or handicaps, 67, 271
Motor Free Test of Visual Perception, 191
mugging, 54
murder, 54
muscular disease, 270

nail-biting, 18, 38, 39
National Association for Mental Health. *See* Mental Health Association
national directories of mental health professionals, 207
National Federation of State Societies of Clinical Social Work, 130*n.*
National Registry of Health Service Providers in Psychology, 130
nausea, 36, 44
Nebraska Test of Learning Aptitude for Young Deaf Children, 184
negative reinforcement, 156
neglected children, 59–60; and residential treatment, 285
neurologists, 95; in inpatient treatment, 281; role in evaluation, 271, 272
neuropsychologist, role in evaluation, 271, 272
New York, 80
nightmares, 15, 28, 29
Northwest Syntax Screening, 191

obesity, causes and treatment, 23, 26–28
obsessive-compulsive syndrome, 47–48
occupational therapist: in inpatient treatment, 281; role in evaluation, 270
ophthalmologist, 272
optometrist, role in formal examination, 272
organic brain syndromes, 68–69
organizational problems, 94–95
orthodontists, 38
otolaryngologist, role in formal evaluation, 271–72
outpatient facilities and services, 99–101, 293
overactivity, 79, 82. *See also* hyperactivity

parent counseling, 170
Parent Effectiveness Training (PET), 153
"parent," in Transactional Analysis, 167–68
parents: attitudes about medication, 172; authority and, 15; children's difficulties and, 79, 88; and discipline or support, 15; and dissatisfaction with therapy, 251–58; and inpatient treatment, 288–93; role in Individualized Educational Plan 273–75; questions asked by, 15–16
Parents Anonymous, 60
Pavlov, Ivan, 155
pediatric evaluation, 292
pediatrician, 105, 119; advice of, 19, 23, 31, 32, 33, 36, 39, 47, 52, 53, 56, 88, 272; referrals from, 205–206, 223; information from, 242; in inpatient treatment, 281
pediatric psychologists, 128
pediatric unit of general hospital, 280
peer group relationships in adolescence, 75
peptic ulcer, 37
perceptual deficiencies. *See* perceptual disability
perceptual disability, 79, 82–83, 270
perceptual disorders. *See* perceptual disibility

perceptual handicap. *See* perceptual disability
Perls, Frederick, 168
personality tests, 145, 187–89
petit mal. *See* epilepsy
phobia, 42–45, 160
phobic reactions. *See* phobia
physical handicaps, 67–72
physical injury (assault), 59
physical therapist, role in evaluation, 270
physical violence, 308–309
physician, 100, 124; in psychiatric emergencies, 303–304. *See also* family doctor
police in psychiatric emergencies, 303, 304, 309
positive reinforcer, 155–56
predelinquent. *See* delinquency, juvenile
priest. *See* clergyman
principal, 19, 104, 268. *See also* school personnel
private clinic, 100–101; some cautions about, 111
private therapist, 100, 277; choosing a, 199–219; fees of, 107; relative advantages of, 109–10. *See also* therapist
problem solving, 94
property damage, mischief involving, 54, 56
psychiatric emergencies, 303–11
psychiatric evaluation, 292, 307
psychiatric hospital and hospitalization, 279–81, 282, 298
psychiatric nurses, 114, 120; fees and insurance, 134; in inpatient treatment, 281; licensing and certification of, 123; training of, 131–33
psychiatric or pediatric units of hospitals, 100, 102, 280–81
psychiatric social workers, 114, 119–20; in inpatient treatment, 281; licensing and certification of, 123; training of, 129–31
psychiatrists, 114, 115, 288; certification, licensing, and training of, 123, 124–26; fees and insurance, 134–35; in inpatient treatment, 281
psychoanalysis, training in, 121–22
psychoanalysts, 122
psychoanalytic approaches, 137, 142–50
psychoanalytically oriented psychotherapy. *See* psychoanalytic approaches
psychodrama, 169
psychological testing, 181–95; in formal evaluation, 270
psychologists, 115, 119; certification, licensing, and training, 123, 126–29; fees and insurance, 134–35; in inpatient treatment, 281; referrals from, 206
psychological treatment in residential treatment centers, 281–83
psychophysiological disorders. *See* psychosomatic disorders
psychosis, childhood (schizophrenia), 61–67; medications and, 176
psychosomatic disorders or psychophysiological disorders, 37, 45, 166
psychotherapist, definition of, 120–21
psychotherapy: in adolescence, 76–77; and anxiety, 46; and childhood psychosis, 67; and delinquency, 59; and elective mutism, 54; and encopresis, 32; and epilepsy, 70; ground rules of, 235–45; and hyperactivity, 89; major schools of, 137–70; and neurotic disturbances, 42; and obesity, 28; and phobias, 43, 45; and stuttering, 53–54; as tax-
(psychotherapy con't)
deductible, 134–35; and tics, 42; value of, 20

puberty, 72, 73
punisher, 156

rape, 58, 309
Ravens Progressive Matrices, 185
reading, 83, 92–96, 98; tests in, 193
rebellion, 17
recreational therapists, in inpatient treatment, 281
reinforcement systems, 158–59, 165
relaxation techniques, 159–60
residency training, 124–25
residential schools. *See* residential treatment centers
residential treatment centers (RTC), 99, 102, 293; advantages and disadvantages of, 116–17; obtaining help through, 298–302
retarded. *See* mental retardation
reward system, 267. *See also* reinforcement systems
rituals of compulsive behavior, 47–48
robbery, armed, 58
rocking, 38, 39
Rogers, Carl, 150
role playing, 169
Rorschach Test, 188
runaways, 58

schizophrenia, childhood (childhood psychosis), 61–67, 149; and behavioral therapy, 160; and humanistic therapy, 153; medications and, 176
school counseling, advantages and disadvantages of, 115–16
school personnel: advice of, 242, 272; role in Individualized Educational Plan (IEP), 273–75. *See also* educators; guidance counselor; principal; teacher
school phobia, 43–45, 166, 179–80
school psychologists, 126, 191, 276
school, public, 101, 263–77; mental health services in, 275–76
school social workers, 104, 206, 276
Science Research Associates (SRA) Achievement Tests, 193
self-mutilation, 64
self-starvation. *See* anorexia nervosa
Sentence Completion Test, 188
separation: in adolescence, 75; fears of, 39; problems related to, 17–18, 48, 65
sexual abuse, 59–60, 309
sexual functioning, 22; problems associated with, 32–35
sexual play, 33
sexual preferences in adolescence, 35
sexuality in adolescence, 72, 73, 74
short attention span, 72, 82, 86, 88
"shrink," definition of term, 122
siblings, fighting with, 15
Skinner, B. F., 155
sleep: difficulties, 45; disorders and medication, 178–79; disturbances of, 22, 29–30; fears related to, 29
Slingerland Screening Tests for Identifying Children with Specific Learning Disabilities, 191
social psychologists, 126
social service organizations, 105
social skills, difficulties with, 79, 86, 87, 88, 89, 96
social workers, fees and insurance, 134–35
spatial relationships, 82–83, 92–93
special education classes, 276

specific learning disability, 80, 82
speech, 90, 92; delayed onset of, 51–52
speech and language pathologist testing by, 191
speech or language specialist, 52, 53–54
speech therapists, in inpatient treatment, 281
spelling, 92, 95, 96
Spencer Memory for Sentences, 191
Spock, Dr. Benjamin, 24, 27, 38, 40, 51, 69
Stanford Achievement Tests, 193
Stanford-Binet Intelligence Scale, 184
starvation. *See* anorexia nervosa
stealing, 54, 56, 57
stimulation, lack of, 40
stomach (ache), 36, 37, 44, 45, 46, 48
store front centers, 100
strategic family therapy. *See* Family Systems Therapy
stress, 37, 71
structural family therapy. *See* Family Systems Therapy
stuttering, 52–54, 160
subacute tic of childhood or adolescence, 41
sugar, 88
suicidal behavior: myths about, 50–51, 307–308; and residential treatment, 283–84; suicide and suicide attempts, 50, 304–305; threats, gestures, and thoughts, 49–50, 304–306
Sullivanian theory, 121
sweating, 46
symbiotic psychosis, 65
symptom, definition of, 143*n.*
synthetic food additives, 88, 175–76

tactile information, 90
Tasks of Emotional Development (TED), 188
teacher, 19, 119; role in help of child, 264–65
temper tantrums, 15
temporal lobe seizures, 69
tension, nervous, 39, 41, 45–46
testing, 181–95, 270
Thematic Apperception Test (TAT), 188
therapeutic communities, 59, 67, 103, 293, 300
therapeutic intervention, 303–11
therapist: definition of, 120–21; unethical behavior by, 255–56, 260; value conflicts with, 254. *See also* private therapist; psychiatric nurse; psychiatric social worker; psychiatrist; psychologist
therapy: and children's complaints about, 258–61; confidentiality of, 241–42; evaluation of, 246–61; treatment goals, 236, 248–49; treatment methods, 237–38; a written contract for, 243–45
thioridazine (Mellaril), 176
Thorndike, Paul, 155
Through the Mental Health Maze: A Consumer's Guide to Finding a Psychotherapist: The Health Research Group, 243
thumb-sucking, 18, 38–39
tics, 38, 41–42; medications for, 180
Transactional Analysis (TA), 137, 167–68, 169
transsexualism, 34
transvestism, 34
treatment, factors in the success of, 138–40
trifluoperozine (Stelazine), 176
truant, playing, 54, 56, 58

unconditioned stimulus, 155
unconscious, 142
United States, 99, 102*n.*–103*n.*

United States Facilities and Programs for Children with Severe Mental Illness, 103*n.*
United Way, 104; referrals and, 223
value conflicts in therapy, 254
Veterans Administration Hospitals, 100
violence: physical or sexual, 308–309; and residential treatment, 285–86
vision: assessment of, 272; impairments to, 67
visual information processing, 90; testing for, 191
visual-motor functioning, 272
visual relationships, 83, 92–93
visual-spatial (perceptual) processing disorders, 91, 92–93
vocational or career counselors, 121
vomiting, 46; self-induced, 25

Wangh, Dr. Mitchell, 171*n.*
Webster, Dr. Ronald, 54*n.*
Wechsler, Dr. David, 185
Wechsler Adult Intelligence Scale (WAIS), 184, 185, 191
Wechsler Intelligence Test for Children—Revised (WISC-R), 184, 185, 191
Wechsler Preschool and Primary Scale of Intelligence (WPPSI), 184, 185, 191
Wechsler tests; descriptions of, 185; and learning disabilities testing, 191
weight loss, 25
Wepman Auditory Discrimination Test, 191
wetting, 52
Why Your Child Is Hyperactive, Dr, Ben Feingold, 88
Wide Range Achievement Test (WRAT), 193
word retrieval problems, 92
writing, 90, 92

yellow pages, mental health professions in, 208, 223